ETHICS OF THE LEGAL PROFESSION

A NEW ORDER

Cavendish
Publishing
Limited

London • Sydney • Portland, Oregon

ETHICS OF THE LEGAL PROFESSION

A NEW ORDER

Sir Fred Phillips
CVO, QC, MCL (McGill), LLD Hon (UWI)

Cavendish
Publishing
Limited

London • Sydney • Portland, Oregon

First published in Great Britain 2004 by
Cavendish Publishing Limited, The Glass House,
Wharton Street, London WC1X 9PX, United Kingdom
Telephone: + 44 (0)20 7278 8000 Facsimile: + 44 (0)20 7278 8080
Email: info@cavendishpublishing.com
Website: www.cavendishpublishing.com

Published in the United States by Cavendish Publishing
c/o International Specialized Book Services,
5824 NE Hassalo Street, Portland,
Oregon 97213-3644, USA

Published in Australia by Cavendish Publishing (Australia) Pty Ltd
45 Beach Street, Coogee, NSW 2034, Australia
Telephone: + 61 (2)9664 0909 Facsimile: + 61 (2)9664 5420
Email: info@cavendishpublishing.com.au
Website: www.cavendishpublishing.com.au

British Library Cataloguing in Publication Data

Phillips, Fred, Sir, 1918–
Ethics of the legal profession
1 Legal ethics – Caribbean area 2 Legal ethics – West Indies, British
3 Justice, administration of – Caribbean area
4 Justice, administration of – West Indies, British
5 Attorney and client – Caribbean area
6 Attorney and client – West Indies, British
I Title
174.3'09729

Library of Congress Cataloguing in Publication Data
Data available

ISBN 1-85941-963-1
ISBN 978-1-859-41963-2

1 3 5 7 9 10 8 6 4 2

Printed and bound in Great Britain by Biddles Ltd, Kings Lynn, Norfolk

To my fellow lawyers everywhere.

FOREWORD

The establishment of the Caribbean Court of Justice emphasises the need for Caribbean jurists to produce literature for the development of jurisprudence in our region. There can be no doubt that the ethics of the legal profession is a burning issue in the Caribbean and elsewhere. There have been many complaints and much discussion. Some of the problems affect the abstract administration of justice; some the contractual and professional relationships between client and legal practitioner. There has been discussion on issues relating to the development of efficient professional operational methods. There has been a re-examination of the philosophy underpinnings of these and related issues. This study by Sir Fred includes well-researched commentary on these and many other issues.

Throughout the Caribbean there has been growing emphasis on judicial reforms. This has been considered necessary for the social stability and economic development of the region. It must be axiomatic that these reforms cannot be successful without similar developments in the legal profession. The importance of the ethics of legal practice has become even more fundamental with the concept that the overriding objective of the court is to do justice with the assistance of the legal practitioners and litigants. This imposes new and different burdens on the legal profession.

An entertaining aspect to the book is the way in which Sir Fred has connected the principles he has examined to ancient learning by referring to well-selected commentaries from distinguished jurists, philosophers and historians. He has given an academic flavour to the subject, and shown the development of legal theory and thought on this subject.

The book tackles a subject which requires elucidation. Discussions on the ethics of the legal profession would be enhanced by reference to this work. It has analysed and classified the subject. The analysis has addressed some essential topics with the particularity of a legal text and the discursive approach of a philosopher. It has demonstrated that the topic is not purely theoretical. It has affected the legal rights of people as demonstrated in the voluminous litigation that it has evoked. The classification of the subjects and the citation of statutes, case law and learned articles makes this book a valuable research tool.

In the treatment of access to justice, this important constitutional principle provides useful insights to policy makers in Government, the judiciary and most importantly to Legal Profession Associations. The analysis of legal aid and fee structures should inform discussion and provide meaningful guidance on these issues. The extent to which the legal profession is or should be immune from suit for losses caused by their professional activity is becoming increasingly relevant as people become more aware of their legal rights. This book connects the discussion to interesting commentary and assessment and a plethora of judicial decisions. The discussion on the professional responsibility of lawyers is informed by consideration of relevant aspects of the law relating to negligence, contract and trust, as well as other topics. The discussion is grounded in jurisprudence and provides important research assistance.

The wasted costs order is one of the judicial responses to enforce discipline and the duty of care in the professional conduct of litigation. Interesting philosophical considerations concerning the justification and practicality of the practices relate to this topic. Sir Fred's interesting evaluation of the basis of the jurisdiction contributes to this important topic.

There are many important topics that have not been given much coverage in any forum. One such topic which is of concern to the public and is relevant to adjudication of complaints against members of the legal profession is the question of confidentiality and legal professional privilege. Sir Fred leads enquiry into public policy issues, statutory duties and the regulatory framework for professional privilege in several particular instances. This study contributes to the subject.

Conflicts of interest is a topic which concerns many members of the public. Much of the theory of ethics revolves around it. However, and perhaps more importantly, it is also a subject which affects the daily routine of the legal practitioner. Sir Fred makes a detailed examination of many practical matters affecting practitioners, such as conflicts in conveyancing issues; conflicts that could arise when there are disputes between two or more clients of the same legal practitioner; and the complex issues that arise during family lawyering. Consideration has been given to some serious ethical, professional and legal issues that arise in cases of gifts and mortgages between lawyers and their clients. The new and complex issues under modern financial services industry are not omitted.

Sir Fred does not evade the concerns of those clamouring for greater access to complaints self-regulation procedures He has dealt with professional self-regulation and discipline in the profession, providing examples and analysis of options by reference to other jurisdictions. In the same vein he has dealt with judicial codes of ethics. He captures codes from several jurisdictions providing the basis for comparative studies. This provides useful research and commentary, and addresses some of the imperatives in the design of such codes.

The chapter on the ethics of the criminal process is tremendously interesting. It is not a topic usually covered in texts. Nonetheless the issues addressed demonstrate that it is worthy of in-depth examination and analysis. He addresses several aspects of the topic and has provided detailed research which must be of great utility. The work contains consideration of the functions of prosecuting and defence counsel, the principles affecting the withdrawal of services, and the legal implications of confidentiality. In the chapter relating to ethics a comparison is made between the English system and newly-independent countries. The work also discusses concepts of fairness of trials, police powers and negotiated justice: subjects which are all topical.

ADR, the new aid to improve justice administration, is given detailed consideration with consideration of current thinking and assessments of the future of mediation.

The entire discourse identifies relevant statute law and case law. It highlights relevant legal literature and pinpoints issues that have informed debate on the subject. Another important and useful aspect is the constant reference to the development of the law in this area. This documentation of the reform process could be instructive to us in the Caribbean and in all developing countries. The style of writing is clear and precise. Although it is a lawyers' book, I think that it can be read and appreciated by anyone with good reading skills.

What is an appropriate audience for this book? This work is useful reading for the judiciary and the legal profession. It is especially instructive for Legal Profession Associations. There is important material for legal academics. In fact I would think that it should become compulsory reading for law students. The material will be extremely useful to the new practitioner as well. In a nutshell it is a useful research tool on its subject matter, and can be used in support of legal research even in litigation. I would think that it would also be of interest to the public.

Sir Fred has been a prolific writer and seems to be going forever. I would like to congratulate him on this important contribution to the literature of the profession.

Sir Dennis Byron

ACKNOWLEDGMENTS

I am greatly obliged to Sir Louis Blom-Cooper for reading the entire manuscript and providing most constructive comments. He also kindly shared with me his views on the jury system and in Chapter 10 I have drawn heavily on an address he delivered on the subject to the British Academy of Forensic Sciences at the Royal College of Physicians in October 2003.

Mr Michael Sherrard, QC, was kind enough to furnish useful comments on Chapter 10 from his vast store of knowledge of criminal law, ethics and procedure. For this assistance I also express my indebtedness to him.

I wish likewise to thank Sir Dennis Byron for so graciously agreeing to write the Foreword. In his capacity as Chief Justice of the Eastern Caribbean Supreme Court, he has embarked on a number of reforming initiatives which have greatly improved the administration of justice in the sub-region and reference has been made to many of those reforms in the text. His deep interest specifically in advancing ethical standards in the profession is well-known and appreciated.

My wife Gloria has suffered from almost total non-communication during my long periods of writing and endured lengthy discussions on points of ethics whenever I wished to obtain an enlightened non-lawyer's view on various aspects of this study. She has also been most helpful in drawing attention to deficiencies and lack of clarity in the text. I am much obliged to her for this indulgence.

I wish to pay special tribute to my publishers, Cavendish Publishing Ltd, for the excellence of their work and their friendly encouragement in making this further volume a reality.

My Secretary, Miss Doreen Applewhaite, has once more exhibited her Job-like qualities in typing and re-typing many drafts. I am very grateful for her input.

I need hardly add that no one who assisted me must in the least be held accountable for any error or defect in the text for which I am alone responsible.

Fred Phillips
October 2004

CONTENTS

TABLE OF ABBREVIATIONS

ABA	American Bar Association
ACLEC	Advisory Committee on Legal Services
ADR	Alternative dispute resolution
CFA	Conditional Fees
CLSA	Courts and Legal Services Act
CPR	Court Procedure Rules
CFY	Contingency Fees
LSC	Legal Services Commission
LSG	Guide to the Professional Conduct of Solicitors (Law Society)
NAFTA	North America Free Trade Association
NCIS	National Criminal Investigation Services
OCCBA	Organisation of Commonwealth Caribbean Bar Associations
ODR	Online dispute resolution
OECS	Organisation of Eastern Caribbean States
OSS	Office for the Supervision of Solicitors
PACE	Police and Criminal Evidence Act 1984
PCC	Professional Conduct Committee
SCB	Solicitors Complaints Bureau
WLR	Weekly Law Reports
WTO	World Trade Organisation

CHAPTER 1

A CRISIS IN LEGAL ETHICS

There is a widespread belief that lawyers are not doing enough to preserve their role as the guardians of the public interest in the independence of the profession and that there is a crisis in the ethics of the profession with various sectors of the profession singing discordant ethical songs. What is the true position?

Like Plato, the layman views lawyers as 'small unrighteous souls'. Like Shakespeare, he would sooner say: 'The first thing we do, let's kill all the lawyers.' With the Gospel according to St Luke, he would exclaim: 'Woe unto you also, ye lawyers.'

The single-firm practitioner has no doubt there is a crisis – one of injustice and inequality. He witnesses his upper-crust colleagues, some of whom are his juniors, becoming more and more prosperous in their large law firms while he is reduced (as it were) to accepting the scraps which fall from his colleagues' table. In a highly acclaimed work by Dezalay and Sugarman[1] the point has recently been made that 'in this new context of transnational deal making and regulation building' the gulf between solo practitioners and their colleagues in large law firms has widened dramatically, so much so that 'traditional models of professionalisation have been rendered invalid'.

On the other hand, the head of the law firm wonders what all the crisis fuss is about. As far as he can see, there is simply a drastic change in the way 'business' (legal business) is conducted. Those who are pressing for adherence to self-righteous codes are old-fashioned and out of date. To him the law is an enterprise which must deliver legal services to clients. The means must justify the ends.

Then there are the older idealists who insist that the ideals they always attributed to a profession, viz, scholarship, integrity, honour (and the rest) are under grave threat; that collegiality and civility are becoming attributes of the past. Lawyers' professionalism, they assert, is on the way out. Lawyers have regretfully reached the stage of advertising and solicitation.

EXCESS OF LAWYERS

Because of the multiplicity of new law schools in emergent countries which strive to teach the common law at home, there are certainly more lawyers in these countries than are sensibly required to serve the populations. Many of them come to the profession because they see a career in law as a way to riches, only to be disillusioned. The result: standards of conduct fall. They find themselves before disciplinary tribunals for ethical lapses. Morale also falls when the new entrants

---

1 See Yves Dezalay and David Sugarman (eds), *Professional Competition and Professional Power: Lawyers, Accountants and the Social Construction of Markets* (London and NY, Routledge, 1995), Preface.

realise that the large law firms will not accept them (despite the fact that those firms continue to recruit others) and that the big corporations are making use only of these large law firms with branches on an international scale. This state of affairs is documented by many North American and British writers whose writings since the last two decades of the 20th century speak volumes of a serious crisis.[2]

GREATER CONSCIOUSNESS

There is greater consciousness today of lawyers' work and responsibilities in that citizens the world over have ideas of their fundamental human rights and are ready to litigate in order to enforce those rights. If, for instance, a lawyer is guilty of a breach of confidentiality, the client is more likely than not to sue. There is even a new wasted costs jurisdiction of which litigants have been prepared to take advantage (this subject is dealt with in Chapter 6 below). People have become aware that if a solicitor performs his functions in a manner contrary to his duty of skill and care or if he is in breach of his duty not to make a secret profit in dealing with his client's property, he can be sued.

GOVERNMENTS' INTERVENTION

It is for these reasons that governments have been intervening, mainly as a populist gesture, in favour of their constituents. Hence also the spate of legislation on legal aid, proper accounting to protect clients' funds, disciplinary matters, the cost of litigation and alternative dispute resolution, mediation, conciliation and arbitration.

BUSINESS v PROFESSION

The legal profession has become a business[3] with a remit to deliver legal services efficiently and cheaply. Lawyers find themselves in a stratified environment – some performing a humdrum and solo practice, others operating in an

2 See CO Houle, *Continuing Learning in the Professions* (California and London, Jossey-Bass, 1980); Charles Wolfram, *Modern Legal Ethics* (St Paul, West Publishing Co, 1986); David Luban, *Lawyers and Justice: An Ethical Study* (Princeton, Princeton University Press, 1980); Robert Nelson, *Partners with Power, The Social Transformation of the Large Firm* (Berkeley, University of California Press, 1988); R Abel and P Lewis, *Lawyers in Society* (Berkeley, University of California Press, 1988); Sol M Linowitz with Martin Mayer, *The Betrayed Profession: Lawyering at the End of the Twentieth Century* (NY, Scribner's Sons, Maxwell and Macmillan, 1994); AT Kronman, *The Lost Lawyer: Failing Ideals of the Legal Profession* (Cambridge, Harvard University Press, 1993); R Nelson, D Trubek and R Solomon, *Lawyers' Ideals and Lawyers Practices: Transformations in the American Legal Profession* (Ithaca, Cornell University Press, 1994); TC Halliday and L Karpik (eds), *Lawyers and the Rise of Western Political Liberalism* (Oxford, Clarendon Press, 1997); A Sarat (ed), *Everyday Practice and Trouble Cases* (Chicago, Southwestern University Press, 1998); Deborah Rhode, *Professional Responsibility: Ethics by the Pervasive Method* (2nd edn) (New York, Aspen Law and Business, 1998).

3 This matter is discussed in Chapter 2.

atmosphere of opulence with their less fortunate colleagues who face a declining market. This is well-illustrated by Professor Harry Arthurs.[4] Writing in conjunction with another expert he states:[5] 'The largest law firms are growing in size, power and relatively, at least, affluence. Solo practitioners and small firms are facing a more radical decline in their prospects, and middle-sized firms are being absorbed, dissolved or, perforce, re-invented.'

THE ENGLISH POSITION

Up to the time of the retirement in the early 1980s of the long-serving and outstanding Lord Hailsham as Lord Chancellor, the profession in England and Wales continued in the even tenor of its way. When, however, Prime Minister Margaret Thatcher appointed a distinguished Scot – Lord MacKay – as her new Lord Chancellor, things began to change dramatically and during his more than 15 years in office he introduced a series of reforms affecting the legal profession, many of which angered both branches of the legal fraternity. In 1984, for instance, he introduced legislation the effect of which was to provide for competition against solicitors in the age-old monopoly in the preparation of conveyances which provided a considerable portion of their income. Their competitors would not necessarily be qualified lawyers and would be known as 'licensed conveyancers'.[6]

The decision to break the solicitors' monopoly in that way led them to press for rights of audience in the superior courts – a facility enjoyed up to that time only by barristers. This concession was duly granted by the Courts and Legal Services Act (CLSA) 1990, under which the Law Society could permit those rights where the solicitor concerned had undertaken the necessary training. The return to office in England of the Labour Government replacing the Conservatives in 1997 provided an opportunity for another Scot – Lord Irvine of Lairg – to assume the Lord Chancellorship. He was, if anything, even more reform-oriented than his talented predecessor and one of his first duties was to issue a White Paper entitled *Modernising Justice*, setting out in some detail the further reforms that the new Labour Government intended to launch.

The restrictive practices which only benefited lawyers would, in the interest of the public, be removed. Standards of service and access to information would be facilitated by the new technology. A Community Legal Service would be established which would in future embrace legal aid, enabling it to assist where the greatest need arose.

---

4 See a powerful argument to this effect by Professor Harry Arthurs in 'Lawyering in Canada in the 21st century' in *Windsor Yearbook of Access to Justice*, Vol 15, 1996, pp 213–15. See also Stager and Arthurs, *Lawyers in Canada* (published in association with Statistics Canada by University of Toronto Press, 1990).

5 Harry Arthurs and R Kreklewich, 'Law, legal institutions and the legal profession in the new economy' in *Osgoode Hall Law Journal*, Vol 34, 1996, p 147. See generally Peter Megargee Brown's *Rascals: The Selling of the Legal Profession* (NY, Benchmark Press, 1989).

6 See Pt II of the Administration of Justice Act 1985.

More money would be spent on the not-for-profit sector with its particular expertise on problems experienced by poor people and on alternative dispute resolution. Conditional fees would be introduced (ie, 'no win, no fee' agreements) and a new 'fast-track' court system would be provided involving fixed-cost hearings to facilitate and speed up justice for people of modest means who would not normally qualify to receive legal aid but could not risk litigation on their own 'because of the unpredictable cost'.[7]

One year later, most of the promises in the White Paper were implemented by the passing of the Access to Justice Act of 1999 ('the Act') which made provision, *inter alia*, for a Criminal Defence Service; for recovering insurance premiums in relation to litigation by way of costs; for the appointment of a Legal Services Complaints Commissioner; and for replacement of the Lord Chancellor's former Advisory Committee on Legal Services (ACLEC) by a Legal Services Advisory Panel.

Among other suggested reforms was one which had been in the air for some time, viz, the offer of barristers' services direct to the public, so that there would be no need for using two lawyers where one would do. In February 2002, the Bar Council approved this suggestion.[8]

Another proposed reform did not, however, fare well. A proposal arising from the Act which had been supported by the Office of Fair Trading in March 2001 was that the Bar should, like the solicitor's branch, be permitted to form partnerships among its members or with solicitors. The Office of Fair Trading had given professional bodies one year to respond to this proposal, but in 2002 it was rejected by the Bar Council on the ground that such an arrangement would undermine the independence of the Bar.

Under s 1 of the Act, the Legal Services Commission (LSC) replaces the Legal Aid Board. The LSC has taken a lead in establishing the Community Legal Service which will consist of legal services providers funded from a range of different sources. A Community Legal Service fund is set up under s 5 of the Act which replaces the existing civil and family legal aid schemes in those cases which cannot be funded in some other way (for example, by a conditional fee arrangement).

The Lord Chancellor possessed wide powers under the legislation; for example, the LSC is empowered to set priorities (s 6) in accordance with directions to be given by him. The exercise of this power has already been the source of some controversy since the Lord Chancellor, although exercising his right in 2001 to increase the rates of legal aid (which had been static for some years), later exercised his discretion in 2002 to freeze the rates – much to the disappointment of both branches of the profession. One commentator, Richard Miller,[9] has underscored the effect of the freeze on the future efficiency of legal aid in England.

7 Cm 4155, *Modernising justice*, presented to Parliament by the Lord Chancellor in December 1998.

8 See *Daily Telegraph*, 4 February 2002, p 9 (article under the caption 'Go ahead to direct access to barristers').

9 Miller, 'Legal aid: back to business as usual', *New Law Journal*, Vol 152, 2002, p 545.

He explains how, in the belief that government's commitment to legal aid was genuine, many law firms had decided to carry on doing publicly funded work for another year when the increase was announced and had undertaken to conform to the new Specialist Quality Mark. They were to be sadly disappointed. In Miller's view, those firms that turned their backs on legal aid will never return to it, especially having regard to the low rates of pay such work yields, in contrast to private work. The result is that only the most junior and inexperienced members of the firms will be available for the service – with unfortunate implications for the quality of work they will produce. This crisis of supply and efficiency will inevitably have special effect on the poor in the community.

CANADA

If the reader needs to be persuaded that the same degree of crisis is being experienced by the Canadian legal profession as in England, I would draw attention to an assessment of the Canadian position as articulated by Professor John Claydon, a legal expert from the Osgoode Hall Law School. This is what Professor Claydon had to say at a Conference at the Faculty of Law of Queen's University on 21 October 1995:

> Although there have been long-standing challenges to the demands of professionalism and ethical behaviour, trends in the legal profession over the past 20 or 50 years, and particularly the last few years, have exacerbated the traditional tensions. The 70s were not the best of times for all of us, but the underlying conditions at least made it possible for us to make professional choices. In the first place, we had a modicum of choice about where we could work. Although more and more lawyers were graduating each year, law firms were expanding, governments were hiring, the public interest field was thriving, and Legal Aid was healthy. And wherever one worked, clients were relatively loyal. These conditions endured into the 80s and while we might not have always been happy professionally I think that at least we felt the professional ideals that gave our role moral content and personal meaning remained essentially intact. Those of us who did not want to operate within the commercial culture could go elsewhere and those who remained in it could by and large retain a sense that it was possible to act ethically in this general way. Clients were diverse, some work was interesting, collegiality existed, and there was some time and opportunity for involvement in public causes and *pro bono* work.
>
> Recently, however, changes in the marketplace have brought into greater relief the distinction between doing good and doing well. There are few jobs in teaching, government and public interest sector for those who do not want to become part of the commercial culture. And even that culture has been affected by government cutbacks, as we see in the current Legal Aid crisis. In the mainstream corporate or commercial culture, increased competition for clients has made it practically more difficult for lawyers to question clients' goals and the means for achieving them. For many lawyers this is a matter of survival; for others, including some in large firms, the issue is more profit. For all, however, preoccupation with the bottom line has not only fostered a concern with keeping clients happy, sometimes at significant ethical cost, but also has tended to undermine other objectives of professionalism, such as nurturing collegiality, mentoring and training young lawyers and involvement in

> public and *pro bono* activities (both because there is not time and the clients might not like it). One recent commentator has referred to the demise of the 'corporate counsellor' – the idea of a commercial lawyer as a responsible counsellor who tries to persuade clients to adopt policies that will comply with the norms and purposes of the legal system and benefit society as a whole rather than one who simply helps the client to negotiate its way through the legal system.

Does this not sound familiar to readers in the other countries of the world?

THE UNITED STATES OF AMERICA

In a powerful and discerning contribution introducing a number of other presentations in a recent volume,[10] Professor Deborah Rhode of Stanford University provides an overview describing a crisis situation in the United States. She calls attention to the certification initiatives of the American Bar Association (ABA) in the second half of the 20th century beginning with the Model Code of 1969, followed by an 'outpouring of codification, commentary and curricular activities', and culminating in the mid-1980s with a revised set of Rules of Professional Conduct. She points out that despite those efforts 'chronic ethical dilemmas remained unresolved' without the stakeholders arriving at a consensus about the nature of the problems and their priorities in so far as professional life was concerned. She gives a forceful account of the economic structures affecting ethics in practice, emphasising the commercialism and competition generated by the large law firms; the working (or lack of it) of the adversarial system; and the need for increasing access to justice by 'more procedural simplification, additional *pro bono* and government-subsidised services' as well as 'greater reliance on qualified non-lawyer providers'. Finally, she bemoans the fact that despite the American Bar Association's request to law schools to pay special attention to legal ethics after the Watergate scandal in the 1970s, most of the schools were prepared to satisfy that request by providing only a single mandatory course which focused on bar disciplinary codes, with the result that there was 'legal ethics without the ethics'.

Two other discerning writers – Marc Galanter and Thomas Palay – have painted an bleak picture of the nature and extent of the crisis as it has been observed in the US towards the beginning of the 21st century. They point to the despondency that has followed the colossal growth and international spread of the large law firms and to the fact that it has caused law practice to descend from the heights of its virtuous and collegiate past. They suggest that there has been a most perceptible decline from a noble profession infused with civic virtues to a business obsessed with the arcane attributes of commercialism for its own sake – 'the bottom line'. They draw special attention to 'the sophisticated account of the decline' provided by Professor Anthony Kronman, former Dean of the Yale Law School, who has gone to the extent of advising young idealistic entrants to the ranks of the profession to eschew the large law firms whose 'harshly economising

10 See *Ethics in Practice, Lawyers' Roles, Responsibilities and Regulation* by Deborah L Rhode (ed) (Oxford, OUP, 2000), pp 3–26. See also generally Charles Wolfram, *op cit*, fn 2.

spirit' and 'increasingly commercial culture' are 'inimical to the commitment to public service that is the hallmark of professional identity'.[11] If the language and behaviour described above do not identify a crisis, then what does?

HOW THE THIRD WORLD COPES WITH THE CRISIS

How these countries cope with the professional ethical crisis we are considering will become more evident as various aspects of the profession's operations are discussed in the following chapters. What must be stressed at this point is that (as suggested above) increased awareness on the part of citizens of their constitutional and other rights will consistently drive governments to enact regulatory legislation in respect of the operation and discipline of the legal profession. Nor must we forget that at this time of globalisation, improved telecommunications and international trade, the changes taking place in the developed countries – and especially in England – will have an impact upon what governments do to regulate the profession's conduct. The profession for its part needs to keep its ears to the ground and be ready to enter into a partnership with government in the interest of social justice. Obviously, political and economic considerations will have a large part to play and tensions between government and the profession are bound to arise, but these must be squarely faced. In all of it, the profession must be prepared to adapt to change while keeping in mind both the interests of its clients and the duties of its members as officers of the court.

CONCLUDING REMARKS

Nowhere is the crisis laid more bare than in a thought-provoking volume written by a former law-firm practitioner[12] who firmly places true professionalism above self-interest. Referring to Mr Justice Robert H Jackson's aphorism that in the US the administration of justice is based on law practice, he states that 'too many of the 80,000 lawyers [*sic*] in the United States show signs of having lost their way'. And then he enquires nostalgically: 'Whoever stops to consider the ancient – and noble – origins and purpose of the law practice we inherited from England?' He replies: 'We simply assume that in a modern world we can do our own thing without any old-fashioned need to glance backward for insights for the future.'

11 See Marc Galanter and Thomas Palay, 'Large law firms and professional responsibility' in Ross Cranston (ed), *Legal Ethics and Professional Responsibility* (Oxford, Clarendon Press, 1995), p 192. See also the severe criticisms of the legal profession by Kronman, *op cit*, fn 2, and Linowitz, *op cit*, fn 2.

12 See *Rascals: The Selling of the Legal Profession*, *op cit*, fn 5.

In bringing down the curtain at the end of the final chapter Brown poses yet another question as to what can be done to restore the law profession to its role of preserving the justice system and our civilisation. This time he finds a response from the 1987 Letters of William O Douglas, that indefatigible spirit who served the US Supreme Court with such distinction for 36 years. Here is Mr Justice Douglas's advice to young lawyers:

> As nightfall does not come at once, neither does oppression. In both instances there is a twilight when everything remains seemingly unchanged. And it is in such twilight that we must all be most aware of change in the air – however slight – lest we become unwitting victims of the darkness.[13]

One of the greatest changes facing the profession today is the way it is being commercialised and this is the subject of Chapter 2.

13 Quoted from *Rascals*, *op cit*, fn 5, p 109.

CHAPTER 2

THE LAW – A BUSINESS RATHER THAN A PROFESSION?

INTRODUCTION

The purpose of this chapter is to consider whether the legal profession has abandoned traditional standards and to what extent it has in fact altered its principles for profit and become commercial.

On this subject there are two camps. The traditionalists claim that 'the bedrock of our programme' from early times has been the professional ideal, the lawyer as an officer of the court compelled as such to maintain a standard of conduct that rises above the standard we would expect from a tradesman engaged in what many now call 'the business of the law'. These traditionalists insist that the law 'is not and never has been a business'. The other camp is occupied by the radicalists who are persuaded that the law is a trade, citing in support of this claim the famous decision of the US Supreme Court in the case of *Bates v The State Bar of Arizona* 1977 433 US 350 the effect of which was that the United States Constitution permits commercial advertising – and by extension any form of client solicitation.

It is that great American judge Louis Brandeis who reminds us that the lawyer's function is to protect the innocent. He considers that the protection of the people presented a great opportunity for those who were expected to be sentinels of the law and ministers of justice. For him, far too much was heard of 'the corporation lawyer' and far too little of 'the people's lawyer'. It may well be that the developments in the field of human rights culminating with the Human Rights Act 1998 in England has restored some of the respect for the people's lawyer, and that ideal of Judge Brandeis has been characterised by David Luban as 'progressive professionalism' (Luban, 1988).

What then truly falls within the definition of 'professionalism'? Nearly a century ago Abraham Flexner gave a definition which is still valid at the beginning of the 21st century. To fall within the category of profession, an occupation should have a store of knowledge of more than usual complexity; have been in possession of 'a theoretical grasp of the phenomenon' with which the occupation deals; be able to apply the theory and practice of the calling to the problems it faces; continue to increase its knowledge in particular fields; make a conscious and deliberate effort to imbue succeeding members of the profession with its ideals; establish recognised admission and disciplinary procedures to ensure proper levels of service and conduct; and develop within the ranks of its members a true spirit of altruism.[1] One additional ingredient in any profession is the fact that its practitioners are specially licensed. The attributes laid down by Flexner as the ideals and ideologies of a profession have also been eruditely

1 In preparing this introductory section, I have relied somewhat on Norman Bowie's seminal paper entitled 'The law: from a profession to a business', in the *Vanderbilt Law Review*, Vol 41, 1988, p 741, in the course of which are set out these attributes of a profession outlined by Flexner.

elucidated by Professor Deborah Rhode[2] in a 1985 article in which she says *inter alia*:

> Over the last century attorneys have variously appeared as 'sentinels', 'ministers' and 'high priests' of justice with eyes well elevated above the 'golden calf'. Though contemporary metaphors are more subdued, legal practice is still idealised as a self-directed calling, informed by 'the spirit of public service'. Such rhetoric appears increasingly removed from the enterprise it purports to describe.

The learned writer continues: 'As the profession's competitive ethos and partisan loyalties grow more pronounced, the pretence that the Bar remains above trade becomes more difficult to accept.'

She asserts that 'within the dominant ideology, professional ideals retain a toe-hold' and that 'concerns for justice and aspirations to a public calling remain a prominent part of the bar's collective conscience'. She also makes the valid point that prescriptions as to how the profession should cease to be commercial 'is a subject on which most commentators are less forthcoming and tend to be more tepid'.

One further attribute of a profession as set out by Flexner is that its members tend to increase and improve their stock of knowledge whereas, according to Metzger, the chief function of a professional is 'to ease the problems caused by the growth of knowledge'.

How is that function achieved? By specialisation on the part of the professional which is employed to protect ignorant clients from exploitation. An example would be the injury caused to an employee by the negligent act of an agent of an employer, when the employee has no idea of his rights. It is specialised knowledge of the lawyer of the law of the tort of negligence that comes to the employee's aid and protects him from exploitation. According to Bowie, 'What has gone wrong with the law is that most lawyers are using their specialised knowledge to enable the rich and powerful to exploit the poor and ignorant while enriching themselves in the process'.[3]

It is that specialisation that has made medicine and law such vital professions. In medicine the days of the general practitioner are numbered. In law, the days of the lone practitioner are waning – the time of the specialist in the large law firm is on the ascendancy.

At the same time as the large law firm has become so prominent a part of legal professional life – and perhaps because of it – key members of our profession now assert that we live in a 'greed era' and that the decline of professionalism has taken on epidemic proportions.[4] This is how a former Chief Justice of the US Supreme Court viewed the trend.

---

2 See Professor Deborah Rhode's admirable article 'Ethical perspectives on legal practice' in *Stanford Law Review*, Vol 37, 1985, pp 589–90, which I have utilised in writing this section.

3 See Bowie, *op cit*, fn 1, p 744. See also the article entitled 'Professionalism' by Richard A Posner in *Arizona Law Review*, Vol 40, 1998, p 1.

4 See Chief Justice Warren Burger's remarks entitled 'The decline of professionalism' adapted from the 23rd Annual John F Sonnett Memorial Lecture delivered at the Fordham University School of Law on 23 January 1995, *Fordham Law Review*, Vol 63, 749 at p 750.

Reference has already been made in the first chapter of this book to the way the large firms have come to be regarded in the crisis that has befallen the profession and in this section we will briefly set out the way those firms operate in the US and how the system has affected the profession in other parts of the world. We shall also look at the way 'legal plans' have entered the market.

LAW FIRMS

The evidence is overwhelming that the law is considered today more as a business than a profession.

It is common ground that lawyers whose desire is to do well gravitate (quite understandably) to law firms which, as we discussed in the first chapter, have in the past two decades been expanding at an unprecedented rate in terms of numbers of staff. It is also generally considered that for most law firms profitability and competition take precedence over collegiality and public-spiritedness. It cannot be denied that large law firms are on the whole concerned mainly with providing quality service to large corporations who can afford to pay their fees to the detriment of the disadvantaged client.

Reference has already been made to what Galanter and Palay had to say about the large law firms[5] and we have discussed Kronman's condemnation of them which he has chronicled in his seminal work.[6]

AM Adams in his assessment of these institutions states that 'the ... most pervasive manifestation of the change in the legal climate is the decline of professionalism and its replacement with commercialism'.[7] PM Brown has in his forthright and critical work levelled stinging criticism at the way the large firms have allowed themselves to be engulfed with greed and lack of principle: 'As the profession becomes a business there follows, as the night the day, a marked decline in public confidence in the American Bar. Lawyers stand – or lie – at the bottom of the barrel.'[8] Linowitz in his work already mentioned has echoed the same sentiments in urging a return to civility and professionalism from the rush to prosperity and incivility.[9]

Professor Harry Arthurs has set the large Canadian law firm in proper perspective in an admirable article on the legal profession in Canada in the 21st century. This is the way he expressed the position:[10]

5 See fn 11 in Chapter 1 above.

6 AT Kronman, *The Lost Lawyer: Failing Ideals of the Legal Profession* (Cambridge, Harvard University Press, 1993).

7 AM Adams, 'The legal profession, a critical evaluation', *Dickenson Law Review*, Vol 93, 1989, p 652.

8 PM Brown, *Rascals: The Selling of the Legal Profession* (NY, Benchmark Press, 1989), p 50.

9 Sol M Linowitz with Martin Mayer, *The Betrayed Profession: Lawyering at the End of the Twentieth Century* (NY, Charles Scribner & Sons, Maxwell and Macmillan, 1994).

10 See the article by HW Arthurs, 'Lawyering in Canada in the 21st century' *Windsor Yearbook of Access to Justice*, Vol 15, 1996, p 202.

> At the other end of the spectrum ... are the large corporate law firms ... They serve mostly institutional clients, such as corporations and governments predominantly in complex business litigation, regulatory proceedings or transactions involving considerable sums of money. Most parties within the firm are specialists; they work collaboratively with each other and with outside experts such as accountants; and they are well supported by associates and juniors, librarians, paraprofessionals, clerical staff and technicians. Because of the high profile of their clients and cases, their technical virtuosity as specialists, and their financial base, lawyers from these firms are usually over-represented in the ranks of the judiciary, governing bodies and professional pantheons. They thus tend to wield considerable power within the profession.

It is not clear to what extent these large Canadian law firms exhibit much predisposition to public-spiritedness in the delivery, for instance, of *pro bono* assistance, about which we will speak later. But there are exceptions.

Chief Justice Warren Burger (in his remarks referred above) spoke to the vulgar type of advertisement carried out by some members of the profession since the *Bates* case. This is how he put it:

> Unfortunately, the shyster conduct in solicitation and advertisement is no longer limited to the 'ambulance chasers'. Today we see television ads, yellow page ads and (believe it or not) ads or billboards forty feet wide and fifteen feet high, touting a lawyer or law firm reaching out for clients with such ads, lawyers usually emphasising that the 'First Conference is Free'. Doesn't this have the ring of 'come into my parlour, said the spider to the fly'?

The learned Chief Justice poured scorn on the idea that the public needs advertisement to gain access to legal service which he considered should be provided by referral arrangements provided by the bar associations and by *pro bono* work. He pointed out at the same time that an empirical survey uncovered that only one in 10 clients found a lawyer through advertisement. Later on in his address the judge recounted that many years ago he had been invited to a meeting of the ABA Committee on Standards where he was asked what action should be taken against lawyers who advertise. He replied that if a client were to make such an enquiry of him he would reply thus: 'Never, never, never, engage the services of a lawyer who finds it necessary to advertise in order to get clients.'[11]

NOVEL BUSINESS WAYS OF DELIVERY

Whether we like it or not, lawyers' services – especially in the US – are delivered today in much the same way as any other business commodity is delivered. The writers who have done most empirical work in this area have expressed the view that in the last decades of the 20th century three developments have transformed legal services delivered to individuals, viz, the 1977 *Bates* decision by the US Supreme Court, the marketing of pre-paid plans, and the computerisation of forms and management tasks. They aver that all management personnel interviewed about these developments confessed unashamedly that their

11 See Chief Justice Burger, *op cit*, fn 4.

techniques were borrowed from the world of business: 'The one clear theme to emerge from the preliminary phase of this project is that business strategies – advertising, sales, efficient management, computerisation and productivity evaluation – have become part of the repertoire of individual – client legal practice.'[12]

FOR-PROFIT PLANS

The writers outline a for-profit plan with Hyatt Legal Services (Hyatt) and Jacoby and Myers – the two main providers of legal service plans. In so doing, it is pointed out that what the providers do is to create a management company which is responsible for purchasing the necessary equipment as well as for arranging real estate expansion, staff training, customer relations and advertising. Additionally, they create a number of store-front shops to deliver the services on a day-to-day basis. It is as if they were selling and marketing any other commodity. Their target is the middle-income group in the community. As the writers claim: 'The opportunity to advertise is the step that made it possible to discuss openly the marketing of legal services. One might claim that advertising professional services brought the discussion of business out of the closet.'[13]

These mini law offices are situated in 'convenient locations' where a general practice is conducted by a managing attorney and his associates – the former's task being the training and hiring of new associates. The main function of an attorney at such a law office is that of being able to handle a heavy caseload of such matters as wills, divorces and bankruptcies – paying special regard to efficiency and profitability – 'think(ing) of cases in terms of dollars and cents; to supervise and evaluate the work of associates; and to incorporate support staff into the organisational culture of the local office'.

PREPAID LEGAL PLANS

Hyatt is the firm which has led the way in promoting legal plans as 'the next fringe benefit'. It is said to have been providing coverage for the sheet metal workers for many years. Hyatt is supported by Signature Group and Nationwide.

Each of these firms sets out to market a pre-paid legal service package to meet the needs of the working middle class. They adopt different techniques towards the same ends. Hyatt goes for specific unions supplying a group plan as part of a bigger package where an employee can decide on legal services through payroll deduction. The employee on coming into the plan is given access to a toll-free number which leads him or her to a lawyer from a small panel of two or three. In the case of Signature, employees are permitted to choose their own lawyer from among older lawyers operating from their own offices. Such lawyers live in the

12 See a detailed and penetrating study of the way professionalism seems to be giving way to commercialisation in R Nelson, D Trubek and R Solomon, *Lawyers' Ideals and Lawyers Practices: Transformations in the American Legal Profession* (Ithaca, Cornell University Press, 1994).

13 *Ibid*, p 69.

same general area as the employee who may, for a small monthly fee, obtain free service in preparing a will, holding consultations, writing lawyers' letters, reviewing documents and having access to a set of other services for a fixed fee. Nationwide's plan employs direct mail, telemarketing and direct sales to sell plans in more than 30 states – marketing 'two products' for individual consumers – a 'one-will' and 'a two-will' package. For a small monthly fee, the consumer can secure a service for a simple will and trust plan, unlimited telephone consultation, unlimited reviews of documents up to six pages in length, unlimited solicitors' letters and one half-hour face-to-face consultation as well as access to an attorney at a discounted rate – the level of discount ranging from 25% to 33% of the attorney's hourly charge, depending on the specific plan chosen.

PERMISSIBILITY OF THESE PLANS

There were decisions of the US Supreme Court[14] that permitted the operation of the legal services to which we have referred above – coupled with the famous *Bates* case – under which private associations were allowed to advise their members on legal claims. Under the 1969 Canons, a lawyer may solicit prospective clients when employed by a qualified legal services organisation. The plans to which we have referred, therefore, have a measure of constitutional protection and do not breach the ABA Ethics Code, although they may be distasteful to the traditionalists.

CANADIAN PLANS

The US plans have been followed in Canada where the plans are considered to have advantages for users.

In Canada, the provincial law societies, which govern the activities of the profession, have, however, expressed concern over some of the plans since they are thought likely to affect the confidentiality and privilege protected by the codes of ethics in the various provinces.

The question has also arisen as to whether some of these plans may not infringe the constitutional rights of individuals to select a lawyer of their choice instead of lawyers who belong to a closed panel chosen for the consumers by a particular employer.

The plans which in the US covered more than 8 million workers by 1986 are likely in Canada in the course of time to become part of the work-package of middle-income earners. They were first introduced into Canada in 1978, initially providing basic legal services in the preparation of wills and conveyances to the United Grain Workers (Stager and Arthurs, 1990).

Subsequently in 1987 the Canadian Automobile Workers introduced a major prepaid plan for over 230,000 workers – a plan intended to provide service in preparing wills, real property transactions, uncontested divorces, bankruptcies,

14 For instance, the cases of *NAACP v Button* (1963) 371 US 415 and *Brotherhood of Railroad Trainmen v Virginia State Bar* (1964) 377 US 1.

traffic violations, consumer issues and landlord and tenant cases. Initially, only those panel lawyers who accepted the tariff annual fee of $60 per employee were retained by the employers, but the Law Society in Ontario objected to the plan on the ground that the constitutional right of the consumer of having a lawyer of his own choice was being infringed. As a result, clients were permitted to retain non-panel lawyers on the understanding that the employer would pay the tariff fee and the client would meet any deficit.

These arrangements may all sound very commercial but what matters is that they provide clients with a service to which they may not otherwise have access, and that the lawyers involved act professionally in dealing with the clients.

POSITION IN THE CARIBBEAN

I was called to the English Bar in February 1956, since when I have been admitted to practise in Guyana, Trinidad & Tobago, Grenada, St Vincent, St Lucia, Anguilla, Barbados, Dominica, Antigua, Jamaica and the Cayman Islands. I have, therefore, had an opportunity of working with and observing other members of the profession in these jurisdictions as well as in Belize, Bermuda and particularly in the Bahamas where I was commissioned to draft company law and trust legislation. In the 47 years since my call in the course of travelling between the various Caribbean countries I witnessed the fusion of the two branches of the profession, viz, barristers and solicitors and the way the profession sought to regulate itself in so far as discipline was concerned.

Since fusion, which took place in the 1960s, all lawyers have been styled 'attorneys' and there have developed partnerships and law firms with various forms of appellation like James Henry & Co, John Doe and Associates, Richard Jones Law Firm, Mark Peters Law Offices, Equity House, Chancery Chambers, Integrity Chambers and Juris Chambers. There is no doubt that many law firms are organised as businesses – more like family businesses – usually two brothers, each with a son or daughter; or father, son and daughter; or father, mother and daughter; or father and daughter. There is a dominant concern over billable hours and 'the bottom-line' in all these offices and it is difficult for a visitor not to consider he or she is in a 'business place'.

At the same time, greater consciousness has developed of the need to act with probity and integrity, since disciplinary regimes have become stricter and more litigants are lodging complaints, as a result of which more lawyers are today being disciplined.[15] There are also codes of ethics which have the effect of making the lawyers more aware of their duties and responsibilities. But there is still more to be done to develop in the members of the profession a keener attitude of public service.

15 See Sir Fred Phillips, *The Evolving Legal Profession in the Commonwealth*, (Dobbs Ferry, NY, Oceana Publications Inc, 1978), Chapters 1 and 4.

In addition, the fact that almost all lawyers in the Caribbean tend to engage actively in politics does not help the profession to live up to the high ethical standards expected of it.

ENGLAND AND WALES

The profession is split into two: the barristers and the solicitors. The barristers are mainly advocates who argue cases in court. They operate as independent professionals from 'Chambers' on a referral basis – several barristers working separately with a clerk who channels work to them and who deals with the solicitors who 'instruct' the barristers.

The solicitors are the litigators who prepare 'the pleadings' and who until towards the end of the 20th century did not have rights of audience in the highest courts. They have traditionally been the conveyancers, but this conveyancing function is now shared with unqualified lawyers trained and certified as 'licensed conveyancers'. The solicitors may be regarded as constituting the business arm of the profession, since it is they who are responsible for the fees of the barristers they have 'instructed' and for negotiating with them via the barrister's clerk.

It should come as no surprise, therefore, that in an empirical study carried out in England in the 1990s, Galanter and Palay should observe: 'Our interviews with lawyers in large London solicitors firms elicited little sense of distress about the increasingly commercial character of law practice. Interviewees unself-consciously spoke of "the law business"' (Galanter and Palay, 1995). Solicitors in English law firms are permitted to enter into partnerships with one another and with such professionals as accountants. The firms have, like their counterparts in the US and Canada, continued to grow in size and to set up offices across international boundaries, taking advantage of business where it can be found. They are professional business entities.

The legal plans in operation in the US and Canada have not taken root in England – no doubt because legal aid (which has always been available) has filled the need.

Two great thinkers of the 20th century have suggested that, far from the law becoming a business, business should become a profession (Bowie, 1988). In Bowie's view the specialisation of lawyers and the growth of large law firms are necessary to meet the 'epistemological requirements of professionalism' and that 'if this makes law a business there is nothing morally objectionable'. It is the contention that when lawyers 'abandon altruistic motivation and become more like traditionally characteristic business persons' the profession should become uneasy. He ends his article thus:[16]

16 See Bowie, *op cit*, fn 1, p 759.

> To ignore the law's impact on the purpose of law, society's central values, and justice – primarily understood as equality before the law – is to abandon one's claim towards being a profession. Society should seek to make business a profession rather than to make law a business.

In similar vein, RH Tawney in 1920 in his *The Acquisitive Society* suggested that business should become a profession on the basis that such a transformation would uplift the morals and standards of business.

Even in the case of the prepaid legal services, those lawyers taking part have consistently contended that their altruism leads them to deal with their clients in exactly the same manner as lawyers in private practice deal with theirs. In other words, professionalism and commercialism work hand in hand.

All in all, one must accept the fact that it is present-day circumstances of economic and social life that have caused the nature and structure of practice to change in the way it has. On that account it is difficult to disagree with Stager that 'various social science disciplines have tended to overlook an important dimension in the study of certain professions such as medicine, dentistry, and law, viz, that these occupations, especially law are both a profession and a business'. (See Stager's useful work *Lawyers in Canada*, 1990, which provides helpful insights on this point.)

CONCLUSION

The literature has clearly revealed that there are many in the profession who cannot come to terms with the ever-growing tendency in our globalised world for lawyers to employ business methods in marketing their activities. Those traditional lawyers find it difficult to accept advertisements and legal plans. They condemn commercialism, competition, lack of civility, probity and collegiality and lack of public spiritedness. But is the position as bad as they make out? In noting the disillusionment of the traditionalist, what must be borne in mind is that we now live in an entirely different world from that which existed 40 or 50 years ago. The modalities of legal practice must take the international economic situation and the World Trade Organisation into account. The world is fast becoming a global village.

The effect of organisations such as NAFTA (to take one example) on the legal profession in Canada, for instance, has never been more forcefully and robustly put into proper perspective than in these words of Professor Harry Arthurs:[17]

> Continental economic integration has produced a number of changes in the structure of the Canadian legal profession. As foreign, especially American, transnational corporations manage more and more of their Canadian operations from headquarters abroad, certain kinds of legal work are affected. For example, prior to 1985, most Canadian subsidiaries of large foreign transnationals were listed on the Toronto Stock Exchange and their shares were held by Canadian investors; they had prestigious Boards of Directors; and they maintained a considerable cohort of Canadian executives. That situation changed considerably between 1985 and 1995.

17 See the article by Professor Harry Arthurs, 'Poor Canadian legal education: so near to Wall Street, so far from God' in *Osgoode Hall Law Journal*, Vol 38, Fall 2000, pp 396–97.

> As the vast majority of these firms were 'taken private' – converted into wholly-owned private companies – their shareholders were bought out and their Canadian boards were downsized or disbanded. The practices of Canadian lawyers who dealt with financing and related regulatory matters, and who served on corporate boards, were obviously affected. As foreign transnationals consolidated more and more of their executive functions at head offices, as the authority and autonomy of their Canadian subsidiaries eroded, further risks emerged for Canadian law firms who provided advice to Canadian head offices, executed strategies conceived in those offices or were in other ways nourished by the 'food-chain' which descended from them. Finally, the takeover of Canadian companies by foreign firms accelerated during the same period, partly as a result of the advent of continental free trade, partly as the result of restructuring in response to longstanding structural problems in the Canadian economy. Once again law firms were affected; in the short to middle term, they perhaps gained mergers and acquisition work; in the longer term, their client base seems destined to shrink. Finally, coinciding with these disturbing consequences of continental economic integration – some would say as a direct result of it – Canada experienced a relatively deep and long-lasting recession through the early and mid-1990s. While arguably some fields of corporate legal practice flourished during the recession and others declined, the overall effects were almost certainly negative.

As regards the law firms, according to Galanter and Palay,[18] the relationship of the large firms with ethics and professional responsibility was up until 1966 regarded as ambivalent when Jerome Carlin extolled their virtues in a book written in that year in relation to a study of the New York Bar.[19] The writers had this to say about those firms: 'In technical skill, collegiality and probity the large law firms seemed to provide a venue for the most elevated professionalism.' And they drew attention to the statement of Geoffrey Hazard in his introduction to Carlin's book that an independent general practice rendering personal service to clients was no longer the mark of identification of a truly professional lawyer. At the same time they felt obliged to expose the other side of the coin in this way: 'Coupled with this high regard is a long tradition of reproach of the large firm for abandoning the professional calling and becoming a mere business.'

In the course of obtaining material for writing this book I sent a questionnaire to 32 Commonwealth countries including the UK, Canada, Australia, New Zealand, countries in the Indian Ocean, Southern Africa, the Mediterranean, the Pacific and South Asia. One of the questions I posed was 'Is it your judgment that in the past 25 years lawyers have tended to involve themselves more in a business than a profession?'.

Of the 27 who responded, 24 answered the question in the affirmative.

My own researches have convinced me that, although there are exceptions, most members of the profession, while following business methods in their offices, have tended to observe professional standards and that the spirit of public service is still alive, although its members on balance will be bound to concede with Anthony Kronman that lawyers today 'are less public spirited and connected

18 See *op cit*, Chapter 1, fn 11, pp 189–90.

19 J Carlin, *Lawyer's Ethics – A Study of the New York City Bar* (NY, Russell Sage Foundation, 1966), pp 168–69.

to their past and more specialized and alienated from their work than they were a quarter century ago'.[20] They will not be able to avoid the indictment that the flourishing 'law firms and the individuals working with them (are) becoming more corporate, more specialist, more completely aware, and more oriented to economic activity'.[21]

The profession must in all this maelstrom keep its eye steadfastly on the altruism ball. In our next chapter we shall try to suggest how best this can be achieved.

20 See Anthony Kronman's 'The law as a profession' in Deborah Rhode's *Ethics in Practice* (Oxford, OUP, 2000), p 38.

21 EH Greenbaum, 'Development of law firm training programs: coping with a turbulent environment' *International Journal of the Legal Profession*, Vol 3:3, 1996, 315 at p 322.

CHAPTER 3

ACCESS TO JUSTICE

FUNDAMENTAL OBSTACLE

> Before the Law stands a doorkeeper. To this doorkeeper there comes a man from the country and prays for admittance to the Law. But the doorkeeper says that he cannot grant admittance at the moment. The man thinks it over and then asks if he will be allowed in later. 'It is possible,' says the doorkeeper, 'but not at the moment.' Since the gate stands open, as usual, and the doorkeeper steps to one side, the man stoops to peer through the gateway into the interior. Observing that, the doorkeeper laughs and says, 'If you are so drawn to it, just try to go in despite my veto. But take note: I am powerful. And I am only the least of the doorkeepers. From hall to hall there is one doorkeeper after another, each more terrible than the last. The third doorkeeper is already so terrible that even I cannot bear to look at him'. These are difficulties the man from the country had not expected; the Law, he thinks, should surely be accessible at all times and to everyone.

This parable is cited by David Luban at p 236 of his famous treatise *Lawyers and Justice* (already alluded to). In a chapter in another monograph entitled 'Speculating on justice: the ethics and jurisprudence of contingency fees',[1] Luban identifies the man from the country as the poor litigant knocking at the door of justice in a dying state coming face-to-face with the first doorkeeper – the fees of the lawyer. Luban may well have added that the two inner sentinels are nothing if not the various forms of procedural and other delays the hapless litigant is sure still to encounter: the statements of claim, defences, replies and rebuttals which are to bedevil him on his lonely way to the seat of justice.

CONSTITUTIONAL DEVELOPMENT

This chapter attempts to explore some practical steps the applicant for access may take on the way to justice – taking as our point of departure the turbulent developments which have manifested themselves on a global basis at the end of the 20th century and the beginning of the 21st century in the matter of providing access to justice.

Shortly after World War II there was the Universal Declaration of Rights, which came into effect in 1953 – although it had been adopted and proclaimed by the United Nations General Assembly on 10 December 1948. Under that Declaration, the United Kingdom undertook an obligation to promote and respect human rights and fundamental freedoms – access to the courts being embraced by a number of these freedoms. In due course this obligation found its way into the written constitutions of not only newly-independent states after World War II but even into constitutions of most of the few remaining overseas dependent

---

1 S Parker and C Sampford (eds), *Legal Ethics and Legal Practice* (Oxford, Clarendon Press, 1995), p 89.

territories. As a result, all the new constitutions are declared or deemed to be 'the supreme law' of the countries to which they relate and jurisdiction has accordingly been conferred on the courts to determine questions relating to the interpretation of the constitutions and to grant redress, by way of declarations, orders, writs and directions in any case in which a person alleges that any of the protective provisions has been, is being, or is likely to be, contravened in relation to him. The result is that in so far as the Caribbean regime is concerned, a formidable jurisdiction has developed by virtue of this access to the courts. The Canadian Charter of Rights enshrined in their patriated Constitution of 1982 (this being one of the latest) has had the same effect in Canada.

In England the European Convention on Human Rights became enshrined into English law by the Human Rights Act of 1998, which became effective in October 2000. This Act gives the courts the power to declare legislative provisions 'incompatible' with Convention rights and provides the executive an opportunity to rectify any defect. The English invented this procedure so that the judge would not be perceived as going outside his turf in declaring legislative acts unconstitutional and void. The device thus preserves the concept of the sovereignty of Parliament while enhancing judicial law-making and sending a message to the public that the judges must not be politicised. It is very English but on the evidence of the last four years it has worked.

THE WORLD ECONOMIC ORDER CHANGES

Not only has the constitutional situation in the world changed noticeably, so has the new economic order. Services which, previous to the second half of the 20th century, were regarded as municipal have become international. The World Trade Organisation (WTO) has made competition – including that for legal services – the name of the game. Thatcherism in the UK and Reaganism in the US have, at the same time as Europe has been undergoing economic revolution, changed the international economic landscape. All this occurred in the last 25 years of the 20th century, when England happened to have as the Head of the legal establishment two Scottish Lord Chancellors – Lords MacKay and Irvine – who were ultra-reformist in outlook. It should also be said that the English judiciary has at the same time been blessed with some distinguished leaders anxious to remove the obstacles to justice for all. The assumption of Tony Blair to office as British Prime Minister in the last decade of the last century also assisted the reforms in no small measure.

In 1998 the New Labour Government published a White Paper[2] outlining plans for reforming legal services and the courts in a way which would build on what had already begun under the Conservative administrations of Margaret Thatcher and John Major – with Lord MacKay as Lord Chancellor.

2 Cm 4155, *Modernising Justice.*

In his Foreword to the White Paper, the former Lord Chancellor Irvine emphasised the need for ready access by citizens to the justice system – to information about their legal rights and their being in a position to resolve disputes and to enforce their rights through the courts at a cost that is predictable and proportionate to the issue at stake. 'The justice system,' he insisted, 'should serve everyone regardless of their means. People should be able to find effective solutions to their legal problems. Justice must not be restricted to the very wealthy who can well afford high legal fees, or to the very poor who may qualify for legal aid.' The Lord Chancellor promised that the reforms would 'remove old-fashioned restrictive practices that only benefit lawyers and focus the courts on serving the public'. In his view, the proposed Community Legal Service would revolutionise ordinary people's access to information about their rights and provide new avenues to good quality legal services, and 'as part of the community legal service, legal aid service spending would be refocused on the people and cases where it is most needed and can do most good'. He promised modern ways of funding litigation through a regime of 'no win, no fee' agreements as well as a new 'fast-track' system in the courts, leading up to fixed-costs hearings which will give access to citizens who do not happen to qualify for legal aid and who dare not attempt to embark on litigation on their own because of the unpredictable cost involved.

In July 1999 the Labour Government passed into law the Access to Justice Act (the Act), in respect of which the long title was:

> An Act to establish the Legal Services Commission, the Community Legal Service and the Criminal Defence Service; to amend the law of legal aid in Scotland; to make further provision about legal services; to make provision about appeal courts, judges and court proceedings; to amend the law about magistrates and magistrate courts; and to make provision about immunity from action and costs and indemnities for certain officials exercising judicial functions.[3]

The Act made the expected provision for a Legal Service Commission (s 1(1)) comprising between seven and 12 members (s 1(3)) with power to establish, maintain and develop the Community Legal Service (s 4(1)); to promote and help in providing general information about the law and the giving of advice as to how the law applies in particular circumstances; to prevent or settle or otherwise resolve disputes about legal rights and duties; to enforce relations by which such disputes are resolved; and to deal with legal proceedings not connected with disputes (s 4(2)).

The Commission is also charged with establishing and maintaining a Community Legal Service Fund (s 5(1)) into which the Lord Chancellor would pay appropriate funds for the funding of services as part of the Community Legal Service that may decide the manner in which and the terms at which the sums are to be paid to the Commission by the Lord Chancellor (s 5(2)).

3 (1999 Cap 22) 27 July.

While all this was taking place at the legislative level, Lord Woolf (the Lord Chief Justice) at the level of the judiciary was busy with other senior judges and senior law officials streamlining the Civil Procedure Rules (CPR) governing the operation of the courts, which were designed to make them more user-friendly while ensuring that the judges 'case-manage' trials to prevent excessive delay with consequential added cost.

THE EFFECT OF THE LEGISLATIVE CHANGES

What then is likely to be the effect of the new legislation and the new Civil Procedure Rules (CPR) on access to justice? The new Community Legal Service Fund is expected to be more flexible and adaptable than legal aid. The service will be achieved largely by contracting out the task of giving effect to specific priorities. Standards will be set and fixed costs arranged on a competitive basis. The new funding assessment will ensure that within each category of case, funding will go to the individuals who need it most.

The scope of the funding will also be widened by refocusing existing spending on types of service not previously available. Thus, the Legal Aid Board was asked to be innovative in developing new ways of delivering information advice and assistance – suggested areas being more use of the internet, digital television, telephone information with advice lines and mobile outreach systems to people in remote areas as well as funding mediation in appropriate civil and family law matters. The crucial point is that lawyers should not be the main beneficiaries from the legal aid funding arrangements and should not have the right (which they had before) of deciding how and where the money is to be spent.

WHAT CHANGES HAVE TAKEN PLACE WITH LEGAL AID OVERSEAS?

In the second half of the 20th century, legal aid came to be accommodated by legislation in most newly-independent Commonwealth countries. A study of seven of these territories has revealed a quite surprising similarity in the terms of the Acts.[4] They all set out the authority to administer legal aid and a list of the civil and criminal matters to be covered; the conditions under which a legal aid certificate would be granted (and this includes how the application should be made) and the level of 'disposable capital' and 'disposable income' (woefully small) required as a prerequisite to the grant of a certificate; the power of the Director of Legal Aid to make enquiries about the authenticity of the data which should be forwarded by applicants; what contributions should be paid by aided persons; how counsel are to be remunerated and at what rates; how they are to be assigned; the fact the court may order a deposit by the applicant of out-of-pocket

4 Community Legal Service Act Ch 112A (Barbados); Legal Aid Act No 36 of 1997 (Jamaica); Act No 25 of 1976 (Trinidad and Tobago); Legal Aid Act No 26 of 1971 (Malaysia); Legal Aid & Advice Act (Cap 160) (Singapore); Legal Aid Act 1967 (South Africa); Legal Act Law No 27 of 1978 (Sri Lanka).

expenses; the fact that the court may order payment of costs by aided persons in certain circumstances; and the fact that costs due to an aided person must be paid to the Director of Legal Aid.

The Acts are long on verbiage but when one studies them carefully one realises that the bureaucratic arrangements are such that those persons who qualify are truly indigent individuals. In other words, only a fraction of deserving people do benefit from legal aid.

The only respect in which all the countries differ is in the way they variously describe the authority responsible for administering the legal aid. In Barbados it is the Community Legal Services Commission; in Trinidad the Legal Aid and Advisory Authority; in Jamaica the Legal Aid Council; in Singapore the Legal Aid Bureau; in South Africa the Legal Aid Board; and in Sri Lanka the Legal Aid Commission. It would provide an interesting exercise to study how much aid is disbursed by each of these grandiosely-named bodies, but it is clear that a country like Jamaica would be quite unable to provide the level of aid granted by South Africa, or by Singapore, which indeed seems to take the matter seriously. For instance, the Law Society of that country provides for assistance to the public in non-capital criminal matters by way of volunteer lawyers under their Criminal Legal Aid Scheme, s 38(1)(g) of the Legal Profession Act (Cap 161) providing that 'the purposes of the society (are) ... to make provision for or to assist in the promotion of a scheme whereby impecunious persons on non-capital charges are represented by advocates'. In that country, too, in capital cases before the High Court and the Court of Appeal, it is the practice of the Supreme Court to assign two lawyers to represent each accused person.

Much therefore depends upon the economy of the country in which access to justice is sought. In Bermuda, with a prosperous economy and a high standard of living, the Government is prepared at present to spend between US$500,000 and $600,000 annually on legal aid under the provisions of the Legal Aid Act 1980 (Title 8 Item 37).

In the Cayman Islands, the Poor Persons (Legal Aid) Law makes provision for legal aid, but in addition to the Government's allocation, the Chief Justice (with the assistance of a Committee) has been contemplating a new scheme under which funds would be provided from lawyers clients' accounts, the interest on which would be used with the approval of the clients for legal aid. In the Cayman Islands, the court does provide assistance in matrimonial and custody matters where the welfare of the child so requires. Assistance is also forthcoming in civil cases where it appears to the court that the claim is meritorious, subject to the costs being recovered from any award of costs to the successful legally-aided person.

In the British Virgin Islands, the Bar Association has displayed commendable public spiritedness in entering into a Memorandum of Understanding with the Government dated 28 December 2000, under which the Government provides the funds and works in close partnership with the legal profession in establishing a legal aid scheme including legal advice, assistance and representation to those persons who might otherwise be unable to obtain such facilities because of their limited financial means. The scheme is administered by a Government Department under the Ministry of Health and Welfare through a five-member Board including the Registrar of the High Court, the Chief Social Development Officer, two attorneys-at-law appointed by the Bar Association and a member of the public to be agreed by the Government and the Bar Association. The scheme covers criminal cases triable on indictment; complex criminal cases triable summarily; domestic violence issues; affiliation proceedings; and juvenile matters as well as matrimonial matters.

The Bar Association provides the Registrar of the High Court with a list of lawyers chosen from various law firms to be selected on a rotational basis – their services to be provided at nominal rates to be agreed between the Government and the Bar Association.

This is an experiment which the Bar Associations in more Caribbean countries might be disposed to follow and to which they should be able in their respective jurisdictions to contribute in a material way. Already there are small voluntary Legal Aid Clinics in various territories and it is hoped that local Bar Associations will do more to expand and develop them.

Meantime, the Organisation of Commonwealth Caribbean Bar Associations (OCCBA) has not been idle in promoting the cause of access to justice. For some time the matter has arisen at their annual meetings, but in August 2002 the body passed what was described as 'The St Kitts and Nevis Declaration on Access to Justice'. In that document, the OCCBA affirmed the importance of improving access to justice in the region and throughout the world; expressed its view that 'there ought to be equal access to justice for all persons, but that far too many persons appear in the courts in serious criminal and civil matters without legal representations'; noted that some governments of the region still have no or no effective arrangements for legal aid, nor do they accord it sufficient priority, funding or scope; and re-affirmed the OCCBA's commitment to *pro bono* work and to encouraging and carrying out projects to improve access to justice.

The Declaration resolved not only that it is unacceptable for any government to have no legal aid system at all, but that it is untenable that governments should limit legal aid only to capital criminal cases. It urged that aid should be extended 'to all serious criminal offences and all civil cases involving child support, custody of children, constitutional redress, judicial review or claiming relief from or compensation for governmental or official abuse of power'.

HOW LACK OF RESOURCES OBSTRUCTS

The powers that be are gradually coming to regard access to the courts as a constitutional right[5] which is only capable of abrogation by express parliamentary

5 See *R v Lord Chancellor ex p Witham* [1997] 2 All ER 779.

enactment; and, as has been asserted by Boon and Levin, 'promoting access to justice and the courts is arguably the distinctive purposes of the legal profession'. It is therefore ironic that it is lawyers' fees and court costs which should operate as the greatest bar to having disputes adjudicated in the courts or other tribunals.

In complicated civil suits, it is always difficult to predict the course that the proceedings will take at the pre-trial stage and the client is often bemused at the multiplicity of interrogatory mini-trials which takes place in 'Chambers' behind closed doors and at the number of affidavits being exchanged. It is difficult for a lawyer in a complicated case to state how long the pre-trial stage is likely to last, since the matter is not entirely in his hands: he must reply to the enquiries and misstatements of his opponent and it may be necessary to do research before replying. Nor can counsel tell how many adjournments opposing counsel will request and how many would be granted. It is of course true that the procedural reforms proposed since 1999 by Lord Woolf have begun to make themselves felt everywhere they have been adopted. Even under the new regime, cases can sometimes take an inordinately long time to come to trial, and the client meanwhile will be paying 'refreshers' to his lawyer for the work done at the pre-trial stage.

The client may recover some or all of these costs if his case succeeds, but even when successful, he may not be awarded costs or he may receive only a fraction of those costs. If the case is lost, he will more than likely recover nothing at all by way of costs, which means he may be called upon to pay both his own costs and those of his opponent. If he is aggrieved by a decision of the chamber judge in the interlocutory stage and wishes to appeal a ruling, the client will find himself saddled with more costs. But, to make matters worse, there are times when lawyers create extra fees for themselves by raising unnecessary interrogatories and the unsuspecting litigant is none the wiser!

FEE STRUCTURE

In all this how does a lawyer arrive at the level of his fees? As far as the Bar in England is concerned, the Bar Council Code cannot be less forthcoming. All r 405 of the Code states is that:

> A barrister in independent practice may charge for any work undertaken by him (whether or not it involves an appearance in Court) on any basis or by any method he thinks fit, provided that such basis or method:
>
> (a) is permitted by law; and
>
> (b) does not involve the payment of a wage or salary.

As regards solicitors, r 57(1) of the Guide to the Professional Conduct of Solicitors (hereafter referred to as 'the LSG') requires an agreement in writing (sub-s (1)) and this agreement must provide for payment of a gross sum, an hourly rate, a commission or percentage, a salary or otherwise and such agreement should stipulate that the quantum of remuneration is not inclusive of any disbursement made by the solicitor in respect of searches, plans, travelling, fees or other matters (sub-s (2)). The agreement must be in writing signed by the person to be bound or his agent (sub-s (3)).

Chapter 14.01 of the LSG lays down that the client in contentious matters is required to make payments on account of costs and disbursements whereas in non-contentious matters the solicitor may require advances on account of disbursements only, unless another arrangement is made with the client. In either case, the solicitor must warn the client that the final costs 'may be greater than the sum paid in advance' and the funds must be placed in a clients' account pending submission of a bill or interim bill or written notification of costs.

CONTINGENCY FEES

Contingency fees are permitted in the US and in all the provinces in Canada. We shall later examine the position in certain newly-independent countries in the common law world. But first let us see what the position is in England where recent legislation, although recognising conditional fees, frown upon contingency fees, which are not recognised except as permitted by the common law. The case of *Thai Trading Co (A Firm) v Taylor* [1998] 2 WLR 893 does permit a solicitor to enter into an agreement under which he may recover his profit costs in a successful suit in certain non-criminal matters such as personal injury, company winding-up or bankruptcy proceedings, and actions before the European Court of Human Rights (s 58 of the Courts and Legal Services Act (CLSA) 1990). Fees are otherwise paid on either a fixed or hourly basis to both barristers and solicitors. However, although s 61 of the CLSA 1990 permits barristers to enter into contracts, the Bar Council is given permission to make rules accepting or rejecting the arrangement. The Council has passed legislation rejecting it.

David Luban sees no difference between contingency fees and conditional fees. He considers them both as speculative. The conditional fee involves speculation with a fee uplift (ie, an agreed premium – usually 10% – added to the normal fee paid in case of success 'to compensate the lawyer for the risk of not being paid in the event of failure'). A contingency percentage fee is, according to Luban, simply the American version of the contingency fee: 'a lawyer retains an agreed-upon percentage of the client's recovery and is paid nothing if the action is unsuccessful.' In this model the percentage can be anything from 40 to 50% representing much more than the lawyer would have been paid if he had charged on an hourly or daily basis. As Luban puts it: 'Technically, then, the percentage contingency fee is simply one species of a conditional fee – the species in which the fee uplift is calculated as a percentage of the res rather than a percentage of the normal attorney's fee.'[6] A similar argument has been made by Michael Zander in these terms:[7]

6 See David Luban, 'Speculating on justice: the ethics and jurisprudence of contingency fees in legal ethics and legal practice', *op cit*, fn 1, p 91.

7 See Michael Zander's article entitled 'If conditional fees, why not contingency fees?' in *New Law Journal*, Vol 152, 2002, pp 747–48.

> The crucial preliminary point is that both conditional fees (CFAs) and contingency fees (CYFs) make the fee dependent on the outcome. So the classic objections to contingency fees apply to both. Public policy does not today condemn a lawyer who conducts a case on the basis that he will be paid if he wins but not if he loses. That is the very essence of CFAs under the Courts and Legal Services Act, s 58 and the Conditional Fee Agreement Regulations 2000 (SI 2000/69). Objections to CYFs founded on this consideration are therefore now outmoded.

Zander also points out that CFAs have 'a serious and perverse incentive for lawyers to increase their costs (whether by conscious or unconscious padding or doing more work) in order to increase the success fee'. In contrast CYFs carry a cap on the proportion of the damages that the lawyer can charge by way of fees.

CANADIAN COURTS LEAD THE WAY

In the 13 Canadian provinces and territories, there are several Canadian decisions worthy of study, on the alleged benefits of contingency fees (properly controlled) in helping to facilitate the entry of persons of modest means into the hallowed halls of justice. But these decisions must be considered against the backdrop of existing disciplinary sanctions when lawyers get out of step with good principles.

David Luban's writings on this subject are expansive and deserve study. In his seminal work *Lawyers and Justice*, to which reference has already been made,[8] Luban makes the statement that surveys of legal aid worldwide have not assisted the poor it is intended to assist. Indeed, he contends that they have borne testimony to the inadequacy and inefficiencies of legal aid programmes and sarcastically remarks that the state has conferred 'the advantages of the legal system on those who can afford to use it and built it on the backs of those who cannot'. He continues: 'The state has not been an innocent bystander observing the regrettable spectacle of economic inequality and poverty: it shares primary responsibility with the legal profession (and its well-off clients) for the fact that the poor have no meaningful access to justice and are made worse off by that fact.'

The leading Canadian cases have also paid special attention to persons of moderate means. Before referring to those cases, however, we will, by way of comparison, examine four of the arguments deployed in England against contingency fees.

First, it is argued that these fees have been employed with very deleterious effects in the US – the so called *argumentum ad Americanum*. It is said that because of the litigious tendencies of Americans, manufacturers are sometimes constrained to cease their operations as a result of being so often sued for one tortious act after another, because of the availability of contingency fees. It is also contended that doctors are compelled to increase the cost of healthcare as a result of malpractice suits, which have the effect of causing their insurance coverage to become higher and higher.

---

8 David Luban, *Lawyers and Justice: An Ethical Study* (Princeton, NJ, Princeton University Press, 1988).

The third argument is that contingency fees conduce to unethical practices by members of the legal profession. This was in fact an argument strongly put to the Benson Commission on Legal Services which persuaded the Commission to advise firmly against the introduction of contingency fees in Britain:[9]

> The fact that the lawyer has a direct interest in the outcome of the case may lead to undesirable practices, including the construction of evidence, the improper coaching of witnesses, the use of professionally partisan expert witnesses, especially medical witnesses, improper examination and cross-examination, groundless legal arguments designed to lead the courts into error and competitive touting.

There is a fourth argument against contingency fees which has been put forward by Lord Denning in his book, *What's Next in the Law*.[10] In that work Lord Denning tells of a Portuguese citizen who was employed by a motor vessel, owned by a company in Texas (US), which was engaged in North Sea operations. While the boat was at anchor at Great Yarmouth in Norfolk and the crew member (the plaintiff) was transferring oil from a drum to a tank, via a pump with compressed air, a valve was disconnected and lodged in his neck, penetrating his spinal cord and causing him complete paralysis in his arms and legs, which rendered him helpless and reduced his quality of life dramatically. The case is *Castanho v Brown and Root* (UK) [1981] AC 557. Lord Denning tells how his employers were willing to settle for £200,000 and costs which 'would be ample compensation by English standards, and also by Portuguese standards'.

Lord Denning then recounted how at that stage 'a firm of solicitors from Texas came on the scene. They went over to Portugal and persuaded the man to drop the English proceedings and get the litigation to Texas'. The English trial judge, however, would have none of this. He was, however, overruled by the Court of Appeal, a course that was endorsed by the House of Lords.

The result: the courts in Texas awarded the man £1,500,000 of which the man received £800,000, the remaining of £700,000 going to the lawyers as contingency fees.

Lord Denning ended his commentary on this case thus: 'That case has a lesson for us in England. Never, never allow lawyers to work on the basis of a "contingency fee".'

He considered it a matter of regret that a man so severely injured should in the American courts receive four times the compensation he would have received in the English courts. It would seem that in a globalised world what the English courts should do is to consider awarding more realistic damages if the clamour for contingency fees is not to become louder. In any event, it is only a question of time before they become a reality.

9 Cmnd 7648, 1979, para 16.4, p 177.
10 Denning (Lord) (London, Butterworths, 1982), pp 105–06.

Many Commonwealth countries do enshrine in their professional legal codes a prohibition against contingency fees in rather summary terms. The following Barbados stricture represents a prototype of a clause found in the Legal Profession Codes in almost every Caribbean territory: 'An attorney-at-law shall not acquire directly or indirectly by purchase or otherwise a financial or other interest in the subject-matter of a case which he is conducting.'[11]

In the Singapore Legal Profession (Professional Conduct) Rules, the prohibition is couched in these words:

> An advocate and solicitor shall not enter into negotiations with a client:
>
> (a) for an interest in the subject-matter of litigation; or
>
> (b) except to the extent permitted by any scale of costs which may be applicable, for remuneration proportionate to the amount which may be recovered by the client in the proceedings.

The prohibition is reinforced by s 107(1)(b) of the Singapore Legal Profession Act (Cap 161), which provides: 'No solicitor shall enter into any agreement by which he is retained or employed to prosecute any suit or action or other contentious proceeding which stipulates for or contemplates payment only in the event of success in that suit, action or proceeding.'

This provision seems to debar even conditional fees – the 'no win, no fee' arrangement.

Are the prohibitions laid down in these emergent countries justifiable?

It is true that contingency fees properly controlled may enable litigants who cannot meet lawyers' fees to obtain access to justice. The Canadian experience where contingency fees now exist in all the country's provincial and territorial jurisdictions would seem to support such an approach. But one must carefully weigh that apparent advantage against the dangers of trafficking in litigation. A study of these dangers undertaken by personal interviews over the past few years with medical consultants as well as lawyers has convinced me that contingency fees must be introduced with caution.

In the course of this study two medical specialists currently practising in Florida who previously practised in another state were interviewed – a cardiologist and a neonatalogist. These specialists consider that now that doctors are permitted to advertise – and do advertise aggressively on radio and television in particular – malpractice litigation by legal firms specialising in that activity has become a thriving growth industry. The lawyers concerned in Florida in their advertisements place considerable emphasis on the fact that the patient will lose nothing by suing a specialist and potentially stands to gain considerable damages – both for personal injury and for pain and suffering. (In California the limit for the latter is $250,000, but legislation recently passed in Florida has capped the limit at $500,000.)

11 See r 64 of the Barbados Legal Profession Code of Ethics 1988 (LRO 1989 E 14).

There can be no doubt that the main beneficiaries of most malpractice suits are the lawyers who specialise in that industry. The result is that unreasonably high damages are claimed and awarded. This in turn causes exorbitant increase in insurance premiums with consequential increased fees.

But according to the doctors themselves, the relation between doctor and patient is affected adversely. The doctor tends to become suspicious of the patient and often ceases to treat him. When he does treat the patient, his fear of being sued leads him often to carry out redundant tests and other investigations, out of the abundance of caution. The doctors complain also that the 'experts' who are called by both sides are often failed clinicians operating as 'hired guns' in a partisan way instead of in a scientific and objective manner.

WHAT ARE THE ARGUMENTS IN FAVOUR OF CONTINGENCY FEES?

One negative argument has already been mentioned, viz, that the argument against contingency fee should apply equally to contingent fees since they are both speculative. A second argument in favour is that in Canada, where contingency fees are employed in all the country's provincial and other jurisdictions, the results have not been deleterious. Indeed in a recent case which came before the courts in Ontario (the last Canadian province to sanction such fees),[12] the presiding judge drew attention to the fact that in a Report by the Canadian Bar Association on the Implementation of Contingency Fees in the Province (15 March 1988), it was stated that the fears of the public were more illusory than real. Here is what the judge said in full:

> Perhaps the major concrete fact that this province has to deal with is that all the other Provinces and Territories in Canada permit contingency fee contracts in varying forms and with varying controls. Their experience would certainly seem to indicate that many of the fears and concerns that gave rise to the original prohibition of contingency fees in Canada are unrealistic in terms of modern society and the practice in terms of modern Canadian society and the practice of law in that society.

The idea of deploying contingency fees has been judicially articulated by Cory J in the Canadian Supreme Court in the case of *Coronation Insurance Co v Florence* [1994] SCJ No 116 (QL) at para 14:

> The concept of contingency fees is well established in the United States although it is a recent arrival in Canada. It's [*sic*] aim is to make court proceedings available to people who could not otherwise afford to have their legal rights determined. This is indeed a commendable goal that should be encouraged ...

Truly legislation can only be undertaken by the very rich or the legally-aided. Legal rights are illusory and no more than a source of frustration if they cannot be recognised and enforced. This suggests that a flexible approach should be taken to problems arising from contingency fee arrangements, if only to facilitate access to

12 Contingency fees were accepted in Ontario in 2002, although up to the time of writing they have not yet been formally proclaimed as being in force.

the courts for more Canadians. Anything less will be to preserve the courts' facilities in civil matters for the wealthy and powerful.

It is interesting that by the end of the 20th century even the English courts had begun to consider a contemporary approach to the question of contingency fees between solicitors and their clients. In *Giles v Thompson* [1993] 3 All ER 321, Lord Mustill in the House of Lords had occasion to examine this matter. He considered that the historical purpose of maintenance and champerty was to control those who trafficked in litigation and that there was now a need to adapt the law to changed circumstances; that the law of champerty preventing contingency fees for solicitors 'survives nowadays, so far as it survives at all, largely as a rule of professional conduct'. In his view, when a court wishes today to consider whether a proposed contingency arrangement is offensive, it must examine two questions:

(a) does the transaction bear the marks of unlawful champerty; and

(b) is the contract validated by the existence of a legitimate interest in the person supporting the action distinct from the benefit he seeks to derive from it?

Put another way:

(a) Is there present in the proposed contingency arrangement the element of officious intermeddling for an improper motive?

(b) Is there a legitimate policy reason for allowing the contingency agreement to be recognised and enforced by the court?

We have already shown that legal aid in poor countries is poorly funded. Their governments give it low priority – especially when times are hard and some jurisdictions are experiencing balance of payment problems. But despite these facts, Bar Associations and governments should, before deciding to embrace contingency fees, ask themselves the questions posed in the preceding paragraph. The fees should be adopted so long as there are satisfactory answers to the above inquiries.

THE FUTURE OF ACCESS TO JUSTICE IN THE CASE OF HARD-PRESSED GOVERNMENTS

In most of these countries, the legal profession continues to urge that steps be taken to enable people to have their rights adjudicated with help from the public purse where they are financially unable to achieve this right on their own. As I have already indicated, such a request does not normally resonate with a hard-pressed government. But it is the business of governments to seek to attend to the welfare of its citizens. On this account, one can only hope that the Bar Associations will continue to press and suggest appropriate remedies.

It is therefore encouraging that the OCCBA at its Annual Meeting held in Basseterre, St Kitts in August 2002 was prepared to make the statement to which reference has already been made earlier in this chapter on the matter of access to justice.

A Declaration of this nature by such a responsible body is worthy of special commendation. But because of the parlous state of the economy in most jurisdictions in this region, it should be followed by some concrete and workable proposal. Indeed, I am satisfied that only a minority of our legal practitioners, faced with such a proposition, may wish to ask themselves the proverbial question: 'Am I my brother's keeper?' But in the interest of humanity, I think it is time all our lawyers develop an ethic of care – an ethic of altruism to which I referred at the end of Chapter 2.

In each territory a Legal Aid Fund should be established to which governments and the private sector could make an annual contribution, along with the profession's contribution to be channelled through the Law Association. The Fund should be administered by a Board on which government, the profession and private sector should be represented. From the Fund, both the poor and people of moderate means should be eligible for aid in serious criminal cases as well as civil matters on a basis to be decided by the respective Boards.

Commitment to legal aid should not be the profession's only contribution. Every practising barrister should, as a condition of receiving his annual Practising Certificate, be required to give at least 40 hours a year to the public on a *pro bono* basis. If the practitioner so prefers, he should contribute to the Legal Aid Fund the annual amount equivalent to the total fee he would have received by charging his usual hourly fee. It is worth noting that in 2000 over 500 barristers in England were engaged in *pro bono* work from death row appeals in criminal cases where aid has been refused.

CONCLUDING COMMENTS

We have in this chapter made an attempt to consider some steps an aggrieved person might take to attain access to justice. Each person needs a solution to his particular legal problems. In the Lord Chancellor's 1998 White Paper (to which we referred at the beginning) it was stated that while some of the solutions would be found by a resort to the courts, in others the litigant would not need such resort. 'Someone charged with a criminal offence should have access to proper legal advice and representation where the interest of justice requires it.'[13] Hence the establishment of a Criminal Defence Service which has been reviewed. As far as civil cases are concerned, it was emphasised that going to court should be the last resort as we will examine when in Chapter 11 we discuss alternative dispute resolution.

Finally, when we think of access to justice, one striking American case immediately comes to mind. It is the case of *Gideon v Wainwright* (1963) 372 US 335; 83 S Ct 792; 9L Ed 799, otherwise known as 'Gideon's Case'. This was a landmark decision taken in 1963 by the US Supreme Court in which a man charged with a felony of house-breaking and larceny appeared in person in court, pleaded not guilty and was convicted. He was sentenced to a long term of

13 See White Paper, *Modernising Justice*, Cmd 4155, referred to at fn 2, *supra*, p 7.

imprisonment. His appeal was dismissed. In desperation he wrote in pencil to the US Supreme Court who assigned counsel to him, the lawyer selected being Abe Fortas, a distinguished and experienced practitioner.

Not only did he succeed in getting the Supreme Court to reverse the lower courts and quash the conviction but Abe Fortas was able to persuade the Court that a right to appointed counsel existed in every case in which the defendant is unable to afford counsel if such defendant is charged with a felony. In 1972, the Supreme Court extended this finding in the case of *Argersinger v Hamlin* (1972) 407 US 25; 95 S Ct 2006; 32 L Ed 2d 530, where it was held that a similar right to counsel existed in a case which is a misdemeanour for which a penalty of imprisonment can be imposed. This right has also been extended to juvenile delinquency proceedings In *Re Gault* (1967) 387 US 1; 87 S Ct 1428; 14 L Ed 2d 527.

Whenever we think of access to justice, we should exalt this case as a triumph and a beacon of altruism. Anthony Lewis, a lawyer-turned-journalist, has written a moving account of the history of this case[14] and *Gideon's Trumpet* should be on the bookshelves of every lawyer as a reminder of the oath to which all members of the profession have subscribed to support the cause of justice.

In the next chapter, our purpose is to deal with the new approach to lawyers' accountability in the discharge of their functions.

14 *Gideon's Trumpet* (New York, Vintage Books, 1964).

CHAPTER 4

IMMUNITY FROM SUIT

We live in an era when the public has been casting an enquiring eye on lawyers and the legal profession. The reverence with which lawyers were once held has dissipated. They do not seem to observe that in the eyes of the public their stocks are sinking lower and lower, as a result of which they simply continue in the even tenor of their way. Many of these professionals become increasingly lax in dealing with their clients' affairs, their main goal being to make as much money as possible in as little time as possible.

One has only to read some of the works of distinguished writers on the legal profession to get a picture of present-day attitudes in the legal profession. I commend to my readers in this connection the following three works:

- *Rascals: The Selling of the Legal Profession* by Peter Megargee Brown;
- *Lawyering at the End of the Twentieth Century: The Betrayed Profession* by Sol M Linowitz with Martin Mayer; and
- *The Lost Lawyer: Failing Ideals of the Legal Profession* by Anthony T Kronman.

This chapter has two purposes. The first is to see the basis on which immunity from suit in matters of negligence by members of the profession has changed in the developed countries. The second is to examine the 'time warp' into which the developing countries have been caught in dealing with the problem, having made statutory provision for the immunity of advocates at a time when it existed at common law in England, Australia and New Zealand. Sadly, the latest decision on the issue by the House of Lords (*Hall v Simons* [2000] 3 All ER 674) has now left them behind and, since it is not vote-catching for governments to make the necessary amendment to the respective statutes, they are likely to remain behind, especially as it is not in the interest of the practising profession that it be deprived of an immunity it once held so dear.

RONDEL v WORSLEY

We shall now address the first case on the subject: *Rondel v Worsley* [1967] 3 All ER 993.

The appellant stood trial at the Old Bailey in 1959 on an indictment for wounding one Manning with intent. He was defended on a dock brief by the respondent and was convicted. At the trial it emerged that the appellant had seriously wounded Manning. However, the appellant (as defendant) pleaded self-defence, although he did not suffer a single scratch and there was no evidence to support such a defence. Despite that, the appellant wished his counsel to call witnesses to prove that Manning's injuries were inflicted by his (the appellant's) hands and his teeth, and not by a knife; that the appellant was in the employ of a Mr Rachman; that when the wounding occurred the appellant was on Mr Rachman's premises in the course of his employment; and that he was not in the habit of using a knife. Significantly, during a hearing in chambers, the appellant, in reply to an enquiry from a judge about the way he inflicted the injuries, had replied: 'I tore M's hand in half and bit off part of his ear.' When the same judge asked him whether he thought calling the specific witnesses would have resulted in his acquittal, he replied in the negative. Nevertheless, he illogically contended that it was because of the failure to call them that he was convicted.

These facts notwithstanding, the appellant brought proceedings in negligence against the respondent six years after his conviction and long after he had served his sentence. The matter was considered by a strong Court of Appeal – Lord Denning MR, Danckwerts and Salmon LJJ – who dismissed the appeal from the order of Lawton J that the claim against the respondent be struck out as disclosing no reasonable cause of action and because there was nothing on the facts before the court to establish professional negligence or lack of skill on counsel's part.

The appellant, without legal aid, appealed to the House of Lords. Before their Lordships the argument was directed to the general question of liability and ranged far and wide. Why should barristers be immune from suit when all other professionals, including solicitors, are liable to suit if loss is caused to their clients? It was urged that for over 200 years no judge or text-writer had questioned the fact that barristers should not be sued in negligence. The status quo should be maintained (see [1969] 1 AC 191).

The court decided so to maintain the status quo on grounds of public policy but Lord Reid, who read the first opinion, sounded the following prophetic note: 'Public policy is not immutable and doubts appear to have arisen in many quarters whether that rule is justifiable in present-day conditions in this country?'[1]

Apart from that substantial ground, their Lordships expressed the following somewhat divergent views as to the occasions when an advocate would be immune from suit. Lord Reid referred to 'their work in conducting litigation' and to 'when litigation is impending';[2] Lord Morris spoke of 'management of a case in court';[3] while for Lord Pearce there was no difference between the liability of a barrister in litigious and non-litigious work as a barrister.[4] Lord Upjohn felt that 'immunity covers litigation at all events in matters relating to litigation and this must start before counsel enters the door of the court'.[5] Lord Pearson put the subject in negative terms and inquired, 'Does the barrister's immunity extend to pure paper work?', that is to say, 'to drafting or advisory work unconnected to litigation'.[6]

1 *Rondel v Worsley* [1967] 3 All ER 993, p 998 C–D.
2 *Ibid*, p 100 J.
3 *Ibid*, pp 1011, 1012.
4 *Ibid*, p 1030.
5 *Ibid*, p 1033.
6 *Ibid*, p 1041.

SAIF ALI v MITCHELL

The next case that came before the House of Lords on lawyers' immunity was *Saif Ali v Sydney Mitchell* [1978] 3 All ER 1040 – a case which was considered to be one of exceptional public importance in which it became necessary for their Lordships to clarify what had been decided in *Rondel v Worsley*.

In that 1980 case, it fell to the House of Lords to examine the extent of a barrister's immunity (if any) against a claim for damages for negligence in the performance of professional duties out of court and generally to reconsider *Rondel v Worsley* (see [1980] AC 198).

The matter stemmed from a road traffic accident which occurred in March 1966 in the course of which a car in which the plaintiff was a passenger collided with a van driven by Mrs S. The plaintiff in October 1968 instructed the defendant firm of solicitors to take proceedings against Mrs S's husband (Mr S) on the basis that he was the true owner and Mrs S was acting as his agent. At first Mr S denied ownership and suggested there might be contributory negligence on the part of the plaintiff. It was at this point that counsel advised that no amendment to the pleadings was necessary to bring an action against Mr S. However, before anything further could be done, the limitation period for the bringing of the action had expired, with the result that the plaintiff was debarred from suing any one. The plaintiff then initiated proceedings against the solicitors alleging negligence, and they in turn brought third party proceedings for an indemnity against the barrister.

The Court of Appeal struck out the plaintiff's claim and the matter reached the House of Lords. The main issue considered by the House was this: was the claim against the barrister so clearly unfounded that it ought to be struck out? The opinions of Lords Wilberforce, Diplock and Salmon are well worth careful study.

Lord Wilberforce outlined that *Rondel v Worsley* gave rise to a restatement of the traditional principle of barristers' immunity in the light of *Hedley Byrne* (see Chapter 5). Previously, an important if not the main basis for the immunity lay in the fact that a barrister could not sue for his fees which 'would have thrown a blanket immunity over all barristers' actions in and out of court, whatever their nature'. He continued:

> This House, however, in 1967 took the inevitable view that this reason no longer applied: liability for negligence might exist in the absence of a contract for reward. Nevertheless, the immunity was held to exist on grounds, essentially, of public policy; mainly on the ground that a barrister owes a duty to the court as well as to his client and should not be inhibited through fear of an action from performing it; and partly on the undesirability of re-litigation as between barrister and client of what was litigated between the client and his opponent. This necessarily involved a removal of the total blanket immunity and a restriction of it to such cases as might fall within the area of public policy.

Such generally was the approach to immunity of the majority in the House of Lords, who felt that the immunity of a barrister should be restricted, viz Lords Wilberforce, Diplock and Salmon. Lord Diplock referred to the fact that any exposition that a lawyer was immune from suit in a blanket way was now 'legal folklore'. He traced the evolution of the movement away from such blanket immunity – *Hedley Byrne* marked an important milestone in the development; *Rondel v Worsley* was another; architects were no longer immune; accountants and building inspectors have been similarly affected. So have professional salvors and borstal officers. In putting the case against extension of immunity, Lord Diplock said:

> The salvor and the surgeon, like the barrister, may be called on to make immediate decisions which, if in the result they turn out to have been wrong, may have disastrous consequences. Yet neither salvor nor surgeons are immune from liability for negligent conduct of a salvage or surgical operation; nor does it seem that the absence of absolute immunity from negligence has disabled members of professions other than the law from giving their best services to those to whom they are rendered.

It is clear that Lord Diplock was ready to upset the applecart and he expressed his disappointment thus that the court was not requested to abolish immunity:

> I find it an unsatisfactory feature of the instant appeal, which has called for a re-examination of the speeches in *Rondel v Worsley* in the light of the subsequent development of the law of negligence by later decisions of this House, that your Lordships have not had the benefit of any argument from counsel in support of a more radical submission that the immunity of the advocate, whether barrister or solicitor, for liability for negligence even for what he says or does in court, ought no longer to be upheld.

The House, therefore, held that public policy required that a barrister should be immune from suit for negligence in respect of his acts or omissions in the conduct and management of litigation. But such immunity was an exception to the principle that a professional person who held himself out as qualified to practise that profession was under a duty to use reasonable care and skill and was not to be given any wider application than was absolutely necessary in the interest of the administration of justice.

The appeal was allowed with the express qualification that a solicitor acting as an advocate in court would enjoy the same immunity as a barrister.

IRONY IN THE HISTORY OF IMMUNITY FROM SUIT

It does not often happen that counsel who argues unsuccessfully in a matter before the House of Lords finds himself as a judge 28 years later called upon to pass judgment on the very point. The records show that Mr Louis Blom-Cooper (now Sir Louis Blom-Cooper QC) had appeared *pro bono* for Rondel in 1967, but in 1995 he was one of a panel of three judges in the Jersey Court of Appeal in a case in which an advocate was sued in negligence.[7] The appellant was seeking

7 See *Picot v Cills* [1995] JLR 33 (CA).

damages for the alleged negligence of his counsel in litigation against a third person and at first instance the judge had struck out the case on the dual ground that not only was the lawyer immune from suit but that continuing the action would constitute a collateral attack upon a subsisting judgment of a court of co-ordinate jurisdiction. By this time *Saif Ali v Sydney Mitchell* had been decided in 1980 by the House of Lords, restricting *Rondel v Worsley* but not overruling it. *Hedley Byrne* had been decided. In *Saif Ali v Sydney Mitchell*, Lord Diplock had expressed his disappointment that, in the light of those developments, counsel had not urged upon the House a more radical approach against immunity, arguments about public policy, however, satisfying Lord Diplock that the immunity should remain for the time being.

In his judgment in the Jersey case of *Picot v Cills* [1995] JLR 33 (CA), Blom-Cooper JA (as he had then become) recalled his radical arguments from the Bar in *Rondel v Worsley* and drew attention to a later House of Lords' decision[8] in which Lord Lowry had pointedly approved his arguments as counsel in *Rondel* on the matter of public policy. This is what Lord Lowry had to say: 'I also believe that the courts in general and your Lordships' House in particular ought to think very carefully before resorting to public policy considerations which will defeat a claim that *ex hypothesi* is a perfectly good cause of action.' And then the noble and learned Law Lord continued: 'In marshalling my thoughts on public policy I have drawn fully upon the argument in *Rondel v Worsley* ... of Louis Blom-Cooper whose submissions, although not rewarded with success in that appeal, strike me as particularly appropriate in the context of the present case.'

In the Jersey litigation, the judge at first instance had struck out the case on the ground that counsel was immune from suit in respect of the actions complained of and on the basis of the collateral attack on the judgment of a court of co-ordinate jurisdiction.

The Court of Appeal reversed the trial judge. It was held that he was wrong to strike out the appellant's action as it was by no means clear whether, if there had been any negligence attributable to the respondent, the conduct complained of was such as to attract the lawyer's immunity from suit.

The two other judges (LeQuesne and Frossard JJA) founded their decision as in the immediately preceding paragraph. Blom-Cooper JA delivered a separate assenting judgment questioning whether the immunity was still good law.

I must confess to being attracted by the argument of Blom-Cooper JA concerning the validity of the immunity. It was based on the fact that striking out the suit was a matter in which the Jersey Court of Appeal had the final say, subject to the grant of leave to appeal by the Judicial Committee of the Privy Council. But Blom-Cooper JA went further. He considered that the case was one for an exercise of the exception to the doctrine of *stare decisis* and he expressed himself in these prophetic terms at p 63:

8 *Spring v Guardian Assurance plc* [1995] 2 AC 326.

> It seems to me not right for any court to opt out of doing what is right and just, on the ground that the resolution of a problematic legal principle must await the arrival of the day, maybe far distant, when the length of an aspiring litigant's purse or the resources of the legal aid fund are to hand, sufficient to finance the costs of litigation all the way up to the final court of appeal. *Rondel v Worsley* was indubitably binding on English courts in 1967 (and would coincidentally at that time have been followed in Jersey). A court, nearly 30 years later, which finds that, in its attitude to professional negligence, society has moved on, cannot properly be unmindful of, or lacking in respect for, the judgment of 10 Law Lords.
>
> They stand impressively, for their day and age. But they cannot indefinitely bind a future generation, or await their Lordships' review of their own previous decision. My assessment is that the common law of England (as adapted to Jersey) can survive without conferring any special privilege on lawyers. Indeed, public respect for the law – particularly where it is made and sustained by judges and lawyers rather than by the elected representatives in Parliament at Westminster or in the States of Jersey – will be enhanced by an acknowledgment from the courts that lawyers are no different from other professionals when it comes to accountability for their professional services to the public.

HALL v SIMONS[9]

The prophecy implicit in the above pronouncement became a reality when in 2000 the House of Lords took the more radical step of abolishing the immunity altogether in *Hall v Simons*, the headnote of which reads as follows:

> In three separate cases, clients brought claims for negligence against their former solicitors. In each case, the solicitors relied on the immunity of advocates from suits for negligence, and the claims were initially struck out as unsustainable. However, the Court of Appeal subsequently held that the claims fell outside the scope of the immunity and that accordingly they should not have been struck out. On the solicitors' appeals to the House of Lords, their Lordships considered whether the immunity should be abolished or whether it could still be justified on public policy grounds, particularly the public interest in preventing collateral attacks on court decisions and in ensuring that advocates respected their overriding duty to the court.

This case is notable for being one of the few matters in the House to have been decided by a panel of seven judges – Lords Steyn, Browne-Wilkinson, Hoffmann, Hope, Hutton, Hobhouse and Millett – all of whom agreed that the immunity from suit for negligence in relation to litigation work should be abolished in civil matters. As to criminal cases, there was a majority of four in favour of abolition, with Lords Hope, Hutton and Hobhouse dissenting. The minority judges had a concern for the limits of immunity in civil cases but were in no doubt that it was not desirable that it should be abolished in criminal matters. They held that it was in the public interest that the immunity of the advocate against claims for negligence should be maintained in criminal cases.

9 *Arthur JS Hall v Simons* [2000] 3 All ER 673.

For the majority, Lords Steyn and Hoffmann gave the leading two judgments, supported by relatively short concurring judgments from Lords Browne-Wilkinson and Millett. They both considered the matter historically under four headings and, in the interest of brevity, it is proposed to examine the way Lord Steyn dealt with it, although Lord Hoffmann's judgment is the more exhaustive:

(a) The Cab-rank Rule – It was a matter of subjective judgment what weight should be put on this rule as justification for the grant of immunity, but in any event it could not justify denying all clients of a remedy for negligence causing them financial loss.

(b) Immunity of Judges, Witnesses and Jurors – Their immunity is based on public policy in encouraging those who participate in court proceedings to exercise free expression; but this has little relevance to immunity of advocates.

(c) Re-litigation – The doctrine of abusive collateral attack can only justifiably survive in criminal cases when the defendant has had his conviction overturned. There is no such need for survival in civil justice where the courts can deal with negligence suits by way of the doctrines of *res judicata*, issue estoppel and abuse of process. The matter of re-litigation should not, therefore, be an obstacle to the abolition of the immunity in all cases.

(d) Counsel's Duty to the Court – In this matter we will let the words of Lord Steyn speak for themselves:

> The view of the House in 1967 was that assertions of negligence would tend to erode this duty. In the world of today there are substantial grounds for questioning this ground of public policy. In 1967 the House considered that for reasons of public policy barristers must be accorded a special status.

The House of Lords had the advantage in the course of the hearing of this case of substantial comparative review. The position in Australia and New Zealand was examined and it was found that their courts have granted immunity along the lines proposed in *Rondel v Worsley*. It was also observed that in the US only judges and prosecutors are granted immunity. The majority, however, regarded the Canadian experience as tending 'to demonstrate that the fears that the possibility of actions in negligence against barristers would tend to undermine the public interest are unnecessarily pessimistic'. Lord Hope, on the other hand – for the minority – would have preferred to adopt the position in Australia and New Zealand. This is what he had to say on that subject:

> My noble and learned friend Lord Steyn has said that he would regard the Canadian experience as the most relevant but I do not see, with great respect, why that should be so. I should have thought that the Australian and New Zealand experience was the more relevant as their jurisprudence is more closely modelled on that of our own jurisdictions and the way in which law is practised there is closer to the way law is practised here than it is in Canada ...[10]

10 *Ibid*, p 721.

CONCLUDING COMMENTS WITH SPECIAL REFERENCE TO THE APPLICATION OF *HALL v SIMONS* TO DEVELOPING COUNTRIES

This radical and far-reaching decision (*Hall v Simons*) brings English law into line with the law against immunity in most other developed countries. The question that presents itself for consideration here is this: is there any reason why the law as set out in this case should not be followed in the developing countries of the Commonwealth?

In present circumstances it frequently happens that senior English counsel are briefed to appear in matters in the courts abroad and it would clearly be desirable that the liability of advocates should be the same, in this globalised world, whether counsel appears in London, England, for a Barbadian resident there or in Barbados for one of the Barbadian's relatives. There is clearly a need for uniformity in a matter of this kind.

But uniformity apart, times have changed and, as Lord Reid properly stated in *Rondel v Worsley*, public policy is not immutable. It is therefore clearly desirable that developing countries should bring their codes and legislation on this matter into line with modern thinking, if they consider that lawyers, like surgeons, architects and salvors should be held accountable for negligence in the performance of their duties.

It is the matter of professional responsibility that is the subject of the next chapter.

CHAPTER 5

PROFESSIONAL RESPONSIBILITY OF LAWYERS

INTRODUCTORY REMARKS

When considering the relative position of barristers and solicitors in England, what is relevant is that they owe a duty to the courts, the profession and the public. In American jurisprudence it was recognised as far back as 1796 that a lawyer could be held liable in damages for failing properly to perform his duties whenever financial loss occurred. This has also been the case in Canada ever since Confederation in 1867. In Canada, Australia and New Zealand (as well as the colonial territories which have since World War II become independent), the English pattern has generally been followed, although Canada has tended to be greatly influenced by the legal system in the US.

The position of lawyers' responsibility was early in the 20th century clearly enunciated by the House of Lords in the case of *Nocton v Lord Ashburton* [1914] AC 932 at p 956, which involved a distinction between a breach of fiduciary duty and a breach by a fiduciary of a duty of care.

It laid down that a solicitor owed a duty properly to advise his client, as a result of which the client could be awarded compensation in equity for breach of that duty. Early in the 20th century, no remedy for such a breach was available at common law. The remedy was later extended by the decision of the House of Lords in *Hedley Byrne & Co Ltd v Heller & Partners Ltd* [1964] AC 465, since when the issue considered in *Nocton v Lord Ashburton* has fallen within the purview of the common law.

In order for negligence to be actionable, it must have caused damage, quite apart from the fact that the person who is alleged to have caused the damage must be under a duty of care to the person who has suffered the damage. But a duty of care is imposed upon a solicitor by virtue of his retainer and he is liable to the client both in contract and tort for the same breach of duty.[1]

BASIS OF CONTRACTUAL LIABILITY

What is the basis of the lawyer's contractual obligations? It is his retainer, which is usually in writing, although it can also be given orally. In England under the LSG a solicitor is generally free to decide whether or not to accept instructions from any particular client,[2] but any refusal to act must not be based on race, colour, ethnic or national origins, sex, creed, disability or the sexual orientation of the prospective client.[3] A solicitor must not act, or continue to act, where the client

---

1 *Midland Bank Trust Co Ltd v Hett, Stubbs and Kent* [1978] 3 All ER 571.

2 LSG 12.01.

3 *Ibid*, 12.02.

cannot be represented with competence or diligence.[4] When instructions are received from a third party on behalf of a client, a solicitor should receive written instructions from the client that he or she wishes the solicitor to act[5] and the solicitor should in that case consider whether both the third party and the person introduced are clients or whether it is only the person introduced.[6] When another solicitor is already acting for the client in the same matter, the solicitor must not accept instructions.[7]

The LSG stipulates how the solicitor should carry out his work, providing as follows:[8]

> A solicitor must act within his or her client's express or implied authority. It is essential at the outset for a solicitor to agree clearly with the client the scope of the retainer and subsequently to refer any matter of doubt to the client. If a solicitor limits the scope of the retainer it is good practice for the limits to be precisely defined in writing to the client.

Other sections of the Guide provide for the solicitor not to take advantage of the client;[9] for dealing promptly with communications relating to the client's affairs;[10] for limitation of liability by contract – warning that 'it is not acceptable for solicitors to attempt to exclude by contract all liability to their clients';[11] for the termination of the retainer;[12] for accounting to the client for funds still held on behalf of the client, for delivery of all papers and property due to the client; and for the retention of papers and property by way of lien pending payment of professional costs owed by the client.[13]

When a solicitor contracts with a client to perform a certain function, the solicitor may be sued in contract for a breach of that obligation even if a court would not regard the breach as a failure to take reasonable care.

There is nothing to prevent a client entering into a more exacting contract with a solicitor than required at common law.[14]

It must, however, be noted that by accepting a retainer to carry out a particular obligation, the solicitor does not guarantee a certain result, unless the terms of the retainer are specific to that effect. Thus, when a solicitor gives a client an undertaking to apply funds to secure a good marketable title to an impending property, such an undertaking was construed as being intended to have the funds applied to secure a title which 'a reasonably competent solicitor acting with proper

4 *Ibid*, 12.03.
5 *Ibid*, 12.05.
6 *Ibid*, 12.06.
7 *Ibid*, 12.07.
8 *Ibid*, 12.08, para 1.
9 *Ibid*, 12.09.
10 *Ibid*, 12.10.
11 *Ibid*, 13.
12 *Ibid*, 12.12.
13 *Ibid*, 12.13.
14 *Bristol and West Building Society v Kramer* [1995] NPC 14.

skill and care would accept as a good marketable title'.[15] This principle is further illustrated in a case in which a solicitor and senior counsel were requested to secure tax clearance for a client. Together they prepared a letter which was forwarded to the Inland Revenue who at first granted the necessary clearance. Subsequently the Revenue withdrew its approval (which by statute it was permitted to do). The plaintiff sued both solicitor and senior counsel, but the court held that they were not liable. They had done what they were required to do and could not guarantee the result.[16]

CONCURRENT LIABILITY IN CONTRACT AND TORT

Quite apart from a solicitor's contractual obligations, he owes a client a concurrent liability in tort – such duty, however, being related to the contractual retainer. The test is always 'what a reasonably competent practitioner would do having regard to the standard normally adopted in the profession'.[17] The decision of *Midland Bank v Hett* (referred to above) was endorsed by the House of Lords in *Henderson v Merrett Syndicates* [1994] 3 All ER 506.[18] This was a case in which managing agents of an underwriting syndicate were held to be liable in contract and tort to members of the syndicate and it was said liability could only be excluded by explicit words to that effect. In giving his judgment, Lord Goff had this to say:

> But for present purposes, more important, in the present case liability can and in my opinion should be founded squarely on the principle established in *Hedley Byrne* itself, from which it follows that an assumption of responsibility coupled with a concomitant reliance may give rise to a tortious duty of care irrespective of whether there is a contractual relationship between the parties, and in consequence unless his contract precludes him from doing so, the plaintiff, who has available to him concurrent remedies in contract and tort, may choose that remedy which appears to him to be the most advantageous.

15 This was decided in *Barclays Bank plc v Weeks, Legg and Dean* [1998] 3 WLR 656. See also to the same effect *Midland Bank plc v Cox McQueen* [1999] Lloyd's Rep PN 223, where the solicitor, having undertaken to secure the signatures of a husband and wife, ended up with the husband's signature but with a fraudulent representation of the wife's signature – the husband having used one of his employees to forge his wife's signature. The courts held that the solicitor was not in breach of his undertaking since the obligation to obtain the wife's signature was not absolute. What was necessary was a reasonable standard of care and this had been fulfilled.

16 *Matrix Securities Ltd v Goddard* [1998] PNLR 290.

17 *Midland Bank Co Ltd v Hett, Stubbs and Kent* [1979] Ch 384.

18 See also *Aitken v Stewart Wrightson Members Agency Ltd* [1995] 3 All ER 449; and *Sumitomo Bank v Bank Bruxelles Lambert SA* [1997] 1 Lloyd's Rep 487, where it was held that not only was concurrent liability possible but that the duties owed in tort could be more onerous than in contract. See to the same effect *Holt v Payne Skillington* [1996] 77 BLR 51, in which the Court of Appeal held that there is a divergence between the duties in contract and in tort, in that an agent and valuer may owe a higher duty of care in tort than in contract. It is submitted that the same principle should apply to a solicitor.

The cases in which concurrent liability has been found to exist are those involving professional relationships and those that relate to commercial transactions where the parties set out their obligations in elaborate contracts do not fall within that category.[19]

'THE IMPULSE TO DO PRACTICAL JUSTICE' IN LAWYERS' LIABILITY

There is a recently developed principle, referred to as the doctrine of 'the disappointed beneficiary', concerning the liability of lawyers to third parties for economic loss. The principle saw its rise in the case of *Ross v Caunters* [1980] 1 Ch 297, the facts of which are as follows:

> A solicitor was instructed to prepare a will for a testator who wished the plaintiff Ross to be a beneficiary. The document was prepared and dispatched to the testator, but the defendant omitted to inform the plaintiff that neither the spouse of the beneficiary nor the plaintiff's husband should sign as one of the two witnesses.

It was held by Sir Robert Megarry VC that a duty of care was owed by the defendant to the plaintiff. The judge did, however, display both sides of the same coin. First he made the following point:

> The solicitor owes no such duty (as he owes to his client) to those who are not his clients. He is no guardian of their interests. What he does for his clients may be hostile and injurious to their interests and sometimes the greater the injuries the better he will have served his client.[20]

Later on in his judgment, however, he made the following apparently contradictory pronouncement:

> A solicitor who is instructed by his client to carry out a transaction that will confer a benefit on an identified third party owes a duty of care towards that third party in carrying out that transaction, in that the third party is a person within his direct contemplation as someone who is likely to be so closely and directly affected by his acts or omissions that he can easily foresee that the third party is likely to be injured by those acts or omissions.

Since that case was decided in 1980, the jurisprudence on the subject of the disappointed beneficiary has developed apace. At first there were halting steps towards following it,[21] no doubt because it was a first instance decision.

It was, however, the case of *White v Jones* [1995] 1 All ER 691, decided by the House of Lords, which put the principle firmly on its feet. In this case, a testator who had originally executed his will in 1986 removing his daughters from his estate became reconciled with them and wished later to include them in the will by providing that each of the two daughters should receive upon his death a

---

19 See *Banque Financière de la Cité SA v Westgate Insurance Co, sub nom Banque Keyser Ullman SA v Skandis Insurance Co* [1991] 2 AC 249; and *Bank of Nova Scotia v Hellenic Mutual War Risk Association (Bermuda) (The Good Luck)* [1992] 1 AC 233.

20 [1980] 1 Ch 297, p 332B.

21 See, for instance, *Kecskemeti v Rubens Rabin & Co* (1992) *The Times*, 31 December.

legacy of £9,000. He so instructed his solicitor who made two appointments to call on him at his home but failed to keep them. He then made a third appointment but the testator died before the solicitor could keep it. The daughters sued the solicitor and the judge at first instance held in favour of the solicitor. The Court of Appeal, however, reversed the judge's decision and they were supported by the House of Lords, albeit on different grounds. The Court of Appeal considered there was no distinction between the case and *Ross v Caunters* which they generally endorsed.

The House of Lords were in favour of the idea of liability but introduced the doctrine of assumption of responsibility.[22] Lord Goff came to the conclusion that since the *Hedley Byrne* principle is founded upon an assumption of responsibility, the solicitor may be liable for negligent omissions as well as negligent acts of commission. He continued:

> I do not consider the damages for loss of an expectation are excluded in cases of negligence arising under the principles in *Hedley Byrne*, simply because the cause of action is classified as tortious. Such damages may in principle be recoverable in cases of contractual negligence; and I cannot see that, for present purposes, any relevant distinction can be drawn between the forms of action.

Since 1995, *White v Jones* has been followed in a number of cases.[23] Of these, the most instructive is *Carr-Glynn v Frearsons* [1998] 4 All ER 225. In this case the testatrix had her will (drafted by the defendants) executed in 1989, leaving her share in a property to the plaintiff. A doubt having arisen as to whether the property was held in joint tenancy or in tenancy in common, the solicitor explained to the testatrix that the gift to the beneficiary would be ineffectual if it were held on joint tenancy without any arrangement being made for severance before her death. The testatrix promised to look into the matter but died before anything could be done. The solicitor should simply have advised the testatrix to have a document of severance prepared in the event that the property was held in joint tenancy. The judge, Lloyd J, held that since the estate could bring an action against the solicitors for the loss of property, no duty was owed to the beneficiary.

The Court of Appeal reversed the judge's order. The court had to grapple with the submission that no remedy could be available to the beneficiary in circumstances where there was a remedy at the disposal of the estate. To answer this suggestion, this is what Chadwick LJ had to say:

> I would find it ... extraordinary ... if the only person for whose benefit a valid claim could be pursued (the residuary legatee) was a person who had suffered no loss, because, absent the respondents' negligence, the property would not have formed any part of the residue and the only person who has suffered a loss (the appellant) has no claim. I am satisfied that it would be consistent with the approach of the majority of the House of Lords in *White v Jones* to fashion a remedy in cases of this nature also, if that can be done without imposing a double liability on the solicitors.

---

22 *White v Jones* [1995] 1 All ER 691.

23 See *Cancer Research Campaign v Ernest Brown & Co* [1997] STC 1425; and *Esterhuizen v Allied Dunbar Assurance plc* [1998] 2 FLR 668.

BREACHES OF TRUST

The cases referred to in the immediately preceding section – relating to the 'disappointed beneficiary' – indicate a disposition by the courts to do 'practical justice' in an equitable context, but we must now examine the circumstances under which a lawyer may find himself guilty of a breach of trust.

Lawyers who hold clients' funds need constantly to remind themselves that they are trustees (albeit bare trustees). They are, however, expected to maintain the standard of care which equity requires of a trustee, viz, that they must take every precaution which an ordinary man (or woman) of business would take in managing similar affairs of their own.[24] And as a professional trustee, a solicitor is held to a higher standard than a non-professional trustee.[25] It is well also to remind ourselves that every trustee has a liability to make good any loss which arises from his breach of trust, provided the beneficiary can trace the necessary causation between the breach and the loss.[26] Flenley and Leech outline, in their admirable volume *Solicitors' Negligence*, the circumstances in which in the 1980s claims by lenders in England increased against solicitors following the decision of the Court of Appeal in *Target* because of the perception that if a client could show a breach of trust on the part of a solicitor, he 'could obtain summary judgment for all its losses without the need to comply with common law rules of causation and remoteness and without facing reductions for contributory negligence or failure to mitigate the loss'.[27]

In this connection, attention is invited to an article written by Lord Millett on the subject[28] in which at p 217 he gives the following word of caution to practitioners:

> Plaintiffs and their advisers have discovered the apparent advantages of alleging breach of trust or fiduciary duty, with the result that a statement of claim is considered to be seriously deficient if it does not contain inappropriate references to these concepts which are often scattered throughout the pleadings with complete abandon.

The question that must be asked in considering this subject is: 'What is the irreducible minimum of duty owed to a client to avoid a breach of trust?' That question is answered by Lord Justice Millett (as he then was) in the well-known case of *Armitage v Nurse*[29] in this way: 'The duty of the trustees to perform the trusts honestly and in good faith for the benefit of the beneficiaries is the minimum necessary to give substance to the trusts, but in my opinion it is sufficient.'

---

24 *Speight v Gaunt* [1883] 22 Ch 727; (1883) 9 App Cas 1.

25 *Bartlett v Barclays Bank Trust Co Ltd* [1980] 1 All ER 139.

26 *Target Holdings v Redferns* [1996] AC 421.

27 See William Flenley and Tom Leech, *Solicitors' Negligence* (London, Butterworths, 1999), p 71.

28 See Lord Millett's article entitled 'Equity's place in the law of commerce' in *Law Quarterly Review*, Vol 114, 1998, p 214.

29 [1998] Ch 241 at p 254.

And what is the nature of the remedy available? The remedy for breach of trust differs from that available in cases of breaches of contract and tort in that it is not necessarily provided to compensate the beneficiary for the loss suffered but to provide an appropriate discretionary remedy; for example, the solicitor may be required to give a full account to the beneficiary. Generally speaking the solicitor's obligation will depend upon the authority which the court reads into the terms of the retainer in respect (for instance) of the disposal of funds. Thus, in the case of a mortgage, the funds would be disbursed only when the property is conveyed to the mortgagor who by that time would have executed a valid charge in favour of the mortgagee who would have been in possession of the charge.[30]

In *Nationwide Building Society v Balmer Radmore*,[31] it was held that a breach of trust was not committed by a solicitor who released a mortgage advance before confirming the purchase price (as was required by his instructions). Nor did it constitute a breach of trust to agree with the solicitor for the lender for the deferment of the balance of the purchase money without the express permission of the lender.

A breach of trust must be fraudulent and deliberate, this principle being borne out by the judgment in *Bristol and West Building Society v Mothew* [1998] Ch 1. Examples are where the solicitor was instructed to apply funds to purchasing and re-mortgaging a property, to report any proposal by the purchaser to arrange a second mortgage and to confirm that the balance of the purchase money was being provided personally by the would-be purchaser. Although he was told the borrower intended to leave £3,350 outstanding to another lender after completion, to be secured by a second charge, the solicitor confirmed that the balance would be met personally without reference to the second charge. Although the statement amounted to a breach of contract, there was no allegation of dishonesty or bad faith – and the solicitor did not realise he was misleading the lender. If such an allegation could have been substantiated, the court would have granted the plaintiff damages for deceit and the solicitor would have been guilty of a fraudulent breach of trust. Indeed it was submitted that the solicitor's authority to complete depended upon his having conformed to all the conditions laid down by the lender and that failure so to conform rendered him incompetent to complete. Millet LJ could not accede to that submission but found that the solicitor's authority to complete 'was not vitiated by the misrepresentation for which he was responsible but of which he was unaware'.

This brings us to the question as to what amounts to dishonesty in a trustee. The principle is that if a trustee fails to manage the trust property in the interests of the beneficiaries, acting in a way which he does not honestly believe is in their interests, he acts dishonestly. But an intentional or reckless breach of trust is not on all fours with the common law action of deceit. In *Alliance & Leicester Building Society v Edgestop* [1994] 2 All ER 38,[32] a solicitor was aware of, and privy to, the

30 See *Nationwide Building Society v Mian* (unreported, Chadwick J, 12 September 1997).

31 [1999] Lloyd's Rep PN 241.

32 See also *Twinsectra v Yardley* [2002] AC 149, where the House of Lords held that a solicitor trustee who turned a blind eye was misguided but not dishonest.

knowledge that his client was making a fraudulent misrepresentation as to the manner of disposal of funds about to be loaned to him. The solicitor, however, concealed his knowledge and the concealment rendered void the solicitor's authority to release the funds. This is what Hoffmann J (as he then was) had to say on the matter:

> The society's instructions authorised the money to be advanced for the purposes of the purchase set out in the instructions and not for some materially different transactions. It also required that the society should, before completion, be notified of matters which ought reasonably to have been brought to its attention. The solicitors knew or ought to have known that the true nature of the transactions had been concealed from the society and I think there can be no doubt that if the facts known to the solicitors had been brought to the attention of the society before completion it would not have made any of the advances.

In the work by Flenley and Leech, the writers referred to 'the deliberate but innocent breach of trust ... familiar to all trust lawyers' and to the following statement made by Lord Millett in *Armitage v Nurse*:[33]

> By consciously acting beyond their powers (as, for example, by making an investment which they know to be unauthorised), the trustees may deliberately commit a breach of trust, but if they do so in the interest of the beneficiaries their conduct is not fraudulent. So a deliberate breach of trust is not necessarily fraudulent. Hence the remark famously attributed to Selwyn LJ by Sir Nathaniel Linley MR in the course of argument in *Perrins v Bellamy* [1899] 1 Ch 797, 798.
>
> My old master, the late Selwyn LJ used to say, 'The main duty of a trustee is to commit judicious breaches of trust'.

HOW DUTIES OF A SOLICITOR ARE TO BE CARRIED OUT

A solicitor has a duty to execute his professional duties personally and may only delegate with consent in exceptional circumstances. One English example occurs when a solicitor is based outside of London when he may request a fellow solicitor to appear on his behalf as an advocate in an interlocutory matter or in open court in London with counsel. There is also implied authority to instruct counsel.[34] In these days of instant email and other electronic forms of communication, it would clearly be possible and desirable to inform the client of any delegation and of the costs involved when the delegation takes place, since there is no privity of contract with such a substitute who is not the agent to the client, although he may be liable in tort to the client.[35]

The retained solicitor continues to be responsible under the retainer to see that a proper degree of skill and care is maintained. He is also responsible personally for paying the cost of counsel or of a professional agent instructed by him on behalf of a client, even if the cost is not received from the client – unless the client

33 [1998] Ch 241.
34 See *Re Bishop ex p Langley* [1879] 13 Ch Div 110.
35 *Robbins v Fennell* [1847] 11 QB 248.

makes an arrangement to the contrary. This includes the cost of experts, professional and other witnesses or agents.[36]

As regards his employees, a solicitor is responsible for their frauds so long as such frauds are perpetrated in the course of their employment.[37]

REMOTENESS AND FORESEEABILITY

We have already considered how under the *Hedley Byrne* principle a lawyer can become responsible for economic loss to a third person as a result of a misstatement or negligent advice despite the absence of any contractual relationship. What we now examine is the manner in which *Hedley Byrne* has been refined by the introduction of the concepts of foreseeability, proximity and reasonableness as well as the assumption of responsibility.

In *Caparo Industries v Dickman* [1990] 1 AC 831, Lord Bridge expressed himself as follows:

> What emerges is that, in addition to the foreseeability of damage, necessary ingredients in any situation giving rise to a duty of care are that there should exist between the party owing the duty and the party to whom it is owed a relationship characterised by the law as one of 'proximity' and 'neighbourhood' and that the situation should be one in which the court considers it fair and reasonable that the law should impose a duty of a given scope upon the one party for the benefit of the other.

This is substantially what Lord Goff had in mind later in *Merrett* when he said:[38]

> However, at least in cases such as the present, in which the same problem does not arise, there seems to be no reason why recourse should not be had to the concept (of assumption of responsibility), which appears after all to have been adopted, in one form or another, by all of their Lordships in *Hedley Byrne* ... In addition, the concept provides its own explanation why there is no problem in cases of this kind about liability for economic loss; for if a person assumes responsibility to another in respect of certain services, there is no reason why he should not be liable in damages to the other in respect of economic loss which flows from the negligent performance of those services.

FURTHER RELATIONS BETWEEN LAWYER AND CLIENT

In the previous sections of this chapter we have underscored the extent to which the lawyer should exercise care not to use his fiduciary position to his personal advantage in dealing with clients.

The conflict of interest situation which every lawyer should guard against will be discussed in Chapter 8.

In the rest of this section our discussion will be confined to those cases where the lawyer employs undue influence over his clients, wittingly or unwittingly, and

36 LSG Ch 20, Principle 20.01.

37 *Lloyd v Grace Smith & Co* [1912] KB 1140.

38 *Henderson v Merrett Syndicates* [1995] 2 AC 145.

a good starting point is what Millett LJ (as he then was) had to say in the case of *Bristol West Building Society v Mothew* [1996] 4 All ER 698 at p 711:

> The distinguishing obligation of a fiduciary is the obligation of loyalty. The principal is entitled to the single-minded loyalty of his fiduciary. This core liability has several facets. A fiduciary must act in good faith; he must not make a profit out of his trust; he must not place himself in a position where his duties and his interest may conflict; he may not act for his own benefit or that of a third person without the informed consent of his principal.

In such matters of conflict, a heavy burden lies on the fiduciary to show that his hands are clean. It is not enough to argue that even if he (the fiduciary) had not acted in an improper and dishonest manner or had made full disclosure to his client, the client would still have pursued the same course. See *Swindle v Harrison* [1999] 4 All ER 705.

IDENTITY OF THE CLIENT

Whether a lawyer has been guilty of exerting undue influence on the client depends upon the identity of the client. Is he foreign and barely able to speak or understand the English language? Is he simply a youth inexperienced or unaccustomed to the ways of business? Is he a seasoned and well-tried business executive? These are considerations, among others, that a lawyer must take into account when exercising his fiduciary functions with the client. The burden of proof becomes greater the less sophisticated the client proves to be when the question comes to be examined as to whether such a client is a victim of undue influence.

When, therefore, the lawyer is minded to purchase the client's property, he must always ensure that the client is independently advised as to valuation. If the client wishes the lawyer or a member of his family to be a beneficiary under his will, the lawyer should insist that the will be prepared by an independent member of the profession and that the client is of sound and disposing mind and memory. If the client is a foreigner, barely able to speak or understand English, the lawyer should see to it before requesting him to sign a document that it is translated into a language the client speaks or understands (if necessary, an interpreter should be used). If the lawyer wishes to provide the client with funds by way of mortgage, he should make certain that the whole arrangement is fair; that the interest charged is not excessive; that there is nothing oppressive about the right of redemption; and that all relevant and material facts are disclosed to the mortgagor client.

CONCLUDING SUMMARY[39]

In this chapter we have seen the extent to which negligence at common law renders the legal practitioner liable in damages in the face of economic loss. We have noted that the lawyer is in such cases liable both in contract and in tort. We have examined a number of cases in which an actionable breach occurs and have taken into account the basis for contractual and tortious liability. In discussing liability, it must, however, constantly be borne in mind that acceptance of a retainer to undertake a particular obligation does not provide a guarantee of a specific result.

We have also briefly considered the position of the 'disappointed beneficiary' with special reference to *Ross v Caunters* and *White v Jones*; and in this connection we have observed the disposition of the courts to do 'practical justice'. At the same time we have been sternly reminded that not every contractual breach is a breach of trust or of fiduciary duty.

We have very briefly reviewed the remedies available for contractual and tortious breaches and contrasted the remedies with those applicable to a breach of trust.

It has been decided that the duties of a lawyer must be executed personally and the circumstances when those duties can be delegated have been stated, the suggestion being proffered that notification of the delegation should always be conveyed to the client in advance.

We have, by reference to decided cases, shown that liability for breach can only be fixed when there is foreseeability of damage and when the lawyer has assumed responsibility for performing a specific obligation in terms of the *Hedley Byrne* decision.

Finally, we have outlined in brief compass the circumstances in which a legal adviser is deemed to exercise undue influence over a client in terms of the client's vulnerability to such pressures.

What general lessons can be learnt from the multiplicity of cases that we have examined? One obvious lesson is that in the last two decades of the 20th century, clients the world over became more worldly-wise as regards their rights than was previously the case – and this trend will surely continue. At the same time, governments and the courts have shown towards the citizenry greater solicitude and vigilance. That combination suggests that the business of lawyering in the 21st century is likely to become more exacting than ever before. Accordingly, those who practice law whether on the contentious or non-contentious side must be prepared to treat their onerous responsibilities with the necessary seriousness.

39 In writing this chapter I have derived much assistance from the following legal treatises: *Jackson and Powell on Professional Negligence* (5th edn) (London, Sweet & Maxwell, 2001); William Flenley and Tom Leech, *Solicitors' Negligence* (London, Butterworths, 1999); Roger Billins, *Solicitors' Duties and Liabilities* (London, Sweet & Maxwell, 1999); and Hugh Evans, *Lawyers' Liabilities* (London, Sweet & Maxwell, 2002).

Failure to appreciate the more rights-conscious nature of our clients and opponents may involve members of the profession in applications not only for negligence but also for wasted costs in the future – the latter being the subject of our next chapter.

CHAPTER 6

WASTED COSTS

IS THE WASTED COSTS JURISDICTION JUSTIFIABLE OR PRACTICABLE?

The jurisdiction of the court to make wasted costs orders against solicitors is of long standing (see, for instance, *Re Bradford* [1883] 15 QBD 635), but a convenient point for discussion of the jurisdiction is the case of *Myers v Elman* [1940] AC 282. This was a case in which judgment for the plaintiff was granted against five defendants for damages for fraudulent conspiracy with costs which could not be recovered. One complaint filed against one of the solicitors (Elman) was that he had permitted the filing of a false affidavit. In respect of this complaint the judge ordered that he should pay one-third of the taxed costs of the action and two-thirds of the costs of the application for a wasted costs order. On appeal to the Court of Appeal, the judge's order was reversed on the ground that in order to make such an order the judge must find professional misconduct established against the solicitor and that in this case the solicitor was not personally at fault. On a further appeal to the House of Lords, the judgment of the Court of Appeal was reversed and that of the trial judge restored. The judgment in the Lords is authority for the following propositions:

(a) The court's jurisdiction to make such an order is something quite separate and distinct from the disciplinary jurisdiction exercised against solicitors.

(b) The disciplinary regime for the profession requires that a solicitor be personally responsible for his action (the subject of the order), but the making of the order does not so require.

(c) The wasted costs order is founded only on a breach of duty owed to the court in the solicitor's capacity as an officer of the court.

(d) What has to be established does not include dishonesty, criminal misconduct, personal obliquity or misbehaviour. All that is required for the making of a wasted costs order is misconduct, default or negligence, provided it is gross negligence.

(e) The jurisdiction is compensatory and not merely punitive.

At that time, the wasted costs jurisdiction was not, however, regulated by specific rules of court. The jurisdiction was put on a statutory basis in the Supreme Court Act 1981 and confirmed by s 4 of the Courts and Legal Services Act 1990 – which came into effect on 1 October 1991. It extends to both civil and criminal proceedings.

Section 51(1) of the 1981 Act makes the costs of all proceedings in the Civil Division of the Court of Appeal, the High Court and the County Courts subject to the court's discretion; and the courts may (by s 6) disallow or order the legal representative to meet the whole or part of any wasted costs as determined by rules of court: 'Wasted costs' being defined as:

> costs incurred by a party—
>
> (a) as a result of any improper, unreasonable or negligent act or omission on the part of any legal representative or any employee of such representatives; or
>
> (b) which, in the light of any such act or omission occurring after they were incurred, the court considers it unreasonable to expect that party to pay.

The jurisdiction is usually invoked when the costs cannot be recovered from the other side.[1]

BASIS OF JURISDICTION

Sir Thomas Bingham (as he then was) speaking for a unanimous Court of Appeal in *Ridehalgh v Horsefield* [1994] 3 All ER 848 laid down in the following terms the procedure to be followed when application for a wasted costs order is made:

> The procedure to be followed in determining applications for wasted costs must be laid down by courts so as to meet the requirements of the individual case before them. The overriding requirements are that any procedure must be fair and that it must be as simple and summary as fairness permits. Fairness requires that any respondent lawyer should be very clearly told what he is said to have done wrong and what is claimed. But the requirement of simplicity and summariness means that elaborate pleadings should in general be avoided. No formal process of discovery will be appropriate. We cannot imagine circumstances in which the applicant should be permitted to interrogate the respondent lawyer or vice versa. Hearings should be measured in hours not in days or weeks. Judges must not reject a weapon which Parliament has intended to be used for the protection of those injured by the unjustifiable conduct of the other side's lawyers, but they must be astute to control what threatens to become a new and costly form of satellite litigation (p 867).

In that case there were six appeals before the court raising substantially (save one) the same question, viz: 'In what circumstances was the court justified in making a wasted costs order in favour of one party to litigation against the legal representative (counsel or solicitor) of the other?' The court considered the matter to be 'a question of great and growing significance' and thought it desirable 'to give such guidance as it could'. Orders had been made in each case and it is from those orders that the five solicitors and one barrister had appealed to the Court of Appeal. A compressed synopsis of the judgment follows.

Their Lordships referred to the adversary system which had served the interest of justice for many years and named five of the safeguards which they considered were needed for the proper functioning of the system in the interest of parties to litigation and the public at large. The safeguards are confidentiality, the payment of costs to the successful litigant by the unsuccessful, the requirement that a lawyer should employ reasonable care and skill in conducting the client's affairs, liability to disciplinary proceedings by the responsible authorities for breaches of conduct, and liability of solicitors and barristers to compensate a party to litigation other than their own clients for costs incurred by that party as a result of acts done

1 *Filmlab Systems International v Pennington* (1993) *The Times*, 9 July.

or omitted by the solicitors or barristers in their conduct of litigation. In *Ridehalgh*, it was 'the scope and effect of this last safeguard, and its relations with the others briefly mentioned, which are in issue in those appeals'. The case was really not, therefore, concerned with the jurisdiction to order legal representatives to compensate their own clients.

Sir Thomas Bingham emphasised the importance of the matter thus:

> The questions raised are by no means academic. Material has been placed before the court which shows that the number and value of wasted costs orders applied for, and the costs of litigating them, have risen sharply. We were told of one case in which the original case lasted five days, the wasted costs application had (when we were told of it) lasted seven days; it was estimated to be about half way through; at that stage one side had incurred costs of over £40,000. It almost appears that a new branch of legal activity is emerging, calling to mind Dickens's searing observation in *Bleak House*: 'The one great principle of English law is to make business for itself ... Viewed by this light it becomes a coherent scheme and not the monstrous maze the laity are apt to think it.'

The Court of Appeal referred to the tension between two existing public interests. The first is that lawyers should not be inhibited from pursuing their clients' interests by fear of incurring a personal liability to their clients' opponents. The second is that litigants should not be financially prejudiced by the unjustifiable conduct of litigation by their own or their opponents' lawyers. It was the reconciliation of these two competing interests that was the *gravamen* of the court's task in *Ridehalgh*.

The court looked at the history of the rules affecting the standards of conduct to be observed to protect against wasted costs orders. The case of *Sinclair-Jones v Kay* [1988] 2 All ER 611 was examined in the context of the amendment of Ord 62 r 8 which in the 1986 amendment to the Rules of the Supreme Court became Ord 62 r 11. By this amendment, where it appears to the court that costs have been incurred unreasonably or improperly in any proceedings or to have been wasted by failure to conduct proceedings *with reasonable competence and expedition*, the court may order (i) the solicitor it considers responsible to repay to his client costs which the client has been ordered to pay to any other party, or (ii) *the solicitor personally to indemnify such other persons against costs payable by them*. In the course of his judgment in *Sinclair-Jones*, May LJ (speaking for the Court of Appeal) stated that the new rule was 'substantially different from the old and was intended to widen the Court's powers' since it was no longer necessary to apply the gross misconduct test prescribed in such authorities like *Myers v Elman*. In the view of the learned Lord Justice, this was a salutary change 'especially as a means of penalising unnecessary delay'.

In the case of *Gupta v Comer* [1991] 1 All ER 289, Lord Donaldson MR spoke of the legislative changes to the 1981 Supreme Court Act which would be capable of 'imposing an even stricter standard than that which Ord 62 r 11 has been held to impose'. Indeed, s 51(6) of the 1981 Act included an amendment which would extend the powers of the court to order wasted costs to civil proceedings in the

Crown Court. Section 11 of that Act made a similar amendment to the Prosecution of Offences Act 1985 applicable to criminal proceedings in the Court of Appeal, the Crown Court and the magistrates' court. And with effect from 1 October 1991, Ord 62 r 11 was amended to supplement the new s 51 of the 1981 Act.

A third case to be approved by the Court of Appeal in *Ridehalgh* as providing guidance for the test to be applied when an order for wasted costs is contemplated is *Re A Barrister (Wasted Costs Order) (No 1 of 1991)* [1992] 3 All ER 420.

The relevant test was stated in this case in these terms:

(a) Has the legal representative of whom complaint is made acted improperly, unreasonably or negligently?

(b) If so, did such conduct cause the applicant to incur unnecessary costs?

(c) If so, is it in all the circumstances just to order the legal representative to compensate the applicant for the whole or any part of the relevant costs?

The judges in the Court of Appeal in *Ridehalgh* were requested to give the three adjectives – improper, unreasonable and negligent – 'specific, self-contained meanings so as to avoid overlap between the three'. Their Lordships declined to accept the invitation but in the judgment they nevertheless outlined clearly what was intended by the three words:

> 'Improper' covers, but is not confined to, conduct which will normally justify disbarment, striking off, suspension from practice or other serious professional penalty. It covers a significant breach of a substantial duty imposed by a relevant code of conduct which would be regarded as improper according to the consensus of professional (including judicial) opinion. Such conduct can be fairly stigmatised as improper whether it violates the letter of a professional code or not.

When is conduct 'unreasonable'? Their Lordships would put into this category 'conduct which is vexatious, designed to harass the other side rather than advance the resolution of the case'. It makes no difference if the legal representative is simply actuated by abundant zeal and has no ulterior motive. The acid test is whether the conduct permits of a reasonable explanation.

The term 'negligent' presented the greatest difficulty. It was submitted to the court that the term as used in the Act was a term of art embracing the well-known ingredients of duty, breach, causation and damage. Thus it was contended that conduct could only be characterised as negligent if it involved an actionable breach of the legal representative's duty to his client to whom he alone owes such a duty. Their Lordships had no difficulty in rejecting this proposition and ruled that 'the expression does not invoke technical concepts of the law of negligence'. They elaborated thus: 'We are clear that "negligent" should be understood in an untechnical way to denote failure to act with the competence reasonably to be expected of ordinary members of the profession.'

Their Lordships also gave guidance on nine main other matters which we must now briefly examine *seriatim*:

(a) privilege;
(b) causation;
(c) reliance by solicitors on counsel's advice;
(d) threats to make applications for wasted costs orders;
(e) timing;
(f) the identity of the applicants;
(g) the procedures to be applied;
(h) discretion; and
(i) pursuing a hopeless case.

PRIVILEGE

As far as privilege is concerned, the question of how and when it can be waived in litigation generally will be canvassed in Chapter 7 below. Whenever a lawyer's client makes the application, privilege is deemed to be waived (*Lillicrap v Nalder & Son* [1993] 1 WLR 94). When in the normal situation, an application is made by the opposing party, the lawyer does not have it in his gift to waive the privilege and his client is often not willing to waive it. If the respondent lawyer suffers from the disadvantage of being unable to reveal what has happened, he cannot properly defend himself. In this connection, the Court of Appeal in *Ridehalgh* had this to say:

> Judges who are invited to make or contemplate making a wasted costs order must make full allowance for the inability of respondent lawyers to tell the whole story. Where there is room for doubt, the respondent lawyers are entitled to the benefit of it. It is again only when with all allowances made, a lawyer's conduct of proceedings is quite plainly unjustifiable that it can be appropriate to make a wasted cost order.

CAUSATION

The court's jurisdiction to make a wasted costs order is exercised only where – as pointed out in the case of *Re A Barrister*, already alluded to – the improper, unreasonable or negligent conduct of a respondent has resulted in a waste of costs. Demonstration of a causal link is vital.

RELIANCE ON COUNSEL

In *Ridehalgh*, the court endorsed the guidance given in *Locke v Camberwell Health Authority* [1991] 2 Med LR 249 that a solicitor cannot abdicate his responsibility by seeking the advice of counsel. He must actively address his mind to the advice he receives from counsel – unless the matter is of a very specialist nature – and in suitable cases apply his own judgment to the matter which is the subject matter of the advice.

THREATS

The court expressed agreement with the decision in *Orchard v South Eastern Electricity Board* [1987] 1 All ER 95 that threats of proposed applications for orders should never be made as a means of intimidation.

TIMING

The normal time for applications to be made is not during the interlocutory stage but at the conclusion of a trial. However, on this aspect it is impossible to lay down rules of general application: *Filmlab Systems International v Pennington* (1993) *The Times*, 9 July.

APPLICANTS

It is open to the court itself to initiate proceedings (this being provided for in the Supreme Court Practice Direction 48 PD 105) but, save in the most glaring cases, the court should be slow to take that step. Glaring cases would include such lapses as failing to appear, lateness and downright negligence in providing documents which lapses result in unnecessary adjournments.

PROCEDURES

The procedures should be tailored to suit individual cases but certain principles should be observed. The time for finalising the matter must be brief – 'measured in hours, not in days or weeks'. The procedure must be simple, without formal interrogatories or other pleadings. It must be fair, every step being taken to conform with the rules of natural justice – which means that respondents must be given an opportunity to reply to any allegations made against them. It is only in this way that a court will be able to decide whether a *prima facie* case exists for an order to be made.

DISCRETION

The judge hearing an application has a discretion to dismiss it at the first of two stages. In the first stage he hears the respondent, *ex parte* or even in writing, as to why an order should not be made. In the second stage, he examines such facts as the quantum of costs alleged to have been wasted and, on a basis of proportionality, assesses the feasibility of making the order. He must of course exercise this discretion judicially and if in all the circumstances he considers the cost of proceeding to be disproportionate to the amount of costs involved, he should refuse the order.

PURSUING A HOPELESS CASE

There is nothing improper in a legal representative acting for a party who insists in pursuing a claim or defence which is obviously doomed to failure.

There is a good deal of learning on this subject, but their Lordships referred only to Lord Pearce's *dictum* in the well-known case of *Rondel v Worsley* [1967] 3 All ER 1993; [1969] AC 191, in which at p 275 he made use of this pronouncement:

> It is easier, and more advantageous professionally for barristers to advise, represent or defend those who are decent and reasonable and likely to succeed in their action or their defence than those who are unpleasant, unreasonable, disreputable, and have an apparently hopeless case. Yet it would be tragic if our legal system came to provide no reputable defenders, representatives or advisers for the latter.

Their Lordships also referred to the cab-rank rule in reference to barristers, making the observation that although solicitors are not traditionally bound by such a rule 'many solicitors would and do respect public policy underlying it by affording representation to the unpopular and unmeritorious'. They continued:

> Legal representatives will, of course, whether barristers or solicitors, advise clients of the perceived weakness of their case and the risk of failure. But clients are free to reject advice and insist that cases be litigated. It is rarely if ever safe for a court to assume that a hopeless case is being litigated on the advice of the lawyers involved. They are there to present the case; it is (as Samuel Johnson unforgettably pointed out) for the judge and not the lawyers to judge it.

This statement was quoted with approval in a recent case from New Zealand in the Privy Council to which reference will be made later in this chapter.

FURTHER CASE LAW ON THE SUBJECT IN ENGLAND, NEW ZEALAND AND CANADA

ENGLAND

The principles stated above as laid down in *Ridehalgh* were endorsed by the House of Lords when it considered the regime of wasted costs for the first time in *Medcalf v Mardell and Others* [2002] All ER (D) 228 (Jun). In this case the Court of Appeal by a majority had made wasted costs orders against two prominent members of the Bar – Bernard Weatherill QC and Josephine Haynes.

This application was made by the other side and accordingly there was no deemed waiver. The former clients of the two lawyers refused to waive privilege and confidentiality, as a result of which counsel were unable to reveal any confidences arising out of their instructions. They took the position that it would be unfair in those circumstances to make the orders against them and that submission was rejected by the majority of the Court of Appeal.

The facts were not in dispute. Counsel was briefed at short notice in an appeal. They were required to prepare amended grounds of appeal including allegations of fraud against the appellant and other irregularities in connection with the way he had conducted the action. Although they did not have before them the evidence on which the allegations were based, they truly believed that details of the evidence would be forthcoming in due course. Unfortunately at the end of the period when such further evidence was to be submitted the original solicitors ceased to act and counsel found themselves without instructions. As a result, new solicitors had to be put on the record and it was not until one working day before the trial that counsel were re-instructed. The upshot was that the evidence could not properly go on the record since it was lodged when neither counsel nor solicitors were instructed, and the evidence proved insufficient. Leave to amend the grounds of appeal was accordingly refused and the appeal itself was dismissed with the appellant being awarded costs.

It was in these circumstances that the appellant made an application for a wasted costs order against the two lawyers on the basis of s 51(6) of the Supreme Court Act 1981 which, as stated above, empowers the court to order payment of wasted costs in the case of improper conduct by the lawyers. Such impropriety, it was contended, involved in this case a breach of para 606 of the Bar Council Rules of Conduct which forbids a barrister to 'draft any originating process, pleadings, affidavit, witness statement or notice of appeal containing *inter alia* any allegation of fraud unless he has clear instructions to make such allegations and has before him reasonably credible material which as it stands establishes a *prima facie* case of fraud'.

The majority of the Court of Appeal (Schiemann and Peter Gibson LJJ) read into the words 'had before him reasonably credible material' the expression 'evidence which can be put before the court to make good the allegations'. The dissenting member of the court (Wilson LJ) was of the opinion that the test was not what material was put before the court but what material counsel had before them. In other words, the word 'material' is wider than 'evidence in proper form'. Wilson LJ also formed the view that counsel was entitled to the benefit of the doubt, since, on grounds of privilege, they were not permitted to inform the court of the material they actually had before them.

The majority of the Court of Appeal was reversed by the House of Lords who restored the opinion of Wilson LJ. In refusing to make the order, the House fully approved the decision of the Court of Appeal in *Ridehalgh*.[2]

The other cases which we now consider address other requirements of the jurisdiction.

2 See an article captioned 'Stemming the tide of wasted costs applications' by Angela Home, in which the author provides a good commentary of the likely effect on future applications for such orders, in the *New Law Journal*, Vol 152, 2002, p 1152.

The first such case is *Davy Chiesman v Davy Chiesman* [1984] Fam 48, in which the Court of Appeal ruled that the court had to exercise its inherent jurisdiction against a solicitor who had failed to inform the Legal Aid Committee of the Law Society of a change in circumstances as he had an obligation to do under the rules, when it appeared or ought to have appeared to a reasonable solicitor that the assisted person no longer had any prospect of success. The solicitor contended that he was acting on the advice of counsel that the case should proceed and that it was difficult for him not to be persuaded by counsel's personality and forcefulness. This is what May LJ had to say about this preposterous claim:

> ... making all allowances for that I cannot avoid the conclusion, differing respectfully from the judge, that this solicitor did abdicate responsibility for his proper part and role in the relevant litigation. I think that he relied blindly and with no mind of his own on counsel's views upon which it must or ought to be apparent to him some question should have been raised. In my judgment this failure by the solicitor to question counsel's advice, let alone to report the situation on his own to the legal aid committee, as in any event I think he should have done, was a substantial failure on his part to fulfill his duty to the court to promote in his particular sphere the cause and administration of justice.

Re Freudiana Holdings Ltd (1995) *The Times*, 4 December was another case which involved full investigation by the Court of Appeal of the issues in the original trial. It is an ideal example of a matter that was not suitable for the wasted costs jurisdiction. The pleadings were 40 pages long, the points of defence covered 35 pages on behalf of counsel and 40 pages on behalf of the solicitors, the reply covering a further 20 pages. Skeleton arguments engaged 100 pages. The court felt constrained to bring the case to a halt at a time when the respondent's costs had reached £400,000, by which time it had become clear that a case of this complexity did not lend itself to the summary procedure laid down for a wasted costs order. The mere fact that the original trial had lasted 185 days and that the respondent lawyers had been discharged on the 85th day should have sent warning signals to the plaintiff's lawyers that the case was not a proper candidate for a wasted cost order. A summary procedure would be quite impossible since this was a matter in which the respondent lawyers were accused of dishonesty and of 'knowing participation in an attempt deliberately to mislead the court and to pervert the course of justice'. It goes without saying that once such accusations were levelled at members of the Bar, every attempt would be made to persuade the court otherwise – with skyrocketing costs.

Two final cases in the English jurisdiction will now briefly be examined – one illustrating unreasonable conduct, the other negligent conduct – sufficient in both cases to attract the making of wasted costs orders.

The first case is *Tolstoy v Aldington* [1996] 2 All ER 556. After a lengthy and successful libel action instituted by Lord Aldington against Tolstoy in which the latter characterised Lord Aldington as a major war criminal responsible for the liquidation of a large number of Cossacks, Tolstoy made an attempt to have the judgment against him set aside on the ground of fraud. His solicitors acted *pro bono* but made no attempt to obtain legal aid. Nor did they take the usual course of sending a letter before action. Tolstoy had in the meantime been declared bankrupt and was, therefore, unable to meet legal costs. The court of Appeal held that maintenance, by which they conducted the case without charge, was not culpable but they did find the solicitors guilty of improper conduct. The court ruled that the case was 'at least potentially vexatious', amounting to a collateral attack on a judgment of a court of competent jurisdiction. It was, in the opinion of the court, clearly an abuse of process since no solicitor could 'reasonably have instituted these proceedings'. Nor did it avail the solicitors that the statement of claim had been signed by counsel. This was a matter in which the solicitors were expected to exercise a judgment of their own. A wasted costs order was made.

The second case is *C v C* [1994] 2 FLR 34, in which the wife's solicitor was negligent in that he failed to ascertain that the husband's assets were far less than he had at first thought. His failure resulted in extensive fruitless investigations involving much wasted expense. His negligence also resulted in the case continuing for 22 days and this caused the wife to be saddled with costs in the sum of £60,000 and the husband £70,000, whereas the award the court made to the wife was only £20,000. The court had no difficulty in issuing a wasted costs order against the solicitors.

THE CANADIAN POSITION

Before 1990, courts in Canada could exercise an inherent jurisdiction to make wasted costs orders in appropriate circumstances – as is the case generally in the common law world.

In the Province of Ontario, for instance, orders were made on the following grounds:

(a) where a lawyer unduly and unreasonably interfered with the conduct of an examination (*Sonntag v Sonntag* [1997] 24 OR (2d) 473 HC);

(b) where proceedings were launched without authority (*Evans v Savarin Ltd* [1988] 27 OR (2D) 705 HC).

It is a matter of particular interest that at the same time as the English Courts and Legal Services Act 1990 and new Rules of the Supreme Court were being promulgated on the matter of wasted costs in England, the Province of Ontario should introduce Rules of Procedure, rule 57.07, PRO 1990, reg 194 to the same effect in Canada.

I have been able to find at least one case in Ontario where a law firm was made personally responsible for costs thrown away. It is the case of *Mans v State Farm Mutual Insurance Co* 32 OR (3d) 786 (1996). In this case M sustained injuries in an accident and retained Mitchell J Kiers of the firm of Neinstein Silverman Wilson ('NSW') to act for her in the proceedings. Not satisfied with the manner in which NSW were representing her she wished to change her solicitor and to retain instead the firm of Richard A Nabi & Associates ('N&A'). In order that such a change could take place, it was necessary that the relevant section of the Civil Procedure Rules be observed. The client may deliver a notice of intention to act in person pursuant to r 15.03(3), or a notice of change of solicitors, pursuant to r 15.03(1), or the solicitor of record may move under r 15.04 for an order removing him as solicitor of record. While the solicitor of record may expect to be served with one of the two notices referred to above, it is up to him to monitor the situation and, in the absence of such a notice, to move for an order in a timely fashion.

The actual facts may be briefly set out. The plaintiff, Jane Mans, after retaining NSW, lost confidence in them and wished to retain another firm. In an affidavit she stated that Mr Neinstein of NSW requested that she pay a retainer, which she did; that thereafter the firm of NSW never gave her any accounting of any funds received on her behalf from any source despite her repeated requests; and that she had always replied promptly to any correspondence received from NSW. She also deposed that she had been told by NSW that they thought the matter could be concluded by way of settlement and had no idea the matter was going to trial. What was even more disturbing is that in her affidavit she averred that:

> I did not know these matters were scheduled for trial until 15 October 1996 when I was informed of this fact by the firm of Richard A Nabi & Associates. I was never informed by the firm of Neinstein, Silverman & Wilson that the trial records in these actions had been passed and/or that the matter had been set down for trial.

The fact is that a trial had been set for 21 October 1996 and the person mainly involved (Ms Mans) was learning about it for the first time one week ahead – even though the solicitors who were replacing NSW had been writing to NSW since 6 June 1996 requesting the handover of the relevant file and giving an undertaking to protect their account at the resolution of the matter. To that letter of 6 June 1996 was affixed a release from Jane Mans stating: 'You are hereby authorised and directed to release to Mr Nabi (of N&A) all documents or information in your possession relating to my case, and this shall be your good, sufficient and irrevocable authority for so doing.'

Up to 10 October the documents had not been released and neither Jane Mans nor the new solicitors had been informed of the trial date set for 21 October 1996. In making the wasted costs order against NSW, Quinn J had this to say:

> The failure of NSW in the letters of June 17 1996 and October 10 1996 to inform N&A that the trials of the two motions were set for October 21 1996 is quite indefensible; and the refusal of NSW to forward their legal account in relation to Mrs Mans, as requested by N&A, is really quite outrageous.[3]

3 32 OR (3d), p 794.

NEW ZEALAND

The case of *Raylee Harley and Glasgow Harley v Robert McDonald* (Privy Council Appeals No 9 of 2000 and No 50 of 2000) is a landmark decision in the matter of wasted costs. It is a matter in which a barrister and solicitor practising in New Zealand were ordered personally to pay jointly and severally a contribution of $NZ65,000 towards the costs of a former client – a Mr Robert McDonald – in circumstances which will be set out at some length in this section. The length of the exposition (it should be explained) stems from the complex nature of the litigation. Broadly, the facts are as follows.

The applicants acted as counsel and solicitor respectively in a suit brought by Mr McDonald against FAI (NZ) General Insurance Company (FAI) and the New Zealand Law Society (the Law Society) to recover money which had been invested with a law firm called Renshaw Edwards which had collapsed. Mr McDonald obtained a summary judgment against the former partners of the firm, but the judgment could not be satisfied because all the partners had been declared bankrupt. He then brought a suit against FAI. Later he joined the Law Society which administers the Solicitors Fidelity Guarantee Fund charged by s 169 of the Law Practitioners Act 1982 with administering the Fund. The purpose of the Fund was to reimburse clients who had suffered pecuniary loss by reason of theft by solicitors or their agents or their employees. There was subsequent further litigation mainly relating to the payment and allocation of the costs (with which we are particularly concerned here).

Mr McDonald was not a pleasant or co-operative client. He was not prepared at any time to meet personally with his lawyers, to whom he gave a Post Office Box Number directing them that all contact with him was to be in writing. He was difficult and strong-willed and given to dismissing his legal advisers on a whim, when, for example, Mrs Harley his counsel – whom he had been pressing to institute proceedings against FAI – suggested that he should await the outcome of a similar suit brought by another law firm against FAI. Mr McDonald summarily rejected that advice and ordered her to proceed immediately. Later Mrs Harley returned his file stating that her commitments precluded her continuing to represent him; under pressure from him, however, she reluctantly decided to continue (she was no doubt later to regret it).

On 8 October 1997, the Law Society offered to settle Mr McDonald's claim for $450,000, but the offer was rejected by Mr McDonald on the basis that he would accept nothing but the full amount. Up to that stage there was no complaint from any quarter about the manner of representation provided by Mrs Harley.

After much interlocutory ado, the action against FAI was dismissed. In the course of the judgment, in which Giles J held that FAI was entitled to costs against Mr McDonald, the judge *of his own motion* raised for the first time the question whether any award of costs to FAI should be paid in whole or in part by Mr McDonald's counsel and solicitor. This is how the judge dealt with the issue:

> I require this aspect (of cost being paid by counsel and solicitor) to be addressed because both in the course of opening and at the time of hearing argument (on 15th October 1997) on FAI's application for dismissal of the claim against it I indicated to counsel for the plaintiff that she needed to reflect carefully on the wisdom of continuing the claim against FAI. I forewarned Mrs Harley that in the event of FAI succeeding, the plaintiff could expect little sympathy in relation to costs ... It is my view that the case against FAI was always weak and that circumstances are such that Mr McDonald should not have judgment against the Society eroded by costs which his counsel could and, in my view, should have avoided by more realistically assessing the wisdom of proceeding.

It was therefore not surprising that when on 28 September 1998 Giles J delivered a single judgment covering both the cost issue and an unrelated issue on a charging order/lien, he made an order that Mr McDonald be indemnified to the tune of $65,000 against the $115,000 he was ordered to pay as costs to FAI. In this connection the judge made the following statements:

> In at least two stages in the course of the trial counsel was provided with an opportunity to review the position with the plaintiff. For whatever reason this was not done. There is the added ignominy, from the plaintiff's point of view, that he was completely unaware that a R46A offer of settlement had been made. A 'hopeless' case was pursued without the plaintiff receiving the degree of objective and independent advice he was entitled to as to the risks of so doing.
>
> The plaintiff was put at risk without being given the kind of objective appraisal required before counsel exposed him to significant financial exposure. To do so was unreasonable, improper and negligent.

Giles J's judgment was endorsed by the New Zealand Court of Appeal who, speaking through Tipping J, devoted much of his discussion (while reviewing the cost issue) to an analysis of the case against FAI which the court all along considered hopeless. The appeal court judge (at para 63) stated the position was not that Mrs Harley prosecuted a hopeless case knowing it to be hopeless, but rather that she did not appreciate how hopeless it was and did not, therefore, advise her client to that effect. As for Glasgow Harley, the solicitor, the judge considered his breach of duty on the same level as that of counsel.

In the Judicial Committee of the Privy Council, Lord Hope, speaking for a unanimous Board, reviewed in great detail the judgments in the two New Zealand courts below and gave an expansive and lucid exposition of the jurisdiction to make a wasted costs order. It is a judgment which should be carefully studied by any judge who is minded to exercise the particular jurisdiction anywhere. Practising lawyers should also pay special attention to this regime.

Their Lordships referred to the prerequisites of the compensatory and penal nature of the jurisdiction and emphasised that allegations of breach of duty relating to the conduct of a case by a barrister or solicitor with a view to making an order for wasted costs should be confined strictly to questions which are apt for summary disposal by the court: such questions as a failure to appear, conduct leading to an otherwise avoidable step in the proceedings, prolongation of a hearing by gross repetition or extreme slowness in the presentation of evidence.

Their Lordships then expressed the following further strictures to be observed when a court is faced with making a wasted costs order:

> But in cases where an order to that effect is contemplated the court must take great care to confine its attention to the facts which are clearly before it or to facts relating to the conduct of the case that are immediately and easily verifiable. Allegations that may raise questions about duties owed to the client by the barrister or solicitor and the conduct of the case outside the courtroom are unlikely to be of that character. They are likely therefore to fall outside the scope of that inquiry. The court must bear in mind that it is not its function, in the exercise of this jurisdiction, to adjudicate on the position as between the client and his barrister or solicitor.

Their Lordships underscored the above warning by indicating that the court should have particular regard in cases of this kind to the factual basis upon which the jurisdiction is exercised. They urged the impossibility of relying on the judge's own knowledge when he is faced with issues about the nature and scope of the instructions given by the client about the conduct of the litigation or the advice that may not have been given to the client by his legal adviser. Their Lordships' own words will highlight the reason for such a suggestion:

> Fairness to the barrister or solicitor requires that notice should be given of allegations about breaches of duty which raise these issues and that an opportunity should be given to them to challenge the allegations, if so advised, by cross-examining witnesses and leading evidence. Bearing in mind the extra cost which an investigation of that kind may involve, and the overriding requirement of fairness to those who are at risk of being penalised, the court may well conclude that further investigation under this procedure is not appropriate.

Their Lordships urged caution in assuming that just because it appears to a court that a case is hopeless there is a failure by the legal adviser to achieve the appropriate level of competence and care, and cited with approval Sir Thomas Bingham's statement on this point in *Ridehalgh v Horsefield*, which is quoted earlier in this chapter under the heading 'Pursuing a Hopeless Case' of the nine points of guidance given concerning a lawyer's duty to pursue such a representation after having duly advised the client of the perceived weakness of the case and received his or her instructions nevertheless to proceed.

In the course of scrutinising the judgment of Giles J at first instance, the Board took cognisance of the judge's promise in his judgments of 12 December 1997 and 19 February 1998 as well as his minute of 10 March 1998 to restrict the limits of the inquiry he proposed to conduct into the costs issue. In the event, however, the judge was confronted with further data in connection with a charging order/lien application which he regrettably heard the same day as the costs order, and in respect of which he gave one composite judgment covering both issues. On this aspect their Lordships stated:

> There is no doubt that he should have left that information (concerning the charging order/lien) out of account when he was dealing with the costs order. Mrs Harley was not a party to the charging order/lien applications. She was not given notice that they might be relevant to the decision on costs, and she had no opportunity to present her account of the facts for consideration by the trial judge. Unfortunately it is plain from the reasons given in his judgment of 24 September 1998 ... for making the costs order that the trial judge went well beyond the limits which he had previously set for his inquiry and that he took into account matters of fact on which Mrs Harley had not had an opportunity to address him or give evidence.

Their Lordships stated that the costs which counsel and solicitor were ordered to contribute were out of all proportion to the costs 'that could reasonably be attributed to the decision to continue with the trial after the warnings which (the trial judge) gave to Mrs Harley that she should consider her position very carefully'. The Board then indicated that the order was made without knowledge of Mr McDonald's insistence that proceedings should be taken against FAI and of the steps which Mrs Harley took to tell Mr McDonald about the Law Society's offer of settlement and to obtain his instructions. In the forceful words of the Board: 'The entire substratum of his decision was based upon a series of mistaken assumptions, all of which were due to the unfair way in which he decided to broaden the scope of his inquiry.'

In affirming the decision of Giles J, the New Zealand Court of Appeal, speaking through Tipping J, had come to the conclusion that although the trial judge did consider matters not germane to the costs inquiry, it was nevertheless open to him, on the material properly before him, to order that Mrs Harley indemnify Mr McDonald for the costs he was ordered to pay to FAI and that a contribution of $65,000 was appropriate.

That assessment did not find favour with their Lordships. They drew attention to the fact that much of Tipping J's judgment concentrated on whether or not Mr McDonald's case was hopeless. (Reference has already been made in the earlier part of this chapter as to what the proper attitude of a court should ethically be to a lawyer who is considered to be pursuing a hopeless case.) However, in respect of the Court of Appeal's confirmation of the judge's position in taking into account the extraneous matters he had considered, their Lordships in the Privy Council had this to say: 'The matters and issues which were not properly before Giles J, but which he nevertheless did consider, played a much greater role in his decision than the Court of Appeal appear to have been willing to recognise' (para 65).

They also took issue with the Court of Appeal that Mrs Harley displayed incompetence in her handling of the case against FAI to such a degree that she was in serious dereliction of duty to the court. On this point they said (at para 66):

> Having analysed the history of the case more fully, their Lordships do not think Mrs Harley's conduct of the case deserves that description. Up to the date of trial at least she was conducting the case in accordance with her instructions. The claim against FAI had not been struck out, and Mr McDonald had still been unable to reach a settlement with the Law Society. It has not been suggested that her conduct was malicious or dishonest or that she deliberately persisted in an action which was an abuse of the court's process ... In the present case the Court's conclusion that Mr McDonald had not given fully informed instructions was based upon assumptions which were not fully tested in the evidence.

Finally their Lordships wished to register their respectful dissent from the proposition of the courts below that a barrister who pursues a hopeless case not appreciating it is hopeless displays such a degree of incompetence as to amount to serious dereliction of duty to the court. Their Lordships were satisfied that the Court of Appeal was wrong to hold that Mrs Harley was on that account in serious breach of her duty to the court. They made the same finding in respect of Glasgow Harley in so far as their conduct as Mr McDonald's solicitors was concerned.

The Board allowed the appeals and ordered that the orders of Giles J and the Court of Appeal be set aside.

CONCLUSION

We have in this chapter looked at the history of the wasted costs jurisdiction beginning with the decision of the House of Lords in *Myers v Elman* in 1940.

We have noticed that the jurisdiction was put on a statutory basis in England in 1981 to cover situations in both civil and criminal cases, mainly when costs cannot be recovered from the other side.

We have looked in some detail into the landmark case of *Ridehalgh v Horsefield*, decided by the Court of Appeal, and approved by the House of Lords in *Medcalf v Mardell*. We have seen how much use has been made of the jurisdiction in the 12 years of its existence – paying special attention to a number of English cases and briefly reviewing the way the regime has been followed in Canada, New Zealand and even in the Caribbean – where it is very much in its infancy, but where it may be more fully deployed in time.

One authority who has carried out an empirical study in England does not consider the arrangement to have been an unqualified success.[4] Evans has illustrated that in a review of all wasted costs cases brought in the first 10 years of the operation of the rules on the subject, he has not found a single case where the cost incurred in the application was justified by the wasted costs sought or recovered. He has also drawn attention to three major flaws in the jurisdiction, viz:

4 See Evans, Hugh, *Lawyers' Liabilities* (London, Sweet & Maxwell, 2002), Chapter 7.

(a) it is too costly a procedure as well as too complex;

(b) since a presiding judge is permitted of his own motion to initiate an order it is conceivable that a non-respondent may find himself having to hire a lawyer to watch his interest although he may have no interest in the suit and does not want it; and

(c) where there is a respondent lawyer from whom wasted costs are being sought, the trial judge involved becomes the judge to hear the application – which makes him judge, jury and witness. It may well be that this procedure will in due course be challenged under Art 6 of the Human Rights Act 1998 since such a tribunal cannot be said to be either independent or impartial.

As it has been well put by Evans:[5] 'We have thus ended up with a jurisdiction in which justice is administered less fairly than in normal litigation but which in practice is far more expensive for the benefits gained.'

The case of *Harley v McDonald* – the New Zealand case referred to in the immediately preceding section of this chapter – lends full support to the argument that there must be a serious flaw in a jurisdiction which enables a judge to encourage or initiate a procedure which can bring such financial and mental distress to lawyer-respondents even though the Privy Council ruled in their favour. The respondents in that case were not granted costs in the court of last resort.

It is true that it can fairly be said that the jurisdiction is still in an experimental stage in England and one expects many further refinements as time goes on. Evans considers that with the advent of conditional fees, the disadvantage of not being able to recover costs from a legally-aided litigant will be obviated and that in consequence there are likely to be fewer applications for wasted costs orders.[6]

The Province in Ontario in 1990 made provision in its Civil Procedure Rules for adapting the jurisdiction to their needs and we have seen that there is already case law on the subject in the province of Ontario.[7]

In so far as the Caribbean area is concerned, the Supreme Court of the Eastern Caribbean States has been the first in this region to enshrine in its 2000 Civil Procedure Rules a clause similar to the English provision. There is no doubt that in this part of the world the jurisdiction can operate as a useful tool to keep negligent and carefree members of the profession 'on their toes', especially in territories where the regime for disciplining practitioners is less well-structured and less efficient than it is in England. It is an experiment that is well worth trying but one expects that the judges will proceed with care and discretion whenever it becomes necessary to invoke it.

The next question to which we turn our attention is that of confidentiality and privilege.

---

5 *Ibid*, p 133.

6 *Ibid*, p 141.

7 See *Danson v Ontario (Attorney-General)* [1990] 2 SCR 1086; and the Ontario Rules of Civil Procedure RRO 1990, reg 194, r 57.07.

CHAPTER 7

CONFIDENTIALITY AND LEGAL PROFESSIONAL PRIVILEGE

(A) CONFIDENTIALITY IN GENERAL

A lawyer is under a general duty of secrecy in respect of all the affairs of his client and the lawyer should always ensure that his associates, juniors and members of his staff accept the same responsibility. Confidentiality holds a central place in the legal system and the lawyer can always draw on three sources for authority to observe it, viz the Codes of Ethics; the common law and equity; and the evidential doctrine of legal professional privilege.

The Codes will be dealt with in Chapter 9 of this book and at this juncture all we need to say is that they abound. Most of them form a schedule or an appendix to an Act prescribing the conditions for the education, admission, and discipline of members of the legal profession. There are however a few countries that do not yet have a code of any kind for lawyers.

In every case the Code includes a section underscoring the lawyer's duty to preserve the secrets and confidences of his clients, revealing them only when forced by law to do so – and the rules are strict.

A few examples will suffice. The Code of Ethics promulgated for the lawyers in the Organisation of Eastern Caribbean States (OECS)[1] as well as those for Trinidad and Tobago,[2] Barbados,[3] Antigua,[4] Jamaica,[5] Bahamas,[6] all provide that 'an attorney-at-law shall scrupulously guard and never divulge his client's secrets and confidences'. Belize goes into more detail, viz:

> An attorney-at-law shall never disclose, unless lawfully ordered to do so by the court or required by statute, what has been communicated to him in his capacity as an attorney by his client, and this duty not to disclose extends to his partners, to junior attorneys assisting him and to his employees – provided however that an attorney may reveal confidences or secrets necessary to establish or collect his fee or to defend himself or his employees or associates against an accusation of wrongful conduct.[7]

This statutory provision reflects the common-law position which has always recognised confidentiality as an implied term in certain professional contracts. As far back as the 17th century Law Commissioner Whitelock included as one of the principal duties which the lawyer owed to his client a duty of secrecy in respect of which he remarked:

---

1 Adopted by the OECS Bar on 15 June 1991 and amended on 9 March 1996.
2 Paragraph 15 of Pt B of Sched 3 to the Trinidad and Tobago Legal Profession Act 1986.
3 Legal Profession Code of Ethics made by the Barbados Disciplinary Committee on 12 December 1988.
4 Section 23(2) of Sched 4 to the Legal Profession Act 1997 (No 9 of 1997).
5 Canon IV(t) of the Jamaica Code of Ethics made by the General Legal Council on 12 December 1978.
6 Rule IV (Confidentiality) of the Schedule to the Bahamas Bar Code of Professional Conduct 1981.
7 Paragraph 66 of the Belize Code of Ethics (Statutory Instrument No 42 of 1991).

> For secrecy, advocates are a kind of confessors, and ought to be such to whom the client may with confidence lay open his evidences and the naked truth of his case, sub sigillo, and he ought not to discover them to his client's prejudice, nor will the law compel him to do it.[8]

This is the duty which has been described as one in which the lawyer has an implied term: 'to keep (his) client's affairs secret and not to disclose them to any one without just cause.'[9]

Public policy permits disclosure in certain restricted circumstances – those always referred to being disclosure of a communication to a lawyer who is being asked to give assistance to a client towards the commission of a crime; when the lawyer has been unwittingly used by his client to perpetrate fraud or some such criminal offence; and when disclosure becomes necessary to establish a defence to a criminal charge.

The duty of confidentiality does not end with the expiry of the retainer. It endures even after that relationship has come to an end and even after the death of the client. A further point in this connection (for instance) is that a lawyer is under a duty not to reveal the contents of a will drawn by him until probate is received, unless he has the consent of the executors.

The duty of confidentiality is an ethical duty which covers all matters revealed concerning the client to a lawyer regardless of whether it relates to the obtaining of legal advice and regardless of its source.

It has been extended in England recently to non-lawyers providing advocacy, conveyancing and probate services.[10] In the US, psychiatrists also have this duty.[11] In England, Ireland and Canada, the doctrine applies in a limited way to priests[12] and psychiatrists as well as to investigative journalists who are immune from having to reveal their sources. In New South Wales (in Australia), there is a professional confidential relationship privilege provided by statute.[13]

PUBLIC POLICY AND CONFIDENTIALITY

Two reported cases will reveal vividly how public policy can override the duty of confidentiality. The first case – *W v Egdell* (1990) Ch 359, CA – provided the courts for the first time with an opportunity of considering the extent of the obligation owed by a doctor to his patient.

---

8 See Sir Bulstrode Whitelock, *Memorials of English Affairs*, Vol 2, 1853, p 454. Quoted by Ross Cranston in *Legal Ethics and Professional Responsibility* (Oxford, Clarendon Press, 1995), p 6.

9 See the case of *Parry-Jones v Law Society* [1969] Ch 1.

10 See s 63 of the Courts and Legal Services Act 1990.

11 See *Jaffee v Redmond* (1923) 116 S Ct (SC 1996).

12 See Jonathan Auburn, *Legal Professional Privilege Law and Theory* (Oxford, Hart, 2000), p 59, in which Auburn asserts that the privilege applied to civil litigation even before the Reformation.

13 See the Evidence Amendment (Confidential Communications) Act 1997.

W had been detained in a secure hospital facility following a plea of diminished responsibility after murdering five persons – the plea being accepted. The court was empowered under the relevant legislation to make W the subject of a hospital order if his mental condition warranted such an arrangement. However, such an order would, under s 37 of the Mental Health Act ('the Act'), only be made if two doctors certified that the patient was suffering from such mental illness or psychopathic disorder as would make detention in hospital for mental treatment appropriate (s 37 of the Act deals specifically with the need for treatment).

At the same time, s 41 of the Act is concerned with protection of the public under which a 'restriction order' may be made for an unlimited period, and in making such an order the court is required to pay special attention to protecting the public from physical harm. Under s 37 it was relatively easy for a patient to effect a transfer from one institution to another and to arrange for a release. However, under s 41 it was necessary to apply to the Home Secretary for a transfer or a release.

W applied through his solicitor to a Medical Health Review Tribunal for a release. The Tribunal had no such powers but could (and did) make a recommendation to that effect to the Home Secretary, who rejected the recommendation, at which stage W's solicitors went again to the Tribunal. For this purpose the solicitors requested a confidential report from Dr Egdell – a distinguished psychiatrist. Upon studying the case, Dr Egdell reported that he did not consider W to be a fit subject for a transfer: he expressed the view that the patient had an abnormal personality and could be of a psychopathic deviant nature with a special interest in 'fireworks' (this is how the patient characterised pieces of steel-piping packed with chemical explosives).

When W's solicitors read Dr Egdell's report they promptly withdrew W's application, the result being that the doctor's report was not placed before the Tribunal. But Dr Egdell decided that a copy of the report should be put on W's hospital file and one sent to the Home Secretary.

In the meantime the Home Secretary had on his own referred W's case to the Tribunal to whom he now sent a copy of Dr Egdell's report. W's solicitors then brought an action before the High Court to restrain Dr Egdell from disclosure of the report. They also sought damages against the Home Secretary for the unauthorised disclosure of the report to the Tribunal.

In the High Court, Scott J rejected the solicitors' application and in so doing he made this statement:

> In my view a doctor called upon, as Dr Egdell was, to examine a patient owes a duty not only to the patient but to the public. His duty to the public would require him in my opinion to place before the proper authorities the results of his examination if in his opinion the public interest so requires. This would be so whether or not the patient instructed him to do so.

The judgment of Scott J was affirmed by the Court of Appeal.

A Canadian case to the same effect – *Smith v Jones* 60 CRR (2a) 46 – should also be noticed. Here the patient was charged with aggravated sexual assault of a prostitute whom he had raped and then murdered. When his counsel referred him to a psychiatrist, the patient described in detail to the psychiatrist how he had chosen the prostitute of small enough stature as to be able easily to overwhelm her and then raped, kidnapped and murdered her. He then volunteered the information that that experience was only 'a trial run' – the suggestion being that he intended to repeat such acts. The psychiatrist diagnosed his patient as suffering from a paraphiliac disorder with multiple paraphilias, in particular sexual sadism, personality disorder with some antisocial features and drug abuse difficulty. The doctor advised defence counsel that the patient was a dangerous person capable of performing other similar offences unless he received proper treatment.

Subsequently, the patient pleaded guilty to aggravated assault and the matter was stood over for sentencing. When the psychiatrist realised that his report was not being brought to the attention of the judge at the sentence hearing, he initiated an action seeking a declaration that he was entitled to disclose, in the public interest, the information in his possession and the judge ruled that the public interest released the psychiatrist from his duties of confidentiality in the matter. On appeal to the Supreme Court of Canada, that court affirmed the decision.

Apart from those referred to (affecting psychiatrists), a few other English exceptions to the duty of confidentiality should be mentioned.

STATUTORY DUTIES OF LAWYERS IN MONEY LAUNDERING MATTERS

There are, however, certain statutory duties which outweigh a client's interest, and what this means is that the lawyer must keep the affairs of the client strictly confidential except when the public interest is threatened.

Towards the end of the 20th century, the English Parliament introduced certain important statutory exceptions to confidentiality, viz money laundering and drug trafficking legislation in 1993. See the relevant sections: 50–53, 55 and 58 of the Criminal Justice Act 1993, which effected certain modifications to the Drug Trafficking Act 1986; the Criminal Justice Act of 1988; the Prevention of Terrorism (Temporary Provisions Act) 1989; and the Criminal Justice (International Co-operation) Act 1990. There was also passed the Drug Trafficking Act in 1994 as well as the Money Laundering Regulations of 1993, money laundering being defined as 'assisting another to retain the benefit of criminal conduct, acquiring or using the proceeds of crime or concealing or transferring such proceeds'.

Such were the exceptions to the fundamental principle of confidentiality created by statute between 1988 and 1994. The Drug Trafficking Act of 1994 created the offence of failing to disclose a person's 'knowledge' or 'suspicion' of money laundering while two later acts (the Terrorism Act of 2000 – amended by the Anti-Terrorism, Crime and Security Act 2001) made it an offence to provide assistance to a money launderer in the retention of the benefit of funds if one knows or suspects that the funds are the proceeds of terrorism. It is also an offence to fail to report knowledge or reasonable grounds for suspicion of money laundering of terrorist funds (acquired in the course of one's professional operations).

Then there is the Proceeds of Crime Act 2002 (POCA) which, in the words of Richard Jones QC,[14] 'clearly demonstrates a political determination to deprive criminals of the benefits of their crimes and to crack down on money laundering in its broadest sense'.

The POCA gives a new remedy of civil recovery against the proceeds of crime. A number of investigative orders are also enshrined in the legislation in respect of giving information by third parties. This Act ranges far and wide and one must readily agree with Richard Jones that lawyers should make themselves acquainted with its provisions. There are many money laundering offences created by the Act; for example, concealing, disguising or transferring criminal property which is described as property which is a person's benefit from criminal conduct or (which) represents such a benefit in whole or in part. The offence is committed if the person charged knows or suspects that it is, or represents, such a benefit. 'Property' includes money, all forms of property, real or personal, heritable or moveable, chose in action and tangible or incorporeal property.

Under the Act, it is not competent for a lawyer to claim that the facts on which knowledge or suspicion is based come under the head of legal professional privilege, if the facts are communicated with the intention of furthering a criminal purpose.

Tipping off provisions are also made in the Act, so that once a person has made disclosure to the appropriate authority he is under no obligation to give an intimation of such disclosure to anyone else which may prejudice the investigations. Such action is itself an offence.

The requirements of the POCA should be of serious concern to all practising lawyers who may hold funds as constructive trustees and it is not surprising that solicitors in England are today having to establish elaborate procedures for testing the suspicious nature of clients' property.

In a recent article,[15] David Dabbs of 22 Old Buildings, Lincoln's Inn, cogently counsels as follows:

> If you are a lawyer who comes into possession of information which implicates your client in certain … fields of criminal activity – and this information was communicated or acquired outside a retainer to defend the client for that offence – then you are under a positive duty to inform the authorities, but in practical terms you will have to determine yourself when that positive duty properly arises.

The author of the article then proceeds to remind his readers of the case of Jonathan Duff reported in *The Times* Law Section of 23 July 2002. This case

14 *New Law Journal*, Vol 152, No 7048, 20 September 2002, p 1394.
15 *New Law Journal*, Vol 151, No 7051, 11 October 2001, p 1531.

concerned an English solicitor who, in the course of reviewing the evidence for the prosecution against a client, realised that the client had purchased cocaine with clients' funds previously held by Duff in his clients' account. Duff took legal advice, after which he came to the conclusion that the duty to make disclosure referred only to suspicion of a person 'engaged in drug money laundering' and that as the cocaine incident was a past event, he was under no obligation to disclose any suspicion to the prosecution under the provisions of s 52 of the Drug Trafficking Act 1994. The court was not, however, persuaded by the argument. Duff was convicted for failing to disclose his knowledge and sentenced to four months' imprisonment even though he acted in good faith.

It is difficult, when one thinks of this case, to quarrel with the following wise caution of Dabbs in his article:

> Perhaps it is time to accept that the fundamental principle of client confidentiality exists now only as a commercial necessity, the intention being to protect a client's legitimate interests either in the completion of a legal transaction, or in the result of actual or contemplated legal proceedings. In all other material respects the lawyer's duty to his client may be qualified or even excluded by his duty to protect the public interest.

There can be no doubt that solicitors and other legal representatives who conduct investment businesses will in the future need to pay special attention to the kind of offence of which Duff was found guilty. More and more countries after 11 September 2001 are making provision for drug trafficking, money laundering and anti-terrorism legislation, since it has been clearly established that these activities are interrelated. It will, therefore, be necessary for lawyers to make themselves fully acquainted with the relevant legislation and to provide the necessary training for their staff to prevent them from falling into the non-disclosure trap wittingly or unwittingly.

In recent years, money laundering has become a menace to our civilisation. The National Criminal Investigation Service in the UK (NCIS) has revealed that in 1997 English solicitors provided only 236 reports (1.9%) of all disclosures under the Drug Trafficking and Money Laundering legislation in respect of information of illicit activities obtained in their professional lives. And of course, lawyers – like everyone else – commit offences by failing to make the necessary disclosures of information in this connection. They can no longer rely on the doctrine of confidentiality and they are clearly expected, in the public interest, to co-operate with the authorities.

Today all enlightened countries collaborate in the grim fight against money laundering and terrorism. That is certainly the case throughout the African, Caribbean and Pacific countries of which a prototype is provided by Antigua and Barbuda in the enactment of such laws as the Proceeds of Crime Act 1993; the Suppression of Terrorism Act 1993; various Money Laundering Prevention Acts and Regulations made under them; and the Prevention of Terrorism Act 2001.

(B) LEGAL PROFESSIONAL PRIVILEGE

This privilege received a shot in the arm by the decision of the House of Lords in *R v Derby Magistrates' Court ex p B* [1996] 1 AC 487. In this case, the House held that the privilege was absolute and, once established without being waived, could not be overridden, even when non-disclosure results in depriving a court of relevant admissible evidence in a charge of murder. This was a case in which B was being tried for the murder of a young girl. At first he confessed to the murder but later withdrew his confession. Later he repeated both the confession and retraction, saying that although he was present, he took no part in the murder, which was the work of his stepfather. He was acquitted. After a civil suit brought jointly against him and his stepfather had resulted in a finding that both were responsible in tort for assault and battery, the stepfather was tried, B then being summoned as a witness.

In the course of the committal proceedings, the stepfather's counsel wished to question B on the likely instructions B had given his solicitors in 1978 when he was answering the charge of murder. He had declined to waive his privilege to disclose documents in both the criminal trial of 1978 and the civil suit of 1991. Thereupon, the defence obtained a witness summons directed to B's former solicitors which was challenged by way of judicial review. The challenge failed before the Divisional Court where McCowan LJ described the balancing exercise carried out by the stipendiary magistrate as flawless.

In granting the witness summons, the magistrate had been guided by a decision of Caulfield J in *R v Barton* [1973] 1 WLR 115, when the idea of a balancing act had first been mooted. He had also felt himself bound by decision in *R v Ataou* [1988] QB 798, CA, in which the Court of Appeal had decided that a judge is required to approach an application for production of documents in two stages. He must first ask whether the client continues to have any recognisable interest in asserting the privilege and, secondly, whether (if so) his interest outweighs the public interest that relevant and admissible documents should be made available to the defence in criminal proceedings.

The Divisional Court had likewise considered itself bound by the decision of the Court of Appeal in *Ataou*.

The House of Lords, however, in this case (*R v Derby Magistrates' Court*) overruled both *Ataou* and *Barton*. Lord Taylor, who gave the main judgment, made this statement in reference to those cases: 'So stated, the principle seems to conflict with the long-established rule that a document protected by privilege continues to be protected so long as the privilege is not waived by the client: once privileged, always privileged.'

Lord Taylor then set out the rationale of the privilege in these forceful and explicit terms:

> The principle which runs through all these cases is that a man must be able to consult his lawyer in confidence, since otherwise he might hold back half the truth. The client must be sure that what he tells his lawyer in confidence will never be revealed without his consent. Legal professional privilege is thus much more than a rule of evidence limited in its application to the facts of a particular case. It is a fundamental condition on which the administration of justice as a whole rests.[16]

QUALIFICATION TO ABSOLUTE DOCTRINE IN FAVOUR OF DISCLOSURE

Shortly after the decision of the House of Lords in the *R v Derby Magistrates' Court* case, and no doubt because of Lord Taylor's endorsement of the absolute nature of legal professional privilege, the House was called upon to rule on the extent to which claims for privilege were recognised in care proceedings under Part IV of the English Children's Act 1989.

The case was *Re L (A Minor)* [1996] 2 All ER 78, the facts of which are as follows. A young child, both of whose parents were drug addicts, was admitted to hospital and placed in intensive care after ingesting a quantity of methadone. The mother stated that the child had swallowed the methadone when her attention was distracted, but the police had a suspicion that the mother had deliberately administered the methadone to the child in the belief that it would assist toothache. At first the mother and father of the child were cohabiting but when they ceased to cohabit a care order was obtained by the local authority. In the course of proceedings to that end the district judge made an order giving the parents leave to disclose the court papers to a medical expert to prepare a report on the possible frequency of the child's consumption of methadone – subject to the report being filed in court and disclosed to all parties. The mother accordingly commissioned a report by a consultant pathologist who produced a report substantially contradicting the mother's account of how the child had come to ingest methadone.

Having become aware of the report, the police sought a copy in order to determine whether the mother had committed a criminal offence by deliberately administering the drug to the child. They applied to the court for a copy. The judge held that she had jurisdiction to order disclosure to non-parties and did so to the police. The mother appealed on the ground that the judge had no such jurisdiction, since the report was protected by legal professional privilege and its disclosure would infringe her privilege against self-incrimination and her privilege against disclosure. The Court of Appeal rejected her contention and she appealed to the House of Lords.

The House dismissed the appeal on the following grounds:

16 *R v Derby Magistrates' Court* [1995] 4 All ER 526 at pp 540/541.

(a) There is a clear distinction between the privilege attaching to communications between solicitor and client and that attaching to reports by third parties prepared on the instructions of a client for the purposes of litigation. The privilege attaching to the solicitor/client relationship was absolute and attached to all communications whether related to litigation or not. The privilege attaching to reports by third parties prepared for a client pertained ONLY to documents or other written communications prepared with a view to litigation.

(b) There was no property in the opinion of an expert witness who could be subpoenaed to give evidence by the other side and could not refuse to answer questions as to his factual findings and opinion.

(c) Care proceedings under the 1989 Act were non-adversarial and investigative proceedings in which the judge had to make a decision in the best interest of the child.

(d) At the time the mother applied for the order, the district judge had no reason to suppose that the report would incriminate her and there was, therefore, no reason to refrain from making the order or to withhold disclosure to all parties on that ground. Further, since the mother voluntarily initiated the process, did not appeal the order when it was made and had filed it with the court without seeking a variation, well appreciating its unfavourable nature, she must be taken to have waived any claim she might have had to privilege against self-incrimination.

Those were the reasons which led the majority in the House of Lords – Lords Jauncey, Lloyd and Steyn – to endorse the judgment of Stephen Browne P in the case of *Oxfordshire County Council v M* [1994] Fam 151, in which it was held that such proceedings are non-adversarial, children's cases being *sui generis* – falling into a special category in which the court must ensure that the result of its findings reflects the paramount interest of the child. The finding was encapsulated by Lord Jauncey in these words: 'Such proceedings are so far removed from normal actions that litigation privilege has no place in relation to reports obtained by a party thereto which could not have been prepared without the leave of the court to disclose documents already filed or to examine the child.'

Although the common law position is that there are no exceptions to the right to claim privilege, there are several derogations from such right which should be noticed. Those that will be considered here are:

- waiver;
- inadvertent disclosure;
- the crime/fraud exception;
- privilege and the revenue; and
- privilege and search warrants.

(a) WAIVER

Jonathan Auburn in a scholarly monograph puts forward the view that the term 'waiver' is unhelpful and should be discarded. In his opinion there is no such thing as waiver in privilege.[17] Rather, there are several exceptions which depend on different fairness considerations such as partial disclosure,[18] problems arising from 'putting in issue'[19] and related rules such as the rule relative to client–lawyer litigation. The current system of classifying waiver leads to an 'intrusion of spurious intent-based arguments' obscuring 'the true scope and bounds of the privilege' and leading 'to a mistaken view of its fundamental nature'. Auburn insists there *are* exceptions and asserts that the system of classification he proposes confirms this. There is a disconnect (he contends) between the principle and the 'exceptions'. The former permits the appearance of strict privilege while the latter detracts from the harshness of the rule. As he succinctly put it: 'This is, to a certain extent, living a lie. But it is a lie which seems to keep everyone happy.'[20]

The privilege is that of the client – only he or she being capable of waiving it. Neither the lawyer nor a third party is in such a position, although a lawyer may exercise ostensible authority to waive. There can, however, be a waiver for a limited purpose and this occurs when a client waives the privilege in criminal proceedings, which concession he is not prepared to extend to a civil suit. See *British Coal Corporation v Dennis Rye Ltd (No 2)* [1988] 1 WLR 1113.

Further, a disclosure of material made in exercise of a taxing master's discretion would only be for the purposes of taxation. See *Goldman v Hesper* [1998] 1 WLR 1128, in which the Court of Appeal confirmed waiver for a specific purpose and in a specific context. It should also be noticed that the courts have held that parties are free to decide the extent of their waiver.[21] When, however, a party permits part of a larger body of privileged material to be disclosed without expressly claiming privilege for the remainder, the privilege might be lost.[22] Privilege may also be lost in respect of a document if an expert refers to it in a report or a witness statement,[23] the underlying principle being one of fairness in the conduct of the trial.[24] If one party were allowed to tender only a section of a privileged communication, there would be a degree of unfairness since the party's action could be misleading.

Waiver was further examined in *Oxford Gene Technology Ltd (OGT) v Affymetrix Inc (No 2)* [2000] All ER 1945, the issue being the amendment of patents in the United Kingdom.

---

17 *Legal Professional Privilege: Law and Theory* (Oxford, Hart Publishing, 2000), p 195.

18 *Ibid*, pp 202–06.

19 *Ibid*, pp 213–30.

20 *Ibid*, p 230.

21 *Great Atlantic Insurance Co v Home Insurance* [1991] 1 WLR 529.

22 *Adelaide Steamship Co Ltd v Spalvins* (1998) 152 ALR 418.

23 *Clough v Tameside and Glossop Health Authority* [1998] 2 All ER 971.

24 See *General Accident Fire and Life Insurance Association Corporation Ltd v Tanter* [1984] 1 WLR 100, QB.

OGT wished to have an amendment of its European patent and for this reason duly served a statement of reasons. The only organisation to register opposition was Affymetrix (A).

OGT, being required by law to reveal all documents relevant to the court's decision, served a list of documents. However, they insisted that inspection of the documents should be restricted to A's solicitors and counsel in the UK, arguing that those documents were covered by privilege since they included legal advice by patent agents, solicitors and counsel in respect of their European patents. A, having looked at the documents, felt they needed help from their clients, but OGT objected to such further disclosure whereupon A moved the court for an order allowing the documents to be disclosed to certain of its personnel.

It turned out that A intended to share the information from OGT with their US counterpart and, if this was done, privilege in the US would be lost. A contended that there was no privilege to be lost since the documents already disclosed to them in the UK were no longer protected by privilege.

In the High Court, the judge held that OGT had in fact lost privilege by handing the list to A but that he would not order the further disclosure when he discovered this would result in a loss of privilege in the US. The matter was then referred to the Court of Appeal.

In the Court of Appeal, Aldous LJ (who gave the judgment of the court) held that it was not necessary for a patentee applying for an amendment to waive privilege. 'Certainly', he said, 'the obligation to tell the court of the facts material to the reason for amendment cannot act as a hidden obligation to waive privilege.'

OGT's contention was that, although there was no waiver, there had been a disclosure to a limited class of person, viz the organisation A. A on the other hand submitted there were two kinds of controlled waiver of privilege, viz:

- partial waiver when there is a waiver of privilege in a part of a document; and
- limited waiver, in which case the document is disclosed for a particular purpose.

The Court of Appeal held that OGT at no stage ever intended to waive privilege by disclosure to its adversary A. The disclosure to A's lawyers was conditional, that is there was to be no extension of disclosure. Although A had not accepted the terms, their inspection was one step in the proposal which was never consummated. In other words, there was an attempt to come to an understanding – but it failed. The documents were, therefore, still confidential and the court held there had been *no* waiver.

(b) INADVERTENT DISCLOSURE

The practitioner will sometimes be faced with a situation in which he wishes to invoke case law precedent for the admissibility or otherwise of an inadvertently disclosed privileged document and, according to Auburn, three subsidiary issues arise in considering such a situation:

(a) Is there a loss of privilege over the disclosed documents? That is, was the privilege waived?

(b) What is the status of privileged documents possessed by an opponent in so far as their admissibility is concerned?

(c) How does the original owner of the privilege restrict the use of the material thus disclosed?[25]

The common law position in this issue is laid down in two cases which together make the law somewhat uncertain. These cases are *Calcraft v Guest* [1898] 1 QB 759, CA and *Ashburton v Pape* [1913] 2 Ch 469, CA. The former decided that the holder of a copy of a privileged document which belongs to his opponent may make use of it in evidence, even though the original is privileged. In the latter case it was held that where the document is obtained by virtue of a breach of confidence, the owner of the privileged document can invoke the court's equitable jurisdiction and seek an injunction to protect its use.

Calcraft and Guest has been criticised both in judicial and academic circles.[26] Auburn considers that there is a need to abandon reliance on what he calls 'doctrinal purity'[27] and to get rid of the rule in that case. In his view, if that rule is to remain, the answer is not to be found in resort to the equitable doctrine propounded in Ashburton which in his words is 'like a plaster that has been applied over a bad shot-gun wound, the plaster then being blamed when the victim does not recover'.[28]

(c) THE CRIME/FRAUD EXCEPTION TO LEGAL PROFESSIONAL PRIVILEGE

Although the word 'exception' is used in this caption, the traditional view is that where crime and fraud are brought into the equation, the lawyer–client relationship does not exist at all, since they fall outside the scope of the professional relationship. That was in fact the *ratio decidendi* in the famous case of *R v Cox and Railton* (1884) 14 QBD 153, which has influenced judicial thinking in the US (where there are many cases on the rule) as well as in the Commonwealth – particularly Australia, New Zealand, Canada and South Africa.[29] In that case it was laid down that:

25 Auburn, *op cit*, fn 17, p 231.

26 Judicial: see *R v Braham* [1976] VR 547 (VIC SC) and *R v Uljee* [1982] 1 NZLR 561. Academic: see DL Mathieson, *Cross on Evidence* (Wellington, Butterworths, 1998), p 411; C Tapper, 'Privilege and confidence' (1972) 35 MLR 83.

27 See Auburn, *op cit*, fn 17, p 258.

28 Auburn, *op cit*, fn 17, p 259.

29 Auburn, *op cit*, fn 17, p 168.

> If the criminal object is avowed, the client does not consult his adviser professionally, because it cannot be the solicitor's business to further any criminal object. If the client does not avow his object he reposes no confidence, for the state of facts, which is the foundation of the supposed confidence, does not exist.[30]

An American case expresses the rule even more directly: 'there can be no such relation as that of attorney and client, either in the commission of a crime, or the doing of a wrong by force of fraud to an individual. The privileged relation of attorney and client can only exist for lawful and honest purposes.'[31]

In a recent case decided by the House of Lords,[32] their Lordships clearly misinterpreted *Cox and Railton*. In a bitter criticism of the judgment in a well-researched article, Newbold[33] has rightly lamented that 'Centuries of jurisprudence to the contrary notwithstanding, the House of Lords have come to the conclusion that the administration of justice is better served by allowing the executive authorities access to potential evidence than by preserving the protection afforded by legal professional privilege'.

The facts of this case are worth stating *in extenso*.[34] A person was suspected of committing a drug trafficking offence, as a result of which the police were investigating him. They decided that he had laundered funds by purchasing a number of properties for members of his family and in that connection they particularly wished to study details of G, a member of the suspect's family, who was a client of the appellant solicitors. It was established that neither G nor the solicitors were aware of the source of funds or of any alleged wrongdoing.

The police applied *ex parte* to a circuit judge for an order under s 27 of the Drug Trafficking Offences Act 1986 (DTOA) requiring the solicitors to produce all files in their possession relative to the transaction. The judge granted the order, which the appellant solicitors resisted on the ground that the files were 'items subject to legal privilege' within s 10(1) of the Police and Criminal Evidence Act 1984 (PACE) and were, therefore, privileged from disclosure under s 27(9)(a) of the DTOA. The Divisional Court dismissed the application for judicial review on the ground that the files were 'items held with the intention of furthering a criminal purpose' and were, therefore, excluded from legal professional privilege under s 10(2) of PACE.

The solicitors appealed to the House of Lords and the issue that arose for determination was whether the intention referred to in s 10 was that of the person holding the items or whether it could be that of some third person, whether or not

30 See to the same effect the decisions in *O'Rourke v Darbishire* [1920] AC 581 *per* Lord Parmoor and *Crescent Farm (Sidcup) Sports Ltd v Sterling Offices* [1972] Ch 553 at 564 *per* Goff J.

31 *Coveney v Tannahill* 1 Hill 33 at 35 (NYSC 1841).

32 *Francis and Francis v The Central Criminal Court* [1988] 3 All ER 775.

33 Article by ALE Newbold in *Modern Law Review*, Vol 53, July 1990, pp 472–84.

34 *Ibid*, p 473.

that third person was a party to that intention. It was held by the House that, in view of the purpose of PACE and the context in which s 10 was included, all documents would be excluded from privilege which were held with the intention of furthering a criminal purpose regardless of the identity of the holder of such documents. In this way conveyancing documents which were intended by a third party to be used for furthering a criminal purpose of laundering the proceeds of illegal drugs were subject to disclosure in the hands of a solicitor even if the solicitor was ignorant of the criminal activity.

Newbold in the article referred to above ends her strident commentary on this judgment with the following words which I respectfully endorse: 'The words of Stephen J in the classic judgment in *Cox and Railton* ring down through the centuries: "every precaution should be taken against compelling unnecessary disclosures." It is tragic that the House of Lords do not appear to have heard them.'[35]

(d) PRIVILEGE AND THE REVENUE

One other ruling of the House of Lords – involving derogation – will be mentioned here. It is the case of *R v Special Commissioner ex p Morgan Grenfel* [2002] UKHL 21. The facts were as follows.

The Revenue sought to challenge a scheme under which for years Morgan Grenfeld (MG) had marketed a scheme calculated to minimise its tax liability. The matter was taken before the Tax Commissioner who ruled that the Revenue were entitled to see papers otherwise subject to legal professional privilege under s 20(1) of the Taxes Management Act 1970.

Morgan Grenfeld was issued with an order requiring production of the legal advice it had sought prior to the establishment of the scheme. Upon Morgan Grenfeld's initiating proceedings for judicial review, the Divisional Court and the Court of Appeal in turn rejected MG's application.

MG appealed to the House of Lords which decided unanimously to allow the appeal. The leading judgment was given by Lord Hoffmann.

The Revenue argued that s 20(1) contained no express exemption from disclosure in respect of the class of documents the Revenue wished to see and that any such derogation would have to be in express terms. This was the argument which compelled the two lower courts to hold in favour of the Revenue.

Lord Hoffmann saw legal professional privilege as 'a fundamental human right long established in the common law'. He continued: 'It is a necessary corollary of the right of any person to obtain skilled advice about the law. Such advice cannot be effectively obtained unless the client is able to put all the facts

35 *Ibid*, p 484.

before the adviser without fear that they may afterwards be disclosed and used to his prejudice.'

In his view, privilege was akin to the right of privacy guaranteed by the European Convention on Human Rights (Art 8). Any intention by the legislature to effect derogation from this right 'must be expressly stated or appear by necessary implication'.

This decision is welcome. It enabled the House to decide that privilege applies outside the sphere of judicial or quasi-judicial proceedings – Lord Hoffmann clearing up that doubt in this way:

> It is not the case that legal professional privilege does no more than entitle the client to require his lawyer to withhold privileged documents in judicial or quasi-judicial proceedings, leaving the question of whether he may disclose them on other occasions to the implied duty of confidence. The policy of legal professional privilege requires that the client should be secure in the knowledge that protected documents and information will not be disclosed at all.[36]

(e) PRIVILEGE AND SEARCH WARRANTS

A matter of interest to practitioners is how privileged documents are dealt with when for any reason a lawyer's office is searched under a warrant. It is instructive to examine two recent cases where this occurred.[37]

In the first of these cases – *R v HM Customs & Excise ex p Popely*[38] – one of the two applicants was an English solicitor who complained in judicial review proceedings that in the course of their search of his premises, customs officers had seized a number of items which were privileged. The officers conceded they had no power to seize privileged articles but explained that when, on cursory review, a document was discovered which appeared to be covered by privilege, such a document would be deposited in a sealed bag for later examination by an independent barrister retained by the Customs Authority. The barrister would review the papers and advise whether or not the material fell within the scope of the search warrant.

The judge had his doubts whether such an arrangement was satisfactory in a case of judicial review which was not in his view 'a fact-finding exercise'. He thought in such cases the proper approach would be for a private action to be brought in which the court would reach a conclusion untrammelled by *Wednesbury* principles.

---

36 Most of the material in this section (d) is drawn from a perceptive article by Ewan Brown, captioned 'Legal professional privilege and the Revenue' in the *New Law Journal*, Vol 152, No 7039, 5 July 2002, pp 1020–21.

37 These two cases are considered in some detail by Colin Passmore in an article 'Search warrants and privilege' in the *New Law Journal*, Vol 150, No 6922, 11 February 2000, pp 161–63. Mr Passmore's three articles have proved a useful source of information. See also *New Law Journal*, Vol 150, No 6922, 11 February 2000, and Vol 151, No 6971, 16 February 2001.

38 Judgment delivered 4 October 1997 by Moses J.

Although ruling that the officers had no power to seize privileged documents which they had reasonable grounds to believe were subject to privilege, he saw nothing unlawful about their collecting the material in sealed bags for later examination by an independent barrister.

The warrant was not, however, rendered invalid – although this did not mean that the seizure of the privileged material might not be unlawful.

The second case is *R v Commissioner of Inland Revenue ex p Tamosius*,[39] the facts of which closely resemble those of *Popely* considered above. In this case the applicant was an American lawyer practising in London whose client had been charged and committed for trial with two counts of cheating the Revenue, the lawyer himself being also suspected of complicity in the offences and of trying to conceal evidence of his client's alleged criminal wrongdoing.

The Revenue accordingly obtained a search warrant for the lawyer's premises, for which purpose they were accompanied by an independent barrister retained by the Department to examine the documents and advise *in situ* whether the material under review was subject to privilege. Those documents which appeared to be privileged were handed back to the applicant's solicitors. Those which, though privileged, were deemed by the barrister to be covered by the crime/fraud exception were deposited in a sealed envelope and taken away.

The appellant challenged the search warrant on three grounds:

- for lack of specificity as to the nature and dates of the particular offence;
- for having counsel accompany the officers involved in the search; and
- for breach of the rule that privilege is absolute, as decided in the *R v Derby Magistrates' Court* case.

In rejecting all these submissions, the judge held that the only requirement of the relevant statute for the issue of the warrant was whether there were reasonable grounds for suspecting that a serious tax offence had been committed and whether there was real evidence on the premises to support the suspicion.[40]

The judge could find nothing irregular or unlawful about counsel accompanying the Revenue, noting that such a procedure was approved by the court in the *Popely* case. He ruled that the seizure of the items was in order and that, in any event, the validity of the warrant was not affected by what was seized under it. The power to seize documents derives from the statute.

39 Judgment of Smedley J delivered on 5 November 1999.

40 There were serious hurdles to the applicant's position since the House of Lords had held in *R v IRC ex p Rossminster* [1980] AC 952 that a search warrant was not invalid because it failed to specify the nature of the offence.

CONCLUDING SUMMARY: APPLICATION OF THE RULES TO DEVELOPING COUNTRIES

In this chapter we have indicated that the duty of confidentiality is broader than the privilege rule. The former relates to all the client's confidences or secrets received by the lawyer – no matter from what source, while the latter is a fundamental right of great importance protecting lawyer–client confidences from being deployed in evidence. David Luban in one of his works has suggested that the lawyer's duty of confidentiality enables the legal adviser 'to proceed to prepare cases without fearing that in so doing he will be forced to compromise his clients' interests'. As far as Luban can see, 'Gideon's lawyer investigated his case more thoroughly than Gideon could himself'.[41]

We have, in our review of some landmark cases on the subject, seen how active the Courts have been in the UK, the US, Canada and Australia in delineating the limits of derogation from the law relating to privilege. We have seen how important this right of the client has become as an instrument of justice in an era of drug trafficking and money laundering in a globalised economy, and the circumstances in which recourse will be necessary to the crime/fraud 'exception' – which the courts have begun to pronounce as not being a true exception but rather in the nature of an *exclusion* from the rule.

Although it is true that many of these issues have not yet been adjudicated in the courts of the newly independent countries in the Third World, we need to realise that it is only a question of time before they will face us. The lawyer like the traveller must be ready for tomorrow.

One final point should be raised. Since we now live in an electronic age, it is the business of the lawyer to use every possible device to preserve the confidentiality of the client's affairs – even after the relationship comes to an end. How will the hacking of computers and the theft of files from them affect that duty? It will be up to the profession to devise means of providing security in order to fulfil its obligations of confidentiality due to the client.

Will the profession be equal to the task? It is a question every lawyer must begin to ponder.[42] Lawyers are also expected to tread warily with problems of conflicts of interest, which we examine in the next chapter.

41 See David Luban, *Lawyers and Justice: An Ethical Study* (Princeton, Princeton University Press, 1988), p 202. See reference to Gideon's Case at the end of Chapter 3 above.

42 See a useful article on this subject by Stephen Mason entitled 'Lawyers and the duty of confidentiality in an electronic age' in the *New Law Journal*, Vol 152, 3 May 2002, pp 662, 663 and 677.

CHAPTER 8

CONFLICTS OF INTEREST AND CHINESE WALLS

THE HISTORY AND BACKGROUND

In a work published more than 70 years ago, Herman Cohen, a Barrister of the Inner Temple in London, expresses in rather quaint language for the 20th century some historical background to the concept of the conflict of interest. He cites a provision from the London Ordinance of 1280 forbidding any 'countor' (lawyer) to undertake a suit if he is partner in such suit or 'to take pay from both parties in any action, but well and lawfully he shall exercise his profession'. The writer then pronounced the sanction in these terms: 'He who takes from both parties and is attainted thereof shall be suspended for three years.' He condemns abandoning one client for another in the same suit thus: 'Where one takes money and then leaves his client and leagues himself with the other party and where one takes money and abandons his client let such person return two-fold and not be heard against the client in that plea.'[1]

The strictures affecting conflict of interest were, therefore, with us for more than 700 years and today constitute one of the most perplexing aspects of a practitioner's life. In recent years it has grown in importance and in complexity. Indeed, globalisation and the interrelated technological nature of everyday life today make it impossible for a lawyer to be sure that unwittingly he may not find himself guilty of a conflict in his dealing with a client or clients. An attempt will, therefore, be made in the course of this chapter to give some examples of the type of problem that the lawyer is likely to encounter. The subject is a vexed one, as will be appreciated from the words of Charles Wolfram – an American ethicist of much repute: 'Conflict of interest problems are probably the most pervasively felt of all the problems of professional responsibility that might haunt lawyers.'[2]

The same writer quite rightly remarks that generally speaking lawyers have not been good at recognising conflict situations, to which should be added the fact that even when they come face to face with glaring ethical problems they tend not to want to face those problems.

II THE NATURE OF THE INTEREST

Wolfram is not enamoured of the term 'conflict of interest', preferring instead alternatives like 'additional interests' or 'compound interests' or 'differing interests'. Boon and Levin regard interests as 'benefits or positions which a person may wish to defend or promote, including those relating to personal or business relationships, financial or property interests or interests in maintaining certain

1 Herman Cohen, *The History of the English Bar* (London, Sweet & Maxwell, 1929), pp 233–34.
2 Charles Wolfram, *Modern Legal Ethics* (St Paul MN, 1999), p 313.

public offices'.[3] It is stated that the driving force behind the rules governing conflict of interest is clients' autonomy – the client in an adversary system reposing trust and confidence in his lawyer whom he expects to do for him or her what that client cannot personally do for himself or herself.

The lawyer is expected in a spirit of loyalty to advance the client's interest and to serve him or her as a fiduciary.

SCOPE OF THIS REVIEW

Because of the expansive nature of this aspect of our study, we must perforce be selective about the situations discussed. We will, therefore, address the following situations in the order set out:

- conflicts with the lawyer's personal interests;
- conflicts when the lawyer acts for the buyer and seller or for mortgagee and mortgagor;
- conflicts between an existing and a proposed client;
- conflicts in family lawyering;
- gifts to a lawyer *inter vivos* and *by will*;
- mortgage transactions between lawyer and client;
- conflicts in the financial services industry;
- joint ventures between lawyer and client;
- conflicts when acting against former clients;
- conflict remedies and procedures;
- client consent to conflict; and
- judicial conflicts.

(a) CONFLICTS WITH THE LAWYER'S PERSONAL INTERESTS

In England a solicitor is expressly forbidden to act for a client if his or her interest conflicts with those of his client. One interesting example of this prohibition occurred where a solicitor was commissioned by a client in advance of the conclusion of the matter in respect of which he was retained to write a book for which he was given the publication rights.[4] On this matter the Law Society Guide expressly forbids a solicitor from acting 'where there is a conflict of interest or a potential for conflict between the client and the solicitor'. It cites as examples 'where a solicitor in his or her personal capacity sells to or purchases from, lends to or borrows from his or her own clients', and emphasises that in those circumstances the solicitor should see to it that the client obtains independent advice. If the client refuses to take that step, the solicitor should withdraw from the transaction (Principle 15.04, para 1 of the LSG).

3 Andrew Boon and Jennifer Levin, *The Ethics and Conduct of Lawyers in England and Wales* (Oxford and Portland, OR, Hart Publishing, 1999), p 268.

4 This relates to the trial of Frederick West for multiple murder.

In the case of *West Building Society v Mothew* [1996] 4 All ER 699, Millett, LJ (as he then was) stated the equitable principle as follows:

> A fiduciary must act in good faith; he must not make a profit out of his trust; he must not place himself in a position where his duty and his interest may conflict; he may not act for his own benefit or that of a third person without the informed consent of his principal.

The point is that whenever a solicitor obtains a substantial benefit from acting for a client other than the remuneration laid down in the 1974 Solicitors Act and the client questions such a benefit, the burden rests on the solicitor to prove that all material facts are disclosed to the client who agreed to permit the solicitor to retain the benefit. That client's decision must of course be made by his free will and not under pressure or undue influence.[5]

It should be noted that the personal ascendancy over the client is more likely to be effective where the client is in the habit of referring the bulk of his legal inquiries to his solicitor for advice and, therefore, has come to lean heavily on such legal adviser for counsel.[6] The solicitor would, by the same token, find his burden even more onerous where the client is young and inexperienced.[7]

(b) CONFLICTS WHEN THE LAWYER ACTS FOR THE BUYER AND SELLER OR FOR MORTGAGEE AND MORTGAGOR

Very disturbing (if practicable) conflicts occur in these cases, as will be seen in this section. Indeed, when the property boom in England which took place in the 1980s collapsed in the 1990s, mortgagees found themselves with large mortgage deficits many arising from the problems of a conflictual nature. Valuers and solicitors acting for both parties were largely responsible for breaches of fiduciary duty while acting for both mortgagees and mortgagors. The words of Millett LJ in *Bristol v West Building Society v Mothew* (1996), underscore the predicament while laying down the principle:

> Even if a fiduciary is properly acting for two principals with potentially conflicting interests he must act in good faith in the interest of each and must not act with the intention of furthering the interests of one principal to the prejudice of those of the other. But it goes further than this. He must not allow the performance of his obligations to one principal to be influenced by his relationship with the other (713b–c).

The Solicitors' Practice Rules in England do prohibit acting for both mortgagee and mortgagor in a private mortgage where the lender is not a company whose business is lending money against security but otherwise allows it provided that no conflict of interest arises. The solicitor should cease to act for both parties should a conflict arise.

5 *Demerara Bauxite Co Ld v Hubbard* [1923] AC 673 and *McMaster v Bryne* [1952] 1 All ER 1362, PC.

6 *Goddard v Carlisle* [1821] 9 Price 1 69.

7 *Savory v King* [1856] 5 HL Cas 627.

As Roger Billins has pointed out in his useful monograph *Solicitors' Duties and Liabilities*,[8] the problem of double representation is by no means a recent phenomenon, the courts having been called upon to examine the matter as far back as 1836 when, in *Taylor v Blacklow* (1836) 3 Bing NC 235, a solicitor who disclosed to the mortgagee a defect in the title of the mortgagor (for whom he was also acting) was compelled to pay compensation to the mortgagor. His duty was to advise the mortgagor to withdraw, failing which the retainer should have been terminated. Under the Solicitors' Practice (Joint Property Selling) Amendment Rules 1997, those solicitors who operate joint estate agencies may undertake conveyancing for both buyer and seller who are clients of a joint estate agency. In the last decade of the 20th century, there was a plethora of cases involving conflict in the circumstances mentioned, one of the most interesting of which was *Mortgage Express Ltd v Bowerman* [1996] 2 All ER 836, the facts of which are as follows.

A Mr Hadi retained solicitors to effect the purchase of residential property for £220,000 from the plaintiffs for whom the same solicitors (Bowerman) were also acting. The plaintiffs were to advance the sum of £180,000. Although the solicitors discovered that the sale to Mr Hadi was a sub-sale and that Mr Hadi's vendors were paying only £150,000 (making a profit of £30,000) the solicitors/defendants never informed the lenders of the said sub-sale. The plaintiffs were the victim of fraud as a result of which they lost £84,000 when Hadi defaulted on his mortgage payments and they were required to effect a sale at a loss.

The court at first instance laid down the following principles to be followed in such cases:

- A solicitor is under a duty when acting for both lender and borrower to inform the lender of any material facts he knows which ought to be disclosed to the lender.[9]
- Whenever a solicitor in investigating title finds facts with a material bearing on the valuation or security of the lending decision, he is under an obligation to advise the client.[10]
- The solicitors were clearly involved in a conflict of interest situation when they encountered the sub-sale which they must have realised would cause the plaintiffs to withdraw their offer of finance.
- In such a case, the defendants had a duty to bring to the plaintiff's notice the irregularities which they knew (or ought to have known) would influence the plaintiff's decision whether or not to continue with the transaction.[11]

8 *Solicitors' Duties and Responsibilities* (London, Sweet & Maxwell, 1999), Chapter 3. I have found Billins' work on this subject particularly helpful in the way he has illustrated conflict situations by reference to the English decided cases and I have drawn heavily on his work in writing this chapter.

9 *Anglia and Thanet Building Society v House and Son* [1987] 260 EG 118.

10 *Schroders v Brook* (1891) 63 LT 837.

11 *Clark Boyce v Mouat* [1994] 1 AC 428.

Independent advice does protect the solicitor, as in the *Clark Boyce* case where the facts were as follows.

A solicitor who acted for mother and son in a mortgage transaction advised the mother to take independent advice which she failed to do, proceeding with the mortgage in any event. She failed in her suit against the solicitor. The Privy Council held that it was no part of the lawyer's duty to advise the mother of the wisdom of the transaction.

Where, however, as in *Mahoney v Purcell* [1996] 3 All ER 61, one of the parties (a frail old man) contracted with a person who was exercising undue influence over him, and the same solicitor acted for them both – as well as the company owned by them both – the solicitor was found liable for breach of fiduciary duty although he had advised the old man to seek independent advice. This was also a case when the solicitor had a wide and general retainer in relation to the man.

(c) CONFLICTS BETWEEN AN EXISTING AND A PROPOSED CLIENT

How does a solicitor deal with a situation where a dispute arises between two persons, both of whom are clients? Does he continue to act for one and terminate his retainer in the case of the other? Under the English Law Society Rule 15.03, he must cease to act for both – subject to one exception, viz if he does not possess any relevant confidential information concerning the other which he received while the retainer subsisted.

It would obviously be necessary for the solicitor to endeavour to find out whether the other client objects – as he or she most likely will. The burden of proving there is no conflict in this case rests on the solicitor. The position would be the same if the solicitor were called upon to act against an organisation the solicitor previously represented.

(d) CONFLICTS IN FAMILY LAWYERING

In a very perceptive paper on this subject in *Legal Ethics and Legal Practice*,[12] Dr Richard Tur made this statement:

> It is, perhaps, too readily assumed that parties' interest are necessarily opposed in divorce. Emotional conflict, of course, is common but in many, perhaps most, cases the parties do have a common interest in the expeditious and economical resolution of their dispute and the welfare of their children, if any.

Dr Tur is right in characterising matrimonial proceedings as costly, lengthy and usually acrimonious. He also correctly puts the procedures down to the formalistic and near-inflexible nature of the adversary system to which many

12 See Dr Richard Tur's 'Family lawyering' in S Parker and C Sampford (eds), *Legal Ethics and Legal Practice* (Oxford, Clarendon Press, 1995), pp 145–70.

lawyers still wish to cling. Happily, as we shall see when we discuss alternative dispute resolution in Chapter 11, the tendency is growing for lawyers to resort more and more to family dispute resolution (FDR) as well. The more that regime develops, the more conflicts of interest will decrease for then the parties will not be represented by partisan agents but by a single mediator who will not be guilty of 'radical individualism'.[13]

(e) GIFTS TO A LAWYER

There is respectable authority for the thesis that a gift to a solicitor is tainted by the undue influence which a lawyer is presumed to exercise over a client. Such a presumption is of course rebuttable, and that burden of rebuttal is heavy: see *Wright v Carter* [1903] 1 Ch 27. The English position – as set out in LSG 15.05 – depicts the reserve with which such gifts are regarded:

> Where a client intends to make a gift *inter vivos* or by will to his or her solicitor or to the solicitor's partner or to a member of staff or to the families of any of them and the gift is a significant amount either in itself or having regard to the size of the client's estate and the reasonable expectations of the beneficiaries, the solicitor must advise the client to be independently advised as to that gift and, if the client declines, must refuse to act.

But this rule would apply even if the client arranges for his wife or sister or brother to make the gift.[14]

The exceptions in this case would seem almost to negative the rule itself. Thus, a gift to a solicitor may be valid where:

- the gift is small or seasonal;
- the gift is a reasonable one, not made under undue influence;
- the solicitor can show that the gift is reasonable and not made under undue influence, in addition to which independent advice has been received from another attorney who was seised of all the facts before giving his advice; and
- the client endorses the gift and acquiesces in the undue influence provided that these occurrences take place after the currency of the retainer and the presumption of undue influence no longer exists. In such a case, the act of affirmation must be unequivocal and the client must be made aware of his right to set aside the gift if so minded.[15]

(f) GIFTS BY WILL

The rules concerning gifts to a solicitor by will from a client are similar to those just referred to, except that (oddly enough) in the case of a gift by will the presumption of undue influence does not apply.[16] This does not, however, relieve

13 See TL Shaffer, 'The legal ethics of radical individualism' *Texas Law Review*, Vol 65, 1987, p 963.

14 *Wills v Barron* [1902] AC 271.

15 *Browne v McClintock* [1873] 2 R 6, HL.

16 *Craig v Lamoureux* [1920] AC 349.

the lawyer of his responsibility to prove there was no undue influence on his or her part.[17]

The solicitor must also show that the testator was 'of sound and disposing mind and memory' and that he was fully aware of the contents of the testamentary disposition. Further, as has already been pointed out in Chapter 5 above when professional responsibility was being discussed, no lawyer worth his salt will fail to advise a client wishing to make him a beneficiary in his will that it would be judicious to have the will prepared by an independent member of the profession. It is not without significance that these common law principles have been enacted in the Singapore Legal Profession (Professional Conduct) Rules (1 June 1998) which provide in s 46 as follows:

> Where a client intends to make a significant gift by will or *inter vivos*, or in any other manner, to:
>
> (a) an advocate and solicitor acting for him;
>
> (b) a member of the law firm of the advocate and solicitor;
>
> (c) any member, director or employee of the law corporation of the advocate and solicitor; or
>
> (d) any member of the family of the advocate and solicitor,
>
> the advocate and solicitor shall not act for the client and shall advise the client to be independently advised in respect of the gift.

(g) MORTGAGE TRANSACTIONS BETWEEN LAWYER AND CLIENT

So long as a lawyer strictly conforms to normative behaviour as between lawyer and client, the former is at liberty to take security against the latter (the client) for, say, bridging finance or for fees outstanding or even for prospective fees for work being done for the client. Provision along these lines is made in s 65 of the Solicitors' (Non-Contentious Business) Remuneration Order of 1994. Authority for this proposition is to be found in *Riddell, Public Trustee v Riddell* [1936] 2 All ER 1600.

Clearly the conditions relevant to the manner a fiduciary deals with his principal must be present, viz there must be no excessive rate of interest nor must the redemption conditions be oppressive. All material facts must be disclosed and a failure in this respect will result in a breach of duty on the lawyer's part even if the other conditions as to rate of interest and redemption are satisfied. In *Swindle v Harrison* [1997] 4 All ER 705, the solicitor was held to be guilty of a breach of duty for failing to reveal to the client that he was making a secret commission from a loan he was arranging on behalf of the clients for the purchase of a restaurant, even though the terms of the loan were in other respects unexceptionable.

17 *Fulton v Andrew* [1872] LR P&D 462.

(h) CONFLICTS IN THE FINANCIAL SERVICES INDUSTRY

It is in this industry that conflicts of interest most frequently occur and it is, therefore, not surprising that an entire volume has been dedicated to the subject.[18]

It is common ground that many financial transactions require the services of an agent, and it is this category of person who will always be subject to fiduciary obligations and who in the words of Lord Herschell 'is not allowed to put himself in a position where his interest and his duty conflict'.[19]

In the ever-changing financial world in which we now dwell, there are, according to Nakayima and Sheffield, three principal conflict situations which beset us, viz:

- those arising from self-interest where a company director transacts business with his own company;
- those arising from dual or multiple agency, where an agent acts for two or more principals in the same transaction; and
- those circumstances where one part of an intermediary obtains information which is relevant to a client of another part of the same business entity.

An excellent example of the way conflicts of interest arise in financial matters is to be found in the landmark case of *Prince Jefri Bolkiah v KPMG* [1999] 2 AC 222. The appellant is the third and youngest brother of the Sultan of Brunei. The respondent is an internationally known firm of accountants which had been appointed to audit the Brunei Investment Agency (BIA), founded in 1983 to manage the General Reserve Fund of the Government of Brunei.

For many years Prince Jefri was the Chairman of the BIA, but when unhappy differences arose between his brother (the Sultan) and himself, the Sultan relieved him of his post and appointed Arthur Andersen as executive managers of the Fund.

Large transfers of capital (special transfers) had been effected from the core funds, but KPMG was not to be concerned with these transfers, being required to accept an annual representation from the Board of the BIA that such transfers were sanctioned by the Government as having been made on its behalf.

For a period of 18 months between 1996 and 1998, KPMG had been retained by Prince Jefri to undertake certain investigations in connection with major litigation in which he was involved – the operation executing these investigations being code, named 'Lucy'. KPMG accordingly provided support services from its forensic accounting department for the litigation – services which in the normal scheme of things would be provided by solicitors – in the course of which it

18 See Chizu Nakajima and Elizabeth Sheffield, *Conflicts of Interest and Chinese Walls* (London, Butterworths, 2002) – a volume which focuses on the identification, implications and control of conflicts in the financial services industry. I have drawn upon this book in writing this chapter.

19 *Bray v Ford* [1896] AC 44 at p 51.

received considerable confidential information about the Prince's assets and financial affairs. That litigation was settled in March 1998 and in May 1998 KPMG was asked to bring Project 'Lucy' to a close.

In June 1998, a Task Force was, however, appointed by the Government of Brunei to investigate the BIA and KPMG was given the assignment of investigating the whereabouts of the destination of the special transfers – this new project being code-named 'gemma'. Having taken legal advice, KPMG came to the conclusion that no conflict of interest was involved since a period of two months had elapsed from the time it ceased to act for Prince Jefri. The accounting firm then decided to make special arrangements for additional protection against the disclosure of the confidential information in its possession concerning the Prince's affairs. Information barriers were erected in the accounting forensic department from 3 July 1998, for that purpose, but Prince Jefri was not informed of the developments, nor was his agreement sought for the new retainer to KPMG. When Prince Jefri learned of the above developments he moved the High Court for an injunction to restrain KPMG from acting under the new arrangements. Pumfrey J granted the injunction but his decision was overturned on appeal by the English Court of Appeal. Prince Jefri then appealed to the House of Lords, who restored the injunction imposed by the trial judge.

The basis of the judgment of the House of Lords, whose leading spokesman was Lord Millett, was not how to avoid the perception of possible impropriety, but how to take all reasonable steps to protect the confidential information in the possession of KPMG from disclosure. In his Lordship's view, a former client is entitled to prevent a solicitor from exposing him or her to any avoidable risk, including the risk of the use of the confidential information to the prejudice of the former client.

The House of Lords departed from the *Rakusen* case of 1912, up until 1999 the leading authority on the point. That case had laid down the applicable test as a 'real probability of real mischief'. Lord Millett was of the view that such a test placed an unnecessarily heavy burden on the former client who would be exposed to avoidable risk not of his own choosing while at the same time not securing the assurances that his or her confidences would be duly or adequately safeguarded.

Nor was the House impressed that the ad hoc arrangements for a Chinese Wall in the *Prince Jefri* case were satisfactory, preferring instead a wall that is part of the organisational structure of the firm (more will be said shortly on the nature of a Chinese Wall).

The *Prince Jefri* case has since been followed in the Canadian case of *Drabinsky v KPMG* [1998] 41 OR (3D) 565, in which once more the confidences of a former client (whose interests would be affected) came into play with the same accounting firm.

A special word of explanation should be said about Chinese Walls as they are currently permitted to operate in England, Canada and in America.

In England they were not provided for by statute until 1983. In the *Prince Jefri* case, we have seen that Lord Millett rejected the suggestion that 'the Wall' provided by KPMG was adequate to protect any leakage of the confidential information it had on the Prince. His Lordship expressed the view that 'an effective Chinese Wall needs to be an established part of the organisational structure of the firm, not created ad hoc and dependent on the acceptance of evidence sworn for the purpose by members of staff engaged on the relevant work'.[20]

In general, however, a Chinese Wall (as defined by Nakajima and Sheffield)[21] is 'essentially a set of internal rules and procedures which are designed to control and prevent the communication and misuse of confidential information between departments of a multiple function financial intermediary'.

It is a device adopted by financial intermediaries who must execute obligations to protect the leakage or communication of information in a situation where such leakage or communication would result in a conflict.

As has been indicated above, legislation was first passed to define Chinese Walls in the Licensed Dealers (Conduct of Business) Rules 1983 which were superseded by the Financial Services Act 1986 (FSA). Rule 2 was in these terms:

> 'Chinese Walls' means an established arrangement whereby information known to persons in one part of a business is not available (directly or indirectly) to those involved in another part of the business and it is accepted that in each of the parts of the business so divided decisions will be taken without reference to any interest which any other such part or any person in any other such part of the business may have in the matter.

Several authorities in the UK have endorsed and adopted this definition and accepted the practice of segregation of information, and the FSA 1986 confirms the use of Chinese Walls by authorising self-regulating bodies to put forward rules having the effect of protecting intermediaries in their dealing with the disclosure of information.

Nakajima and Sheffield speak of the formalisation of the 'walls' thus:[22]

> Although Chinese Walls are not physical constructs in practice, the procedures making up the 'wall' are often formalised. A written policy statement prohibiting any communication of non-public, price-sensitive information to the firm's investment officers, who trade in the securities markets, is a basic element of many, if not most, Chinese Walls. This statement outlines procedures to be followed in the event of such information being accidentally communicated. In addition it stipulates sanctions for breaches of the firm's internal rules. The Chinese Wall is an internal device, which is policed by the compliance departments of individual firms. Some firms have attempted to avoid frequent inter-departmental transfer of personnel, or have prohibited the involvement of certain personnel who are likely to come into possession of inside information, in certain activities. A continuing educational and

20 [1999] 2 AC 222 at p 239.

21 See Chizu Nakajima and Elizabeth Sheffield, *Conflicts of Interest and Chinese Walls* (London, Butterworths, 2002), p 109.

22 *Ibid*, pp 110–11. Reproduced by permission of Reed Elsevier (UK) Ltd trading as Lexis Nexis UK.

> training programme, giving personnel an understanding of insider dealing and other conflict of interest problems, is another feature of many Chinese Walls. Nonetheless, the characteristics of individual Chinese Walls will necessarily vary according to the size and nature of the intermediary's business.

The FSA 1986 did not have the effect of exempting a firm from common law liability which was the result of breach of fiduciary duty. However, where a Chinese Wall existed, a firm could be relieved of liability for the breach of specific rules.

In a work of this kind it is not practicable, in the interest of space, to explore the attempts to make further statutory provision for Chinese Walls in the English parliamentary environment. What is proposed, however, is to give a brief outline of the attitude of the English courts to the efficacy of the 'walls' in the three most important cases on the subject which have so far reached the courts (apart from the *Jefri* case already discussed).

First, *David Lee & Co Ltd v Coward (A Firm); Supasave Retail v Coward Chance (A Firm)* [1990] 3 WLR 1278, a case in which separate actions were brought by two liquidators who sought a declaration from the court in the following circumstances. The case arose from the merger of two solicitors' firms which had acted for the liquidators of David Lee & Co and Supasave Retail in proceedings by the liquidators against Coward Chance (now Clifford Chance). William Prior in London were first retained as solicitors by the liquidators while Dibb Lupton in Leeds were retained by the accountant/defendants, Vick, Mark and Stead. The two firms of solicitors having merged on 1 May 1990 – the day before Dibb Lupton took itself off the record for the Mark defendants – the defendants objected to Dibb Lupton being retained as solicitors for the liquidators who wished the merged firm to act for them.

The grounds for the defendants' objection were that confidential information about their defence would be passed by the merged firm to the liquidators. The firm of solicitors contended that a Chinese Wall had been erected between the members of the firm who had previously dealt with the defendants' matters and those who were representing the liquidators. When the Law Society refused to rule on the problem until the court had done so, the liquidators issued a summons praying for a declaration from the court.

The Vice-Chancellor, then Sir Nicholas Browne-Wilkinson, was not persuaded about the effectiveness of the 'wall'. He found as a fact that very sensitive confidential information had been imparted to Dibb Lupton which could leak to the liquidators as a result of the merger. Nor was the judge impressed by the paucity of data provided by the merged firm to justify the security of the 'wall'. Sir Nicholas found for the defendants on the dual ground that (a) there might well be leakage of the information as a result of casual chatter and social interaction, and (b) that no evidence was adduced which showed that the staff were briefed as to the sensitivity of the matter.

Secondly, there was *Re A Firm of Solicitors* [1992] 1 All ER 353, a case considered by the English Court of Appeal, the facts being somewhat similar to the one just discussed. In this case, the court considered the *Rakusen* decision and created a new test, viz 'whether a reasonable man informed of the facts might reasonably anticipate such a danger (the communication of confidential information)'. Parker LJ, who gave the majority judgment, stated that in endorsing the injunction imposed by the trial judge he was also supporting Sir Nicholas Browne-Wilkinson's suggestion that there was always the possibility of a casual conversation having the effect of breaching the 'Chinese Wall'.

The third case to be considered is *Re A Firm of Solicitors* [1997] Ch 1.

In this case, the plaintiff was a client of solicitors called Bristows, Cooke and Carpmael, of which a Mr Cohen was a partner. Mr Cohen left that firm to join another called Hammond Suddards. The plaintiff was pursuing patent litigation with Bristows. The defendants in this case now wished to retain Mr Cohen in his new firm, but the plaintiff moved the court for an injunction to restrain Mr Cohen from accepting the retainer. Mr Cohen established to the satisfaction of the court that he had had no involvement whatever in the matter while at Bristows nor was he in possession of any confidential information in connection with the plaintiff's affairs.

In refusing the application for injunctive relief, Lightman J took the opportunity to elucidate the law on the use by solicitors of confidential information:

- the court would intervene to protect confidential information which remains confidential and which is relevant to the subject matter of the particular retainer;
- the retainer is not, *per se*, sufficient to protect the client from the solicitor acting against him in the future;
- where a firm is involved, all members in possession of confidential information must refrain from using it once it is obtained in the course of the retainer; and
- the burden is on the solicitor to prove there is no risk of him imparting confidential information or indeed that he possesses such information.

THE US PROBLEM

In the US it is mandatory for security firms to set up Chinese Walls to control the flow of confidential information within the firm. This was statutorily provided by the Insider Trading and Securities Fraud Enforcement Act 1988 (ITSFEA) which added a new s 15(f) to the original Securities Exchange Act 1934.

The decision of the Federal District Court in the case of *SEC v Texas Gulf Sulphur* 401 F 2d 833; 2nd Cir 1968 came as a great surprise to American financial intermediaries. The finding was that r 10 b-5 deemed it fraudulent for non-public data concerning issuers of securities to be utilised for purposes of trading on the market if full disclosure was not made. Thus was established what came to be known as the 'abstain and disclose rule', under which the holder of such information was under a duty to disclose it. If unable to disclose on grounds of confidentiality or because he elected not to disclose, he was debarred from trading in the securities or to recommend them for trading.

US financial intermediaries found themselves exposed to serious sanctions. As a result Chinese Walls were established on a wide scale and became a defence to liability under the rule.

A second decision – *Re Merrill Lynch, Pierce, Fenner and Smith Inc* (1968) 43 SEC – was an administrative action brought against Merrill Lynch in these circumstances. Merrill, being the managing underwriter for an offering of convertible debentures, received certain negative information about the issuer which was confidential. His underwriting staff disclosed the information to a number of their customers who promptly proceeded to dispose of their shareholdings in the company concerned.

By way of settlement of the administrative suit, Merrill was compelled to adopt a policy statement forbidding any such disclosure in the future and proposing an appropriate Chinese Wall.

Legislation was eventually enacted in the US in 1980 (via 5.14(e) and SEC r 14 e-3) by which it was rendered illegal for any person who acquires confidential information about a pending tender offer to trade in the company's securities.

According to Nakajima and Sheffield, during the 1980s 'Chinese Walls were rightly recognised in the US as affording multiple function financial intermediaries the best possible protection against suits based on misuse of confidential information'. The writers concede that the Walls are 'not impregnable' but consider that so long as they are supported by proper compliance mechanisms, they are considered 'the most efficacious way of dealing with conflict problems'.[23]

The suggestion has been made that the pragmatic solution to the conflict of interests of multiple function firms is to reinforce the Walls by internal devices such as the 'no recommendations policy' and a 'stop list'. The former is a practice where the firm refrains from making a recommendation in cases where it is likely to receive inside information; the latter being an arrangement under which the securities of a unit about which the firm receives sensitive information are placed on a restricted (stop) list, only to be removed when the information reaches the public domain.

23 *Ibid*, p 114.

(i) JOINT VENTURES BETWEEN LAWYER AND CLIENT

What is the position of a client who enters into a joint venture with his solicitors? Is the solicitor required to advise him on the merits of the venture or to suggest he take independent advice?

These questions have been authoritatively answered by the English courts in the case of *Hanson v Lorenz and Jones* (1986) 136 NLJ 1088. The facts are as follows.

The client and his lawyers fell out after they had embarked on a joint business venture and the client brought an action against the lawyers on the ground that they had put themselves into a conflict position and should, therefore, hand over to him the profits they derived from the business.

The client failed at first instance and again on appeal. In the Court of Appeal, May LJ, after pointing out that it was no part of a lawyer's business to advise a client on the prudence or imprudence of a business transaction, stated:

> What was intended was a joint venture between the plaintiff on the one side and the firm of solicitors and their company on the other. Provided that the plaintiff as the client knew and understood the terms of the proposed joint venture by implication, whether the proposed enterprise was prudent or not, was not a matter for them.

There is, of course, a duty on the part of a solicitor not to make a profit from his dealings with the client – as, for instance, when a solicitor obtains a commission for professional work done on behalf of a client. He may, however, keep such a commission if the transaction takes place with the full knowledge and concurrence of the client after the solicitor has made full disclosure of all material facts.[24]

(j) CONFLICTS WHEN ACTING AGAINST FORMER CLIENTS

The general rule is set out in Principle 15.02 of the English Law Society Guide in this form, viz that any information acquired by a solicitor while acting for a former client is confidential and should not be disclosed without the client's consent. However, it is the duty of a solicitor to inform an existing client of all matters relevant to the retainer.

If the solicitor is to divulge to a later client any confidential information relevant to his retainer which he acquired from his former client, the solicitor must obtain the consent of that former client – and the consent must be informed consent – of which more will be said later. Most of the cases on this aspect of former client conflict deal with accidental or inadvertent leakage and we shall deal with a few of them here.

We have already considered the case of Prince Jefri Bolkiah which, apart from illustrating how conflicts arise generally in financial matters, also demonstrates the circumstances under which conflicts occur between present and past clients.

24 *Browne v IRC* [1964] AC 244.

Prior to that case, it was a principle of the common law that there was no impediment to a solicitor acting in a case where one partner in a firm had acted for one side and another partner subsequently decided to act for the other side. This was laid down by the English Court of Appeal in the case of *Rakusen v Ellis Munday and Clarke* [1912] 1 Ch 831. The facts of this case were as follows.

Munday and Clarke, though said to be partners, apparently looked after their own clients. The client, Rakusen, consulted Mr Munday in connection with a claim against S&H Rakusen while Clarke was on holiday. Confidential information was imparted to Munday of which Clarke was unaware. Later, Rakusen changed his solicitors and Clarke appeared for the other side against the former client of the firm. It was at that stage that Rakusen moved the court for the imposition of an injunction to restrain Clarke from acting. The trial judge granted the injunction but his order was reversed by the Court of Appeal.

The principle laid down by the court in this case was that there is no absolute rule of law that a solicitor may not act against a former client. It was also held that a restraint will apply only to avoid any significant risk of disclosure or misuse of confidential information belonging to the former client.

This was the common law position from 1912 until the decision of the House of Lords in the *Jefri* case of 1999 (which we have already considered earlier in this chapter). What *Jefri* decided was that a line must be drawn between the position of a former client and that of existing clients, where conflicts are concerned. In the case of *the former* client, the court's jurisdiction is not based on real or perceived conflict of interest since the fiduciary relations between solicitor and client ends with the termination of the retainer. The jurisdiction is, instead, based on the protection of the confidentiality, for it is the solicitor's duty to keep the client's confidences intact and not merely to take all reasonable steps to do so: the client being entitled to prevent exposure from any avoidable risk of confidential information being disclosed to the client's prejudice – either wittingly or unwittingly.

The burden is on the plaintiff to establish that the solicitor is in possession of information confidential to the client and that such information may be relevant to the new retainer in which the interest of the other client may be adverse. This burden is not a heavy one. The position is quite different where the court's intervention is sought on behalf of two existing clients with conflicting interests. In such a case, the question is not one of the confidentiality of client information. 'It is,' according to Lord Millett in the *Jefri* case, 'based on the inescapable conflict of interest which is inherent in the situation.' In his Lordship's view, 'a fiduciary cannot act at the same time both for and against the same client ... A man cannot without the consent of both clients act for one client while his partner is acting for another in the opposite interest'.

The rules of former-client conflicts are well developed in American jurisprudence. In his *Modern Legal Ethics* (Chapter 7), Charles Wolfram discusses them at considerable length, in the course of which he states that the problem of defining the circumstances under which a lawyer might bring an action or otherwise take a legal position on behalf of a present client against the interest of a former client has of recent times 'been the subject of frequent litigation and significant legal development'.[25]

It has been widely accepted in American, Canadian and UK law systems that any claim for a lawyer to be disqualified on grounds of former-client representation must satisfy two requirements, viz:

- both representations must be adverse in some material respect; and
- the issues must be substantially related.

There is, of course, no rule prohibiting a lawyer from bringing an action against a former client on a matter totally unrelated to the former representation.

(k) CONFLICT REMEDIES

Very briefly, what are the remedial and procedural sanctions that follow conflicts of interests when they come to light?

First, disciplinary actions which provide for violations of proper behaviour on the part of members of the profession are common in all jurisdictions in respect of glaring conflicts. Then there are judicial remedies in respect of disqualification motions and mandatory injunctions. The remedy of damages applies in cases where injury is caused to a client by a conflicting representation. We shall consider these in turn.

DISCIPLINARY PROCESSES

Many codes of conduct provide that multiple representation is not permitted unless the lawyer can adequately represent the interests of each client who must individually consent to such representation after full disclosure of the possible effects of such representation. These conditions are enshrined in the various Codes of Ethics and breach of those Rules may render the lawyer subject to sanctions for professional misconduct. See, for instance, rule 29 of the Barbados Legal Profession Code of Ethics 1988 and paras 25–31 of the Singapore Legal Profession (Professional Conduct) Rules 1999.

JUDICIAL REMEDIES

In the US, England and Canada, there have of recent years been many cases involving requests for disqualification of lawyers in conflict situations – particularly where the interests of one client conflict with that of a former client, but such disqualifications where they occur do not necessarily reflect breaches of discipline. See *Cinema 4 Ltd v Cinerama Inc* 528 F 2d 1384, in which the United

25 See Charles Wolfram, *op cit*, fn 2, section 7.4.1, p 358.

States court referred to '*prima facie* impropriety' and 'undivided loyalty'. It ordered a disqualification of a lawyer and his firm despite findings of *bona fides*, and a consequential pronouncement that the court was satisfied that dual representation was inadvertent and unknowing.

In England, a good example of such application is to be found in the case of *Re T and A (Children)* in the Court of Appeal (unreported but published in *The Times Law Report*, 1 February 2002). This was a case in which the applicant sought unsuccessfully to disqualify the lawyer from appearing for a guardian *ad litem* on the ground that the same lawyer's firm had appeared for him in the past, although the lawyer had no recollection of the case that was supposed to have occurred some 13 years previously.

Three Canadian cases must be mentioned. The first case is *Sun Life Trust Co and Bond City Financial Ltd* (35 OR (3d) Pt 1-83), in which the plaintiff brought proceedings as the first mortgagee of a property. The company represented that S of the C&C law firm who was formerly a partner of GT had acted for the defendant F Corporation in previous proceedings concerning F's interest as a second mortgagee and should, therefore, be disqualified and removed as the solicitor of record for the plaintiff. The motion was, however, refused on the basis that, while at the former law firm of C&C, S's involvement was such that he was precluded from receiving any confidential information.

The second case is *Aptowitzer et al v The Queen* (23 OR (3d) Pt 4 315). In this case the solicitors previously acted on behalf of C Ltd (the defendant), but their role was limited to entering appearance and filing a statement of defence in the first action. In the second action, the solicitors acted for C&L Ltd – a different litigant.

Once more the motion to disqualify was dismissed on the ground that the matter in which the solicitor was acting was neither the same nor a related issue. Further, no confidential information had been received in the course of the former retainer.

The third and final case is *Moffett v Wetstein* (29 OR (3d) Part 5 371). This was a further application to the court to disqualify a solicitor/defendant based on professional and taxation services provided by the defendants to the plaintiff regarding certain investments.

The plaintiffs were represented by the law firm of MT and by T, a former partner of that firm. T was also a former partner in the defendant accounting firm PMT. While he was a partner in PMT at the time the conduct complained of took place, he was not involved in that conduct. However, T would be exposed to financial liability if the plaintiff's action was successful.

PMT had also been represented in the past by MT. PMT moved for an order removing MT as solicitors of record for the plaintiffs on the basis of an actual and/or apparent conflict of interest.

The motion was dismissed. Before a disqualifying conflict of interest can be found, a solicitor and client relationship must have existed between the solicitor sought to be removed, and a party presently adverse in interest to the position the solicitor has been retained to represent. Further relevant confidential information must have been received in the context of that relationship. There was no solicitor and client relationship between T and PMT at the time he was a partner at PMT. It would, therefore, be inappropriate to remove him or MT as solicitors of record on that basis.

An example of the application for an injunction is to be found in *Drabinksky v KPMG* (41 OR (3d) Part 7 565) (already referred to) in which the plaintiff moved for an injunction restraining the accounting firm KPMG (of which the plaintiff was a client) from further participating in a pending investigation into the financial records of L Inc (a company of which the plaintiff was a senior officer) and from producing copies of the plaintiff's documents in KPMG's possession to L Inc or to any other person.

In this case the motion was granted on the same grounds as it was granted in the *Jefri* case discussed above.

(l) CLIENT CONSENT TO CONFLICT

To what extent may a lawyer in an obvious conflict situation with a client depend upon the client's consent to protect him from any appropriate sanction? It would be simplistic to attempt to answer this question by invoking the doctrine of client autonomy or the principle of the freedom of contract, with the result that there would be little or no restriction on such consent. Such an arrangement would be disingenuous in the extreme, in the context of a lawyer's professional responsibility and specifically his fiduciary relations with clients. Professional rules, statutory regulatory provisions affecting the profession and judicial decisions all contrive to make blanket consents to conflict somewhat of a mirage. It is on that account that there will be many conflictual situations which are incapable of being cured by simple consent.

We shall, therefore, look briefly at some non-consentable conflicts situations in which a so-called consent would be largely nugatory – having no effect on either disciplinary proceedings or disqualification. It would amount to the permissibility of accepting the consent of an impaired citizen or a person not fully informed of the implications of the so-called consent. The burden would be on the lawyer to prove that each client has consented after full disclosures, but it is not sufficient that the conflict was consentable. What must be established is that there has been full information about the conflict and consent on the basis of such information.[26]

There are times when a client should be advised to seek independent advice from a lawyer who is in no way connected with either client or the lawyer involved in the conflict situation. This will always be necessary when the conflict is potentially dangerous.

The client's consent must always be explicit and not in any way qualified.

---

26 See Wolfram, *op cit*, fn 2, Sections 7.2.3 and 7.2.4, pp 341–49.

The consent should only follow disclosure if the client fully understands and appreciates the implications of consenting and has reached his consenting decision freely and is not under pressure of any sort.

The client must have full capacity to consent. He must not be an infant or a person of unsound mind. Nor must he be an illiterate person who is unable to grasp the circumstances in which a conflict is liable to arise.

Finally, in such situations of conflict there is always a possibility that a consentee may, upon further reflection, wish to revoke his original decision to consent. How is the lawyer to deal with such a revocation? Clearly, it is for the lawyer to act upon it by withdrawing from representing all parties, since he is likely to be in possession of confidential information which it would not be fair to use in any further representation.

(m) JUDICIAL CONFLICTS

In a recent article in the *Journal of the Commonwealth Lawyers' Association*,[27] Mr Michael Beloff QC gave an account of an incident in which he was involved when he had been appearing in the High Court representing the Broadcasting Standards Commission to defend a judicial review brought against them by the BBC. The former organisation had alleged that the BBC had wrongly interfered with the Commission's privacy by secret video recordings of its counters. Mr Beloff told how on arrival in court he found that the judge who was to preside had failed to appear and was replaced by another.

He states that when later that day he happened to find himself travelling on foot with the judge who was originally due to preside, he enquired as to what had caused the change. 'Ah,' said the judge, 'a member of the Commission whom you represent is a Bishop, from whom I have recently taken communion in church'. Hence his inability to sit.[28] This incident bespeaks the extreme sensitivity with which the English judiciary carry out their work today where possibilities of perceived bias are concerned.

On a wider plane, of course, we must not lose sight of the fact that for centuries Britain was the only country in the developed world where there was an in-built conflict giving the lie to the doctrine of the separation of powers. This is the situation under which the Lord Chancellor has combined the functions of Head of the Judiciary, a member of the Cabinet and Speaker of the House of Lords (the Upper Chamber of the Legislature). This triplication has given rise to critical comments from academics and others for many years. Even a senior Law Lord has recently been publicly moved to speak in rather strident terms of the anomaly[29] and it is good to see that – as this section is being written – the Labour Government in the UK has awakened from that country's long slumber and is

---

27 'The Commonwealth Lawyer' *Journal of the Commonwealth Lawyers' Association*, Vol 11, No 3, December 2002, p 15.

28 *Ibid*, p 15.

29 Lord Steyn in the Neil Lecture delivered in Oxford in March 2002. See also the Queen's Speech from the Throne of 26 November 2003, in which it was expressly stated that provision had been made for the abolition of the current post of Lord Chancellor.

about to take corrective action which will enable the judiciary not only to be independent but to be seen to be independent.

The anomaly has been exacerbated by the fact that s 6(1) of the Human Rights Act 1998 makes the following provision in respect of the independence and impartiality of tribunals: 'in the determination of their civil rights and obligations everyone is entitled to a fair hearing ... by an independent and impartial tribunal established by law.'

In addition, the new European Union tribunals have made some landmark rulings on the English judicial position.

Findlay v UK [1997] 24 EHRR 221 is a case in which there was a successful challenge against the English Court Martial system while McGonnell's case 28488/95/TLR was another in which the European Commission on Human Rights held that the Bailiff of Guernsey lacks sufficient impartiality to adjudicate a litigant's dispute, he being the embodiment of a breach of the doctrine of the separation of powers. He is not only the Speaker of the local Parliament and the Chief Executive in the jurisdiction but also the chief judicial officer.

Finally we come to the *Pinochet* case,[30] which reached the House of Lords in the following circumstances. Senator Pinochet, a former Head of State of Chile, had come to England for medical attention. While there he was arrested on a warrant issued by a magistrate at the instigation of the Spanish authorities to enable his extradition to Spain to face trial for crimes against humanity, he was alleged to have committed while in office in Chile. Pursuant to the international warrants of 16 and 25 October 1998, Metropolitan Stipendiary Magistrates had issued two provisional warrants for his arrest under s 8(1)(6) of the 1989 Extradition Act. Upon his arrest he applied to the Divisional Court to quash the warrants. The warrant of 16 October 1998, was quashed. When the same fate befell that of 23 October 1998 the authorities requested a stay to enable an appeal to be taken to the House of Lords on the question, certified by the Divisional Court, 'as to the purpose, interpretation and scope of the immunity enjoyed by a former Head of State from arrest and extradition proceedings in the UK for acts committed while he was Head of State'.

Amnesty International had sought leave to intervene – which had been granted. Lord Hoffmann, one of the five members of the court hearing the case, was a Director and Chairman of Amnesty International Charity Ltd (AICL).

When the House of Lords gave judgment on 25 November 1998, the appeal was allowed by a majority of three to two, Lord Hoffmann being among the majority.

At that time, neither Pinochet nor his legal advisers were aware of Lord Hoffmann's involvement with AICL and when it was discovered the Home Office was informed while a petition was also sent to the House of Lords requesting that

30 *In Re Pinochet* [2001] 1 AC 119.

the order of the House be set aside or that Lord Hoffmann's opinion be declared to be of no effect. The only ground advanced was that Lord Hoffmann's links with Amnesty International were such as to give the appearance of bias.

The House, having considered the petition, decided on 17 December 1998 to set aside the former decision of 25 November 1998. Lord Goff's words sum up the whole story:

> I have already stated that there was no allegation made against Lord Hoffmann that he was actually guilty of bias in coming to his decision, and I wish to make it clear that I am making no finding of factual bias against him. But I consider that the links, described in the judgment of Lord Browne-Wilkinson, between Lord Hoffmann and Amnesty International which had campaigned against General Pinochet and which intervened in the earlier hearing to support the case that he should be extradited to face trial for his alleged crimes, were so strong that public confidence in the integrity of the administration of justice would be shaken if his decision were allowed to stand. It was this reason and the other reasons given by Lord Browne-Wilkinson which led me to agree reluctantly in the decision of the Appeal Committee on 17 December 1998 that the order of 25 November 1998 should be set aside.

Since the *Pinochet* case, applications from lawyers and clients in England for judges to recuse themselves have become somewhat of a growth industry. One example will illustrate the extent of the problem.

Sion Jenkins, a deputy head teacher from Hastings (England), was indicted for the murder of his stepdaughter and convicted. He appealed to the Court of Appeal where one of the judges on the three-judge panel was Mr Justice Penrys-Davey who had attended the same Grammar School as the convicted man. However, not only had the judge attended the school, but he had kept in touch with the authorities there and made financial contributions to its activities over the years.

In the *Locabail* case,[31] the court had laid down certain guidelines, one of which was that a judge who had a continuing professional or personal association which might impair his judicial impartiality should so declare in advance of the trial. The appeal court construed that test to mean 'if there was a real danger, or possibility, of bias'. It was also felt that if there is any doubt, then the matter should be resolved in favour of disqualification.

In the Jenkins case, Penrys-Davey J mentioned this possible appearance of conflict to his two colleagues who did not consider it necessary to inform the defence. When eventually towards the end of the trial senior counsel for Jenkins raised the matter and suggested that in the circumstances the case should be sent to the House of Lords for determination, Kennedy LJ, the president of the court, dismissed the request as 'absurd' while at that time admitting that the matter had been raised with him by Penrys-Davey J.

It seems unfortunate that the defence was not advised of this development and it may well be that further guidelines are necessary to make it obligatory on the

31 *Locabail v Bayfield Properties Ltd* [2002] QB 851.

presiding judge in a case like this to inform the defence and to seek their concurrence in the judge continuing to sit.

CONCLUDING REMARKS, WITH SPECIAL REFERENCE TO CONFLICT IN THIRD WORLD COUNTRIES

From what has been pointed out above, there is no doubt lawyers everywhere should continually be on their guard to avoid conflicts of interest in their professional activities and that they must be alert to withdraw from a case in which a clear possibility of conflict becomes evident.

The issues that face the profession can often only be resolved on an intuitive basis and members of the Bar are advised that whenever it is felt that a certain course of conduct is questionable, the answer should always lie in ceasing to act if a retainer has already been accepted, or in refusing to act where the retainer is contemplated.

Whenever banking institutions are engaged in mortgage transactions in many developing countries, the bank frequently requires that the mortgagor (the borrower) should retain the bank's solicitor. This puts the solicitor in difficulties because if he is to act for the bank he cannot reveal to the bank any confidential information he may have on the borrower or vice versa. It also makes life just as uncomfortable for the borrower who may well have as his solicitor of choice a trusted adviser in whom he has always put his trust.

In the case of family matters lawyers are called upon – for reasons of costs – to represent both husband and wife in undefended divorce proceedings, only to face serious conflicts when the question of settlement of property becomes an issue.

Conflicts in matters of judicial adjudication have begun to assume new proportions since the *Pinochet* case to which reference has been made earlier in this chapter. Some lawyers both in the developed and developing world have since that case tended more and more to play the 'Hoffmann card' and in future it will be up to the judges and magistrates to address the matter of judicial bias soberly and maturely in deciding if and when they will recuse themselves. The reasonable man must, however, never be left in doubt as to the impartiality of the judge. The obvious approach is for a judge, if he thinks there might be a perception of bias, to declare his or her interest at the very start of the proceedings – as suggested in the Penrys-Davey case discussed earlier.

Our very next chapter will address the regulatory and disciplinary aspects of the profession.

CHAPTER 9

SELF-REGULATION AND DISCIPLINE IN THE LEGAL PROFESSION

INTRODUCTORY REMARKS

This chapter is divided into three parts.

Part I treats of the various ways in which the Bar is regulated in a sample of selected countries of the common-law world.

Part II addresses the matter of discipline in the profession embracing the court's inherent duty not only to admit but also to suspend or disbar lawyers as officers of the court, and examines the part played by Bar Associations in that exercise and in sanctions generally. These matters will be considered in the context of Codes of Ethics including the existing American, English and Canadian Codes. An attempt will be made to show how these codes, though differing in legislative form, are substantially similar in content in different parts of the world.

Part III discusses the subject of separate Codes of Ethics for Judicial Officers. Should superior court judges be guided by the same codes as would be applicable to magistrates and judges of inferior tribunals? Are the purposes of codes for practising lawyers different from those for judicial officers? Should judicial codes provide for sanctions as legal codes normally do? These are issues that will be examined in this Part.

PART I – SELF-REGULATION

NATURE OF INTERNAL REGULATION

It is the hallmark of every profession that its members should have a say in its internal regulation, and the legal profession is no exception.

THE BARRISTERS

Oddly enough, for more than six centuries regulation of the barrister's profession in England was covert – in the interstices of the minds of the profession who during that period operated without any written or organised indicia as to how its members (most of whom were originally ecclesiastics) were expected to conduct themselves. The rules of conduct were traditionally transmitted by word of mouth, namely, through personal apprenticeship and pupillage. Such rules as existed had their basis in tradition and rulings by the judges when considering rules of procedure. After 1894 (when the Bar Council was established), the rules were informally made by resolutions of that body, to be later confirmed in General Meeting, and sometimes by ad hoc rulings of the Council.

The training for the Bar was proposed by the judges and implemented by the four Inns of Court: Middle Temple, Inner Temple, Gray's Inn and Lincoln's Inn – the training being supported by a system of pupillage under which, before a barrister was released to the unsuspecting public, he would spend a year with a 'pupil-master' in 'chambers' during which he was expected to learn by example, what might be termed 'training by osmosis'.

Women were grudgingly admitted to the Inns in 1919. Originally the Inns of Court did not require the trainees to pass any written examinations and it was not until 1852 that such a requirement was introduced with the creation of a Council of Legal Education. Pupillage itself only became compulsory in 1956 and then only for those who would practise in England.[1]

As far as discipline was concerned, that was a matter for the Inns of Court, but in the words of Anthony Thornton:[2] 'The Inns did discipline its members from time to time but recorded instances are largely associated with drunken or riotous behaviour, landlord disputes arising out of the occupation of rooms or chambers within the Inns, and financial improvidence.'

Thornton attributes the degree of collegiality among barristers from the 19th century to the circuit system which developed out of the Industrial Revolution – a system still in existence today under which both Bench and Bar travelled (and still do) to the main centres of population dispensing justice *ambulando* – what was referred to as 'going on circuit'. This gave the lawyers the opportunity to travel with the judges and to share the Circuit Mess and Grand Council – institutions designed to give the Bar exclusive rights of audience on circuit.[3]

The Bar Council was eventually given statutory recognition as the representative entity for barristers by the Courts and Legal Services Act 1990, s 27(3) of which provides that the right of audience as a barrister would only be accorded to those persons who have been called to the Bar by one of the Inns of Court in England.

However, it was not until 1980 that the first Code of Conduct for barristers was approved by the Bar Council, following the recommendations of the Benson Commission on Legal Services which reported in 1979. Paragraph 104 of that Code stipulates: 'The general purpose of this Code is to provide the requirements for practice as a barrister and the rules and standards of conduct applicable to barristers which are appropriate in the interests of justice.'

The Code includes 17 Appendices setting out sets of Rules applicable to a number of situations such as (*inter alia*) Continuing Professional Development (App C), Practising Certificate (App D), the Terms of Work on which Barristers offer their Services to Solicitors (App G), Complaints Rules (App J), Disciplinary

1 This was the year I was called to the Bar by the Middle Temple and because I was to practise in the West Indies I was not required to undergo pupillage although I did practical work in a post-final training course.

2 See A Thornton, 'Responsibility and Ethics of the English Bar' in Ross Cranston (ed), *Legal Ethics and Professional Responsibility* (Oxford, Clarendon Press, 1995), pp 54–57. I have found this essay useful in the course of writing this section.

3 *ibid*, p 56.

Tribunals Regulations (App K), Hearings Before the Visitors (App M) and Fitness to Practice (App O).

Before the Bar Council Code came into existence, the only unofficial Guide provided for recruits and others at the Bar was a volume compiled by Sir William Boulton known as *Boulton's Conduct and Etiquette at the Bar*. Sir William had been the Secretary of the Bar Council for many years and his work, which went through six editions over a 22-year period beginning in 1953, was for many years of great ethical assistance to those who tried to master the techniques of serving as a barrister.

THE SOLICITORS

The solicitors' profession in England was regulated for centuries and Alison Crawley and Christopher Bramall have posed the question as to what constitutes the relation between regulation and legal professional ethics. They reply to their own question is as follows: 'despite that it is a maze ... we would assert that underlying the maze, there are the fundamental principles of legal professional ethics which can be found, in one form or another, in most jurisdictions.'[4]

The Law Society is the representative body for the governance of solicitors – just as the Bar Council is for barristers. The Law Society is, however, much larger and more complex than the Council and much more centralised in organisation. Both have rule-making powers but whereas the Bar Council is capable of having its rules brought quickly into operation, being subject only to the review of the former Lord Chancellor's Department, the procedures of consultation with the Lord Chancellor's Department and the Master of the Rolls prolong the process for the Law Society.

The Solicitors' Act 1974 is the statutory basis for solicitors' practice, but that legislation has been supplemented by a number of Rules made by the Law Society, such as the Solicitors' Practice Rules and the Accounts Rules.

It is this rule-making power that confers a claim to autonomy on the Society. The Bar makes a similar claim to autonomy on the same ground.

The current Codes, principles and rules which govern the practice of solicitors are to be found in the Eighth Edition of the *Guide to the Professional Conduct of Solicitors* published in 1999 which runs into 893 pages. The volume (referred to in this book as 'LSG') has been characterised as 'the Highway Code for Solicitors' and deals not only with the rules and principles of professional conduct, but with regulatory requirements, private practice, the position of employed solicitors, legal aid, the international aspects of solicitors' practice, relations with clients and obligations to non-clients.

4 See A Crawley and C Bramall, 'Professional rules, codes and principles affecting solicitors (or what has professional regulations to do with ethics?), in Ross Cranston (ed), *Legal Ethics and Professional Responsibility* (Oxford, Clarendon Press, 1995).

It gives guidance in such areas of practice as litigation and advocacy, alternative dispute resolution, insolvency practice, succession – testate and intestate, conveyancing, property transfers, investment business, financial regulation and professional indemnity. The main purpose of the Guide is clearly to assist solicitors (old and new) in the conscientious discharge of their professional duties. As the President of the Law Society stated in his Foreword to the 1999 Edition: 'Whatever changes take place, one thing remains certain: a proper standard of conduct is an essential hallmark of our profession and vital to the administration of justice. The Guide is intended to help solicitors maintain that standard.'[5]

APPLICATION TO DEVELOPING COUNTRIES

The Guide may be read with advantage by attorneys-at-law who practise outside of England and Wales, especially in the newly-independent countries of Asia, the Caribbean and the Pacific, if for no other reason than that the English laws governing barristers and solicitors still have application to some newly-independent countries. See Karen Nunez-Tesheira's book *The Legal Profession in the English Speaking Caribbean* (published by the Caribbean Law Publishing Company Jamaica in 2001) in which at pp xx and xxi she names Anguilla, Antigua and Barbuda, Dominica, Grenada, St Kitts and Nevis, and St Vincent as countries in which English legislation affecting some legal professional matters still applies. Note in particular that the Solicitors Act 1974 and the Solicitors Remuneration Order of 1972 still govern solicitors' fees today in an independent country as far removed as St Kitts and Nevis. See the decision of the Privy Council in a recent case[6] affirming a decision of the Eastern Caribbean Appeal Court ruling that the English legislation in question formed part of the laws of St Kitts and Nevis.

In these parts of the developing world, young lawyers (and even old ones) do not have the good fortune to have at their elbow the type of information and guidance to be found in the Guide. Many of them learn from their mistakes. For this reason, the LSG is recommended as required reading for new entrants to the profession in newly independent countries. They must of course read it critically and appreciate that while much is common, much is also very different in their respective countries.

The regulation of the profession is in those countries usually a joint effort between government and the profession, and whenever ground rules (or revised ground rules) are being established, governments always call upon members of the fused profession to provide their views on draft legislation.

To this extent, lawyers in developing countries do have a say in how they are governed and it would be of advantage to those lawyers to have the data which the Guide provides in order to be able to make a useful contribution. Indeed, many of the matters dealt with in existing codes and legislation are covered by the

5 See LSG, 8th edn, p xi.
6 *Zuliani v Viera* (1944) 45 WIR 188.

LSG, but the legislative provisions, especially where they take the form of statutes, tend to lag behind modern thinking and developments – as, for instance, in matters of publicity and advertisements as well as in money laundering and confidentiality.[7]

A few territories have managed to keep their laws governing the profession reasonably current and one such country is Mauritius. A Code of Ethics which came into effect there in 1997 was made and approved by the Mauritius Council of Legal Education pursuant to the Law Practitioners' Act of 1984. However, even before the Code of Ethics came into effect, barristers in the country were required to observe the rules of professional etiquette of barristers of the High Court of England – and this in an *independent Republic* in the Commonwealth which obtained self-determination two decades ago!

The strength of the English inheritance is manifest from the fact that, in the Mauritius law, barristers must still be 'instructed' by attorneys-at-law, as barristers in England are 'instructed' by solicitors (para 3.6 of the law). The language in the Mauritius law is the identical language of the English Bar Code; for example, 'barristers in independent practice'; 'employed barristers'; 'non-practising barristers'; and 'the cab-rank principle'.

A study of almost all the codes reviewed from the developing common law world yields the same result. Even where there are no codes – as in Vanuatu – it is an unwritten law that the profession follows as far as possible ethical rules in force in England.

PART II – DISCIPLINE

THE BAR

A new disciplinary procedure for the Bar in England came into being in 1997 under which a complaint goes to a Lay Complaints Commissioner who is empowered to dismiss it if it does not disclose a *prima facie* case of misconduct or inadequate professional service (IPS). If it does, further investigation will take place in the form of documentary evidence from the barrister and his instructing solicitor. If there is a *prima facie* case of IPS, the matter is referred to the Professional Conduct Committee (PCC) who must decide whether a *prima facie* case exists of IPS or misconduct. If the answer is the affirmative, the PCC refers the complaint to *either* an adjudication panel (in the case of IPS) or a disciplinary panel (in the case of misconduct) for either an informal hearing if the breach is minor or

7 See, for instance, the Barbados Legal Profession Code of Ethics 1988 made on 12 December 1988 under s 18 of the Legal Profession Act; the Jamaica Legal Profession (Canons of Professional Ethics) Rules 1978 made on 29 December 1978 made under s 12(7) of the Legal Profession Act 1972; the Belize Legal Profession (Code of Conduct) Rules 1991 made under s 18 of the Legal Profession Act 1988. All these Codes as well as the Trinidad & Tobago and the OECS Codes can do with substantial revision. At the same time see the extent to which Singapore has upgraded its rules on the matter of publicity in the Legal Profession (Publicity) Rules 1998 made on 1 December 1998.

it is IPS; or a summary hearing in case of a serious breach. The disciplinary panel is chaired by a High Court Judge or a circuit judge. It is a tribunal of the Inns comprising, in addition to the Chairman, three practising members of the Bar and a lay member.

In the case of IPS, the sanctions include an apology to the client, repayment or reduction of fees or compensation of up to £2,000.

In the case of misconduct, the tribunal may impose a fine, cause a withholding of fees, suspend or disbar the offending barrister.

SOLICITORS

The client sends his complaint to the firm to which the solicitor belongs (when it is sent to the Office for the Supervision of Solicitors (OSS) it is in any event referred to the firm). In case the matter is not resolved by conciliation in the firm, it is sent either to an investigating unit at the OSS or to the Compliance and Supervision Committee. At this level, the matter may be considered either by the Client Relations Sub-Committee which deals with IPS or the Professional Regulation Sub-Committee which deals with matters of misconduct and can impose sanctions in that connection. In cases of serious professional misconduct, the matter is referred to the Solicitors Disciplinary Committee – a statutory body.

The sanctions for IPS are similar to those imposed by the Bar, although in the case of solicitors there may be an order for auditing the accounts. The Disciplinary Tribunal may impose a fine or order suspension or disbarment.

The public is fundamentally suspicious of having lawyers disciplined by other members of the profession. These functions at one time fell upon the Solicitors' Complaints Bureau (SCB) – a creature of the 1974 Solicitors Act – but as a result of public pressure the duties of that organisation were taken over in 1996 by the Office for the Supervisior of Solicitors (OSS) which Boon and Levin have described as representing 'a last chance to retain a measure of self-regulation for solicitors in the field of complaints'.[8]

The Legal Services Ombudsman who supervised the work of the SCB consistently complained that the body had failed in its duty to achieve customer satisfaction with the way complaints were being handled, and it is therefore hoped that the OSS will fill the bill more efficiently, since it is empowered to compel the disclosure of files and since it has disciplinary powers to rebuke solicitors; to refuse practicing certificates or lay down conditions on which they should issue; to disallow costs in appropriate cases; and to recommend that disciplinary action be taken against offending solicitors.

POSITION IN THE DEVELOPING WORLD

There is an undoubted laxity in certain parts of the world with which some lawyers without proper supervision perform their work. Has the time not come

8 Andrew Boon and Jennifer Levin, *The Ethics and Conduct of Lawyers in England and Wales* (Oxford, Hart Publishing, 1999), p 127.

for such an appointment like a Legal Services Ombudsman to be made in those countries that can afford it? It may well be only a matter of time before such action will take place. If individual territories find it economically unfeasible, surely it is something that a group of territories adjacent to each other can do, for example, the Organisation of Eastern Caribbean States (OECS). Take the case of that chain of nine jurisdictions comprising the Eastern Caribbean Supreme Court in which the Chief Justice is physically located in St Lucia, in the centre of the chain. How will such a dignitary with a minute staff handle complaints about the conduct of lawyers from litigants in all the territories? In them all (except St Lucia, Antigua and Barbuda), there is provision in the Supreme Court Act for lawyers to be disciplined by two judges, but there is no direction as to the route to the two judges.[9] On this account it has taken 35 years since the Supreme Court Act was passed in 1967 for the first two cases to be brought against practitioners in 2002 (and these resulted in minor punishments).[10] Since there are *puisne* judges stationed in all the jurisdictions, would it not be a more sensible arrangement if local complaints could be addressed to the senior resident judge? That judge should then establish whether a *prima facie* case is made out before forwarding the matter to a Disciplinary Committee to be appointed by the Chief Justice. Surely the local judge should even have the power to reprimand and/or to impose a fine on a lawyer who was guilty of a breach of ethics?

Most of the codes of conduct studied contain a mixture of the hortatory and the forbidden. They also tend to state specific sections, breach of which renders the offender subject to mandatory charges of professional misconduct, and other sections the breach of which attract charges of misconduct.

THE NATURE OF PROCEEDINGS

A question that frequently arises for consideration is whether disciplinary proceedings are civil or criminal matters. A supplementary question is what burden of proof is required. The object of disciplinary proceedings is to protect the public and to help to maintain high standards for the profession with a view to public confidence in the legal profession being maintained. On the other hand, punishment *per se* is at the heart of criminal proceedings, which are matters for the courts. Thus, it was held in a Canadian case, *Stevens v LSUC* [1979] 55 OR (2d) 405, that charges brought to a disciplinary body should not be treated like counts in a criminal indictment. It was also held in *Re Sugg v LSUC* [1989] 68 OR (2D) 278 that a doctor could be struck off the Medical Register even though acquitted by a court on the same charge.

It is suggested that the proper approach to rules of evidence in disciplinary matters is that taken by the Ontario courts which have decided that the rules applicable should be those referable to civil proceedings, with the lawyer being a

9 I happen to know that litigants would like to have someone to whom to forward such complaints, since I was asked more than once while chairing two Constitutional Commissions in the OECS how such complaints may be made.

10 See Civil Suit No 73 of 1999 (St Vincent and the Grenadines) and Civil Suit No 84 of 2000. In the first of these suits, the offender was suspended from practice for one month while in the latter case the lawyer was fined $5,000 with costs.

compellable witness. Thus a provision compelling a lawyer to testify at his or her trial does not offend the section in the Charter of Rights which forbids a person from giving evidence which would tend to incriminate him or her.

The Canadian courts have also held that disciplinary proceedings may continue at the same time as criminal proceedings against a lawyer, since to adjourn the former would prejudice the public interest. If, however, the two sets of proceedings are unrelated to each other, there would be grounds to await the end of the trial.

THE NATURE OF THE PENALTIES

In almost all common law jurisdictions, the court or a disciplinary tribunal may suspend a law practitioner, and order that his or her name be erased from the Roll, or make such other order as it thinks fit; for example, it may give a reprimand or impose a fine.

WHAT CONSTITUTES PROFESSIONAL MISCONDUCT?

The kinds of offences that constitute professional misconduct vary from jurisdiction to jurisdiction[11] but they include such acts as:

- misappropriation of clients' funds;
- creating false documents;
- forgery;
- suborning perjury;
- failing to honour undertakings; and
- failing to maintain proper books of record.[12]

HOW DOES PROFESSIONAL MISCONDUCT DIFFER FROM CONDUCT UNBECOMING?

The former arises from acts or functions executed in the course of the lawyer's professional service, the latter from acts performed in his private capacity. The Law Society of Upper Canada in an amendment to its Rules of Professional Conduct in 2000 defined 'conduct unbecoming a barrister or solicitor' as follows:

> 'conduct unbecoming a barrister or solicitor' means conduct in a lawyer's personal or private capacity that tends to bring discredit upon the legal profession including, for example:

11 The Ghana Code of Ethics (1994) set out 50 acts which constitutes misconduct.

12 These are among 26 acts set out (for Canada) by Gavin MacKenzie in *Lawyers and Ethics: Professional Responsibility and Discipline*, Carswell, 2001, 26.24.

(a) committing a criminal act that reflects adversely on the lawyer's honesty, trustworthiness, or fitness as a lawyer;

(b) taking improper advantage of the youth, inexperience, lack of education, lack of sophistication, ill-health, or unbusinesslike habits of another; or

(c) engaging in conduct involving dishonesty.

ARRANGEMENTS FOR BRINGING DISCIPLINARY PROCEEDINGS

These differ from jurisdiction to jurisdiction and in the interest of space we will briefly set out what they are in three jurisdictions: Mauritius, Singapore and Vanuatu.

MAURITIUS

The procedure in this country is as follows:

- The Attorney-General may, either *proprio motu* or on receipt of complaint under sub-s (2), inquire into any act done by a law practitioner.
- Any person who is aggrieved by an act done by a law practitioner in the exercise of his profession may report the matter to the Attorney-General.
- Where the Attorney-General is of opinion that an act done by a law practitioner, whether or not an inquiry under sub-s (1) has been made, is of such a nature as to call for the institution of disciplinary proceedings, he shall submit a detailed report on the matter to the Chief Justice and a copy of the report to the person against whom the proceedings are to be taken.
- The Chief Justice shall, on receipt of a report under sub-s (3), appoint a day for the hearing of the matter.
- The Registrar shall cause notice of the day appointed for the hearing, together with a copy of the report, to be communicated to the law practitioner.
- Nothing in this section shall be construed as limiting the inherent powers of the Supreme Court to deal with matters of professional discipline of law practitioners.

Procedure at disciplinary proceedings is as follows:

- Any proceedings under s 13 shall take place:

  (a) before at least three judges; and

  (b) unless the court otherwise directs, in public.
- Any witness for proceedings under sub-s (1) shall be examined on oath.
- The court may, after considering the evidence laid before it:

  (a) suspend the law practitioner for such period as it thinks fit;

  (b) order that the name of the law practitioner be erased from the Roll; or

  (c) make such other order as it thinks fit.

SINGAPORE

In this case we set out this brief account of the system in existence with statistics.

Under the Legal Profession Act (Cap 161), the Singapore Law Society is empowered to take action against lawyers. All complaints are investigated at first instance by an Inquiry Committee of the Law Society and this Committee may impose a fine or refer more serious cases to be dealt with by a Disciplinary Committee. The following chart at Table I shows the number of cases referred to the Inquiry Committee for the five year period 1997–2001 and their outcome:

TABLE I

Year	Sep 96 to Aug 97	Sep 97 to Aug 98	Sep 98 to Aug 99	Sep 99 to Aug 00	Sep 00 to Aug 01
No of complaints dismissed	59	35	36	31	32
No of complaints resulting in imposition of penalty	21	12	17	13	5
No of complaints referred to Disciplinary Committee	7	23	5	4	2
Total Number of complaints with by Inquiry Committee	87	70	58	48	39

Figures are extracted from the Law Society Of Singapore Annual Reports 1997 to 2001. As at 31 August 2001, there were further complaints pending.

VANUATU

In this small jurisdiction in the Pacific the Law Council by Order appoints a Disciplinary Committee (hereafter simply 'the Committee') to hear complaints against legal practitioners and employees: see the Legal Practitioners Act (Cap 119) (s 7). This Committee consists of not less than five persons, viz a judge; not less than two legal practitioners nominated by the Attorney-General; not less than one person not qualified to be registered as a legal practitioner; and such other persons as the Law Council shall consider suitable. Any person who wishes to complain concerning the conduct of a legal practitioner or an employee does so by lodging a complaint in writing with the Secretary of the Committee containing specific allegations of misconduct.

The Committee, which has the same powers as the Supreme Court to summon and examine witnesses and to order the production of documents, may require the Secretary to investigate and report on a complaint before considering it further. If the Committee finds a legal practitioner has committed misconduct, it may:

(a) order that he be struck off the roll;
(b) suspend the practitioner for such period as is considered fit;
(c) impose a fine to be paid into the Revenue;
(d) order the practitioner to pay compensation to the complainant; or
(e) reprimand the practitioner.

In the case of an employee, if the Committee finds misconduct, it may order that no practitioner either on an indefinite basis or for a fixed term employ the employee (s 9).

A person found guilty of misconduct may, within 15 days of the communication to him of the finding, appeal to the Supreme Court, which is empowered to dismiss the appeal or to set aside or vary the decision of the Committee. Counsel to represent the Committee may be appointed by the Attorney-General.

PART III – JUDICIAL CODES

THEIR DESIRABILITY

In some judicial quarters doubts have been expressed as to whether it is desirable to promulgate or prescribe judicial codes. If a man or woman is appointed as a judge, the appointment itself is a vote of confidence that he or she is above reproach. The very fact, so runs the argument, that a judge is required to subject himself or herself to a code suggests there are doubts about his or her probity and integrity. There are others who attack the idea from a constitutional angle. All modern constitutions provide for the appointment, promotion and discipline of judges and a code suggests he or she may be disciplined in some way – perhaps by a quiet word from a Chief Justice or by a verbal rebuke. Any such sanction would run foul of the constitution which already provides a special regime for dealing with disciplining judges through the Judicial and Legal Service Commission. There is not much in the first argument, but there would be some substance in the second if in fact an attempt was made in the code to usurp the functions of the relevant Commission or to create a parallel regime for discipline in the case of judges. Such, however, is not the intention.

The fact is that the promulgating of a code for judges is intended to achieve two purposes, viz to remind the judges constantly of what is expected of them; and to assure the public that the judges are expected to serve the public in an independent and impartial manner – that being a right due to the public.

In this day and age, the citizens of most countries are aware (or should be aware) that the 1948 Universal Declaration of Human Rights laid down that 'everyone is entitled in full equality to a fair and public hearing by an independent and impartial tribunal'.

That Declaration contemplated criminal proceedings in the main.

It is also common ground that the European Convention on Human Rights (ECHR), signed in 1950 and brought into force in 1953, claimed the same equality for civil matters. Art 6 provided as follows: 'In the determination of his civil rights and obligations or any criminal charge brought against him, everyone is entitled to a fair and public hearing within a reasonable time by an independent and impartial tribunal established by law.'

This, it will be recalled, was followed by the United Nations Convention on Civil and Political Rights which came into force in 1976 – and to this all Caribbean jurisdictions have since subscribed. It must also be noted that it has become the norm for all independent countries – certainly those in the Commonwealth from Asia, the Pacific or the Caribbean – to enshrine in their new constitutions a clause in terms of s 10 of the Universal Declaration of Human Rights referred to earlier. Canada legislated for a Federal Bill of Rights in 1960 and for a full Charter of Rights in 1982, as has South Africa in its post-apartheid Constitution in the mid-1990s.

In June 1998, the Latimer House Commonwealth Guidelines suggested the creation and adoption of a Code of Ethics for judges 'as a means of ensuring the accountability of judges'. It is encouraging to note that in the small jurisdictions of the Organisation of Eastern Caribbean States (OECS), the Chief Justice, Sir Dennis Byron, shortly after the Guidelines were released, instructed one of his senior judges to prepare a draft. The Chief Justice also commissioned a one-man Task Force in 2000, comprising Mr Reginald Dumas, a distinguished former diplomat from Trinidad & Tobago, to examine, *inter alia*, the working of the Judicial and Legal Service Commission and matters connected herewith. Mr Dumas strongly recommended that enforceable codes for both the higher and lower judiciary should be introduced as soon as possible and such a code has since been promulgated for superior court judges. It is a tribute to the OECS Chief Justice that he should have selected a layman of the high calibre of Mr Dumas for this important task and Mr Dumas deserves the thanks of the legal and judicial fraternity for producing a first-class report which all judges in this area should read for its insights and in order to appreciate the need for a code.

During 2002 and 2003, I managed to secure similar codes from South Africa, Mauritius, Kenya, Pakistan, Uganda and Guyana. (There are doubtless others already prepared or in the course of preparation.) Why have they all come into existence at this time? I attempt what I consider an answer.

KENYA

In the case of Kenya, the Code is said to be applicable 'to all judicial officers and more particularly to the magistrates because some of the penalties prescribed by this code cannot be meted out against judges and, secondly and more so, because about 90% of the people who appear in courts do so in the magistrates' courts'.

PAKISTAN

In so far as the Pakistan Code is concerned, 'an attempt is made to indicate certain traditional requirements of behaviour in the Judges of the Superior Courts, conducive to the achievement of a standard of justice worthy of the nation'.

UGANDA

The Ugandans proclaimed as follows in putting out their Code:

> Now, therefore, we the Judges of the Supreme Court and the High Court of Uganda now assembled this 21st day of July 1989 in an effort to transform the judicial institution so that it can regain, live up to and maintain its proper role of an independent, impartial and honourable organ of government, do hereby adopt this code of conduct to be known as 'The Code of conduct for judges, Magistrates and other judicial officers 1989' as some guidelines to our conduct as Judges and to the conduct of Magistrates and other Judicial officers.

NIGERIA

The Nigeria Code applies to all categories of judicial officers throughout the Federation, 'Judicial Officer' being defined as:

> a holder of the office of Chief Justice of Nigeria, a justice of the Supreme Court, the President or justice of the Court of Appeal, the Chief Judge or judge of the Federal High Court, of a state or of the Federal Capital Territory, Abuja, the President or judge of a Customary Court of Appeal of a State and of the Federal Capital Territory, Abuja, and includes the holder of a similar office in any inferior court whatsoever.

It prescribes that 'violation of any of the rules contained in this Code shall constitute judicial misconduct or misbehaviour and may entail disciplinary action'.

GUYANA

The Guyana draft Code states that the 'principles and rules (of the document) are intended to establish standards for ethical conduct of judges by which they agree to be bound'.

MAURITIUS

Mauritius is explicit as to the purpose of its Code, expressing its *raison d'être* as follows in the Preamble:

> And whereas consistently with the United Nations Principles on the Independence of the Judiciary, it is essential that judges, individually and collectively, respect and honour judicial office as a public trust and strive to enhance and maintain confidence in the judicial system.

And then it concludes:

> The following Guidelines and Principles are intended to establish standards of ethical conduct of judges. They are Guidelines to be applied in the light of all relevant circumstances and consistently with the requirements of judicial independence and the law. They are designed to provide guidance to judges and to afford a structure for regulating judicial conduct. They are intended to supplement, and not to derogate from, existing principles which bind the judge.

THE US

The Code of Conduct for the United States Judges was initially adopted by the Judicial Conference on 5 April 1973 and was then known as 'the Code of Judicial Conduct for United States Judges'. Subsequently in March 1987 the word 'Judicial' was deleted. The Judicial Conference in September 1992 made substantial amendments to the Code and s C of the compliance section was revised in March 1996. The US has been in the forefront of countries which have always seen the need for such codes, ever since the American Bar Association adopted the first Code of Judicial Ethics in 1924 which inspired such instruments throughout the US and in other parts of the world.

CANADA

In 1983, Martin Friedland, a Professor of Law at the University of Toronto, produced a volume entitled *A Place Apart: Judicial Independence and Accountability in Canada*. After considering the US Federal Judicial Code of Ethics as well as the American Bar Association Code in all their joint aspects, he expressed the view that it was time the Canadian establishment take a leaf out of the book of its neighbour to the south. Work began in 1994 when the Canadian Judicial Council set up a Working Party consisting of four council members to prepare a Code. After much consultation within and outside the judiciary involving more than 50 meetings with organisations and judges at various levels in all parts of the country culminating in a special judicial seminar on the matter, the Canadian Judicial Council in 1998 published the volume entitled *Ethical Principles for Judges* – a volume which is very highly recommended for study and possible adoption.

Its purpose is to provide ethical guidance for the judges. It is laid out in the form of Statements, Principles and Commentaries describing the very high standards towards which all judges should strive. The Statements are characterised as 'principles of reason' to be applied in the light of all the relevant circumstances and consistently with the requirements of judicial independence and the law. They are not intended as a 'Code' or 'a list of prohibited behaviours' as in the case of a lawyer's Code of Professional Conduct which normally attracts sanctions. Above all, nothing in the document is intended to limit or restrict judicial independence in any way.

Judges are the guardians of judicial independence, not as a privilege of judicial office, but 'as the constitutionally guaranteed right of every citizen to have disputes heard and decided by impartial judges'.

There is this final exhortation in the Canadian Ethical Principles:

> The intention is that judges will accept these Statements, Principles and Commentaries as reflective of their high ethical aspirations and that they will find them worthy of respect and deserving of careful consideration when facing any of the issues addressed to them.

OECS

In regard to the OECS Code of Judicial Ethics, its purpose is stated as being to provide guidance to judges and nominees for judicial office. It also provides standards of conduct 'for application in proceedings under the Courts Order, although it is not intended that disciplinary action would be appropriate for every violation of its provisions'. It explains:

> Whether disciplinary action is appropriate and the degree of discipline to be imposed should be determined through a reasonable application of the text and should depend on such factors as the seriousness of the violation, the intent of the judge, whether there is a pattern of improper conduct, and the effect of the improper conduct on others or on the judicial system.

SOUTH AFRICA

The reader is also invited to study carefully a Code issued in March 2000 in South Africa by the Chief Justice, the President of the Constitutional Court and the Judges, the President of the different High Courts and the Labour Appeal Court and the President of the Land Claims Court. This document is replete with learning. It is a set of guidelines 'intended to assist judges in dealing with ethical and professional issues which may confront them during their judicial careers'. They are intended to inform the public about the judicial ethos in that country. In preparing the document, regard was had to the Constitution of South Africa, to the common law, case law and international standards as well as the views of the judiciary: 'It should be emphasized that professional ethical rules derive much of their binding nature from their general acceptance by members of the profession.' The judicial ethical rules very much resemble the Ethical Principles for Judges promulgated by the Canadian Judicial Council (referred to above). They are set out in two groups, viz those which apply to judges in respect of their judicial duties and those which apply in respect of their extra-judicial activities.

NOTE ON JUDICIAL CODES

It would be wise if future judicial codes could give guidance on a judge's post-service employment position. Some members of the Bench do not observe the rule that a member of the profession is no longer a barrister, solicitor or attorney-at-law once he becomes a judge. Thus, a judge of a superior court should never permit the title 'QC' to appear after his name on court documents (or at all). By the same token, no High Court or appellate judge should practise law after retirement from the Bench.

No less distinguished a jurist than Lord Bingham, the Senior Law Lord in England at the time of writing, has drawn attention to this aspect of judicial ethics in an informative paper in *Legal Ethics and Professional Responsibility*,[13] in which he has pointed out that a lawyer on appointment to the Bench 'becomes solely a judge with the result that on retirement he lacks the qualification to practise', to which he adds 'I would for my part be very sorry to see the role eroded'.

There is, of course, nothing inappropriate in an ex-judge serving as an arbitrator, legal consultant or advisor, Company Director, Law Professor, Chairman or Member of Commissions of Inquiry, Public Service Boards, Civil Service Boards of Appeal or any such bodies. An ex-judge is also eminently qualified to serve as a Governor-General, as in the cases of Sir John Kerr and Sir Ninian Stephens in Australia or Sir Clifford Husbands in Barbados (at the present time), those dignitaries having had distinguished service on the Bench.

CONSCIENTIOUS PERFORMANCE OF FUNCTIONS

Judges must perform their functions conscientiously and diligently not only when presiding in court but when performing all other judicial tasks. They should always be punctual and work in a programmed and organised way. The legal profession and the public should not get the impression that a degree of disorder or anarchy exists in the administration of court arrangements and procedures.

IMPARTIALITY

It goes without saying that the judge must at all times strenuously strive for total impartiality. But what constitutes impartiality? The test is whether an informed person, viewing the matter realistically and practically and having thought the matter through, would come to the conclusion that a lack of impartiality exists.[14] It must also be borne in mind that 'true impartiality does not require that the judge have no sympathies or opinions; it requires only that the judge nevertheless be free to entertain and act upon different points of view with an open mind'.[15]

JUDICIAL DEMEANOUR

A judge should adopt a well-balanced attitude towards all parties with whom he deals in court. He should be decisive and maintain firm control of any court over which he or she presides, treating everyone with the greatest courtesy and respect. A Judge should never permit himself or herself to lose his or her temper. A judge

13 R Cranston (ed), *Legal Ethics and Professional Responsibility* (Oxford, Clarendon Press, 1995), p 51.

14 See Grandpré J in *Committee for Justice and Liberty v National Energy Board* [1978] 1 SCR 369.

15 A passage from p 12 of the Canadian Judicial Council's Commentaries on Judicial Conduct published in 1991 cited with approval by L'Heureux-Dube and McLachlin JJ of the Supreme Court of Canada (Gonthier and LaForest JJ concurring) in *RDS v The Queen* [1997] 3 SCR 504.

should always be punctual and should not be tardy in delivering judgments, indicating a timeframe within which it is hoped judgment will be delivered and explaining to the parties when it is not possible to fulfil the promise.

As far as possible, a judge should ensure that the close members of his or her family also comport themselves in such a way as not to give the public cause for concern about the judge's position of impartiality and independence in the discharge of his duties.

CONCLUDING SUMMARY

Although in this chapter we have not specifically given the details of lawyers' codes in the US, it is appropriate that in this summary we should point out that the codes – both legal and judicial – that have been promulgated elsewhere owe their origins to the happenings in that regard in the US, as we shall now explain.

When the first US 'Canons of Ethics' were promulgated by the legal profession in 1908, they served as internal norms to govern and regulate the profession. They were fraternal exhortations – a kind of collegial expression of the 'narrative' by which lawyers were guided in the defence of due process. They served to proclaim the profession's internal autonomy.[16]

In 1964, as a result of persistent clamour about their vagueness and outdated nature, an ABA Committee was appointed to study and make amendments to the Canons. The new Code was adopted by the ABA House of Delegates in August 1969 to take effect from 1 January 1970. The 1908 Code had embraced the basic core values of loyalty and confidentiality to the client and candour to the court. The new Code of 1970 came into being because members of the profession by that time had approached the courts to assist them to secure a firmer grip on errant members of their craft.

The 1970 Code of Professional Responsibility was promulgated in three sections:

- Canons;
- Ethical Considerations; and
- Disciplinary Rules.

Unfortunately, the Code of 1970 came under fire almost as soon as it became a reality. By 1977 a further Commission was formed to revise the Code and this resulted in the 1983 Model Rules of Professional Conduct embracing a Preamble, Scope and 52 Rules, each of which is followed by an Explanatory Comment.

It will be observed from what has been stated in this chapter that legal codes in developing countries are all the product of an external legalising process – albeit with an input from members of the profession, usually via the Bar Association.

16 See Geoffrey C Hazard Jr, 'The future of legal ethics', in the *Yale Law Journal*, Vol 100, No 1239. See also Charles Wolfram, *Modern Legal Ethics* (St Paul, MN, West Publishing Co, 1999), 2.6.2–2.6.4, 53–60.

The legal codes in most developing countries form part of an Act of Parliament which includes hortatory 'canon-like' sections and preachments alongside firm disciplinary rules capable of enforcement by a court of law or other tribunal. To this extent, those countries are still at the stage of the US 1970 Code of Professional Responsibility, and I have in the course of my researches only found one jurisdiction in the Caribbean which is actively considering early revisions. Others may follow in its wake. In the case of the Legal Code for Jamaica and the OECS Code for Judges, the term 'Canons' is still employed.

As for Judicial Codes, the words of exhortation are described as 'Guidelines' in Canada and South Africa; as 'Articles' in Pakistan; and as 'Rules' in Kenya, Nigeria and Uganda. Singapore also provides a Code for the judges of both Superior and Subordinate Courts, but the document is 'classified'.

In the next chapter we consider the ethics of the criminal process in some depth.

CHAPTER 10

ETHICS OF THE CRIMINAL PROCESS

RESPECTIVE FUNCTIONS OF PROSECUTOR AND DEFENCE COUNSEL

The prosecutor and the defence counsel have a duty, which they each exercise in different ways, to foster and promote the administration of justice. They act in divergent ways because their roles differ.

Professor David Luban, an American arch-libertarian, propounds a doctrine of classical liberalism. In his view: 'the state exists to protect its citizens in their pursuit of their own goals and not to pursue goals of its own ... Individuals have rights against the state ... The greatest danger to citizens is the state itself.'[1] According to Luban, justice requires that the prosecutor restrain his zeal while defence counsel operates as a 'wild card' injected into the proceedings of the state, and that zealous advocacy of those accused of crime is 'the greatest safeguard of individual liberty against the encroachment of the state'.[2]

Another equally distinguished American ethicist is not, however, persuaded that a defendant is as isolated and helpless against the state as Luban makes out. This writer – William Simon – while accepting the protection of proof beyond reasonable doubt and even the zealous advocacy of the defence when warranted, considers the case for special protection to be overstated.

Simon would pay more attention to the position of the victim which he considers is often overlooked.[3]

In England – the bosom of the common law – it will be illustrated later in this chapter[4] that the protective advantages which have traditionally been hailed as such a benefit to accused persons obtain more on the books than in practice. In fact the illustrations to be given later will reveal that the so-called advantages are being slowly, but surely and effectively, eroded. Successive Home Secretaries have in recent years, under the guise of judicial suggestions for reform, taken it upon themselves to make changes characterised as being intended 'to restore the balance' or 'to create a fairer balance'. In the process they have made 'equality or arms' a myth, since the advantageous protections were originally designed to redress the acute imbalance in terms of resources and experience that a prosecuting authority has always enjoyed.

---

1 David Luban, *Lawyers and Justice: An Ethical Study* (Princeton, NJ, Princeton University Press, 1988), p 63.

2 *Ibid*, p 62.

3 See Simon, 1993, p 1704, in which he states that the libertarians have overstated the case for the dangers of the State and underplayed the dangers to society posted by the criminal defendant. He disagrees with Luban that no tangible harm is inflicted on anyone when a criminal evades justice and that 'no one's life is materially worse off by acquittal as such'.

4 See under 'Concluding Comments' at p 151 below.

The extent and mood of such changes can best be illustrated by reference to the formal words of the caution signalling the arrest of an accused. Until relatively recent times the caution was in the following familiar terms: 'You are not obliged to say anything, but anything you do say will be recorded in writing and may be given in evidence.' This, of course, was consistent with the major principle that it is the duty of the prosecution in a criminal trial to prove the guilt of the accused beyond reasonable doubt and that the accused was (at his own risk and by his own choice) entitled to remain silent until the end of the trial.

The erosion of the rights of an accused is today evident in a new caution including this injunction: 'It may harm your defence if you do not when asked reveal matters on which you might subsequently wish to rely at your trial.'

In 1996, the UK Parliament introduced an Act[5] which made provision for a wide range of prosecution and defence disclosures by the prosecution *and the defence*, including a scheme for preparatory hearings before trial in long and complex cases; for judges to make binding rulings on points of law or the admissibility of evidence at the pre-trial stage; and for the re-trial of a case which results in an acquittal, if the acquitted has been tainted by a conviction for interfering with witnesses or jurors in that case.

In a well-researched essay on the rights of an accused, Andrew Ashworth has made the following pertinent statement:[6]

> The criminal justice system has moral dimensions other than the moral force of the law against those who do wrong. Among those other moral dimensions are that the rights of victims and witnesses should be respected, and that citizens who are suspected of, or charged with, offences must be dealt with in a way which respects their rights.

These changes do not stand alone. The current English position is that if the accused fails to give evidence at his trial, the jury may be told by the judge that the circumstances of the case would entitle them to draw adverse inferences against the accused.

There is no obligation on the defence to reveal the truth if defence counsel is or becomes aware that the prosecution is in error in suggesting that the accused is a person of good character when in fact he has a criminal record. However, the defence may not, through counsel or otherwise, make affirmative favourable references to the record of the accused or overtly rely on his 'clean sheet'. Silence is all that is required. This is one of the special advantages available to defence counsel which has so far not been touched.

---

5 See the Criminal Procedure and Investigations Act 1996.

6 Ashworth, 'Ethics and criminal justice', in Ross Cranston (ed), *Legal Ethics and Professional Responsibility* (Oxford, Clarendon Press, 1995).

WHEN MAY DEFENCE COUNSEL WITHDRAW HIS SERVICES?

If the client makes a confession of his guilt to his counsel but insists in entering a plea of not guilty, it is said that the lawyer should withdraw if time permits because, in the words of a seasoned Canadian jurist, it is highly doubtful if counsel could plead the case effectively and affect warmth for his client without being plagued by his conscience that he is acting the role of a base dissembler.[7]

That statement about withdrawal in the previous paragraph is not valid today. On what basis does the client make such a 'confession'? Is he expected to be au fait with all the elements of a particular crime? What if he is mistaken (as he is very likely to be) about the ingredients of the particular crime? What makes the lawyer a judge of the client's cause? Surely this is a matter for the court after the admissible evidence has been led? Is not the client to be presumed innocent until the contrary is proved to the satisfaction of the judge (and jury)? What 'guilt' has the client confessed – is it a legal or moral guilt? Does he understand the difference?

What these questions suggest is that it would be ethically improper for a lawyer to decide to withdraw from representing a client in a criminal case simply because the client asserts he is 'guilty'. Unfortunately, as we shall see later in this chapter, the codes of conduct in newly-independent countries – when discussing when a lawyer may withdraw – seem to assume that every client is competent to declare his guilt, whatever the offence with which he or she is charged.

It is to correct this misapprehension that Gavin MacKenzie in his well-researched treatise[8] refers to the ethical position of the defence lawyer and makes the valid comment that the most difficult ethical problems of criminal defence lawyers involve the resolution of conflicting professional responsibilities. Munroe Freedman has likewise spoken with a loud voice on this matter.[9] So have David Luban[10] and Charles Wolfram.[11]

DUTY OF CONFIDENTIALITY

All these ethicists have underscored the fundamental fact that the doctrine of confidentiality will affect the lawyer's candour with the court. Thus, if the lawyer is aware that his client intends to give perjurious evidence in a matter in which he is legal representative, is he ethically permitted to bring this information to the notice of the court? Munroe Freedman leads the way with a resounding no, since in doing so the lawyer would be abandoning his fiduciary duty of confidentiality

7 Statement made by Mr Justice Walter Schroeder in a 1963 lecture entitled 'Some ethical problems in criminal law' (1963 Law Society of Upper Canada Special Lectures).

8 See Gavin MacKenzie, *Lawyers and Ethics: Professional Responsibility and Discipline* (Carswell, 1993), at 7.6.

9 Freedman, 'Professional responsibility of the criminal defence lawyer: the three hardest questions' *Michigan Law Review*, Vol 64, 1966.

10 See generally Luban, *op cit*, fn 1.

11 See generally Wolfram, *Modern Legal Ethics* (St Paul, MN, West Publishing Co, 1999).

and forfeiting the trust placed in him by the client to whom he must steadfastly maintain loyalty and fidelity in taking care of his affairs. Terrorism and drug trafficking on an international scale have necessitated statutory exemptions to this principle – and these have been referred to in Chapter 7 above during our discussion of confidentiality and privilege.

DOES COUNSEL DELIVER JUSTICE?

Some legal experts go as far as to say that in representing an accused person the defence lawyer is under no generalised obligation to deliver justice. Martin Erdman is said to have declared in relation to the persons defended, 'I have nothing to do with justice' and that 'Justice is not even part of the equation'.[12] Such a statement would appear to be seriously at odds with the declaration of the American jurist who described a criminal trial as 'the centre of ideals of every Western Government'.[13]

Unfortunately, Luban does not accept that the criminal trial is 'the centre of ideals'. In commenting upon the statement that accused persons are granted many advantages when they are arraigned in a criminal trial, he expresses strong doubts as to whether they are permitted to exercise those rights which are sometimes set out on paper but are largely non-existent in practice. We shall now briefly examine that claim by reference to the English situation.

THE ETHICS OF THE ENGLISH SYSTEM

No branch of the English legal system has been more stridently criticised in the past three decades of the 20th century than the criminal system – and with justice. The criticism has come from judges, from practising lawyers, from academics, from members of the media, as well as from the public in general and victims in particular. The police – the gateway to the system – have frequently been weighed in the balances and found wanting – although efforts have been made to improve their performance. The period since 1970, with the various examples of miscarriages of justice that have occurred, has been described by a discerning practitioner as 'probably the darkest hour of British criminal justice'.[14] The interrogation practices of the police are in need of drastic overhaul and such practices have been vilified by many empirical studies in England.[15] What is distressing is that although many litigants receive heavy damages every year from police misconduct, disciplinary proceedings are not usually taken against the

12 Quoted by MacKenzie, *op cit*, fn 8 at 7.2.

13 Thurman Arnold, *The Symbols of Government* (New Haven, CT, Yale University Press, 1935), p 128.

14 See a very informative article by Patrick O'Connor in [1992] Crim LR 464 entitled 'Prosecution disclosure, principle, practice and justice' at p 466.

15 See, for instance, I McKenzie, R Morgan and R Reiner, 'Helping the police with their inquiries: the necessity principle and voluntary attendance at the police station' [1990] Crim LR 22; and M McConville, A Sanders and R Leng, *The Case for the Prosecution* (London, Routledge, 1991), Chapter 3.

officers. It was as a result of the public outcry about police conduct that two Royal Commissions were set up to examine criminal justice – the first in 1981 (the Phillips Commission – mainly prompted by a miscarriage of justice in the Confait case); the second in 1990 (the Runciman Commission).

The Phillips Report[16] recommended sweeping changes in police powers, as a result of which the Police and Criminal Evidence Act (PACE) 1984 was enacted and a new Crown Prosecution Service established by the Prosecution of Offences Act 1985.

The Runciman Report[17] was a great disappointment. The mandate of this Commission was, *inter alia*, to give meaning to the rights of the citizen in the context of the adversarial system while at the same time dealing with miscarriages of justice. But this is what a learned criminologist had to say about it:[18] 'The Report of the Royal Commission on Criminal Justice (Runciman Commission) is a sham. It is a document that is slipshod in its use of empirical evidence, slippery in its argumentation, and shameful in its underlying political purposes.'

The English case law is littered with miscarriages of justice: Rowland (1947); Evans (1950); Bentley (1952); Stafford and Luvaglio (1967); Murphy, McMahon and Cooper (the Luton Post Office murder) (1970) and Lattimore, Salih and Leighton (the Confait Case 1972). It is, however, to four more recent miscarriages that I wish to make a brief reference as demonstrating further grave denials of justice.

The Guildford Four[19] and the Maguire Seven[20] were convicted of IRA offences. In the former the accused were convicted and appealed, but their appeals failed even though other IRA defendants awaiting trial claimed responsibility. In addition, certain police interviews were said to have been contemporaneously recorded whereas later detention records contradicted the police version as to the time and length of the interviews. In the case of the Maguire Seven, there were two sets of tests for the presence of nitroglycerine – a chemical used in the manufacture of bombs, but the police only disclosed the one that proved positive, withholding evidence of the negative result of the other test carried out by another forensic expert in the same laboratory.

Another case in which police lapses were revealed is that of Judith Ward.[21] This conviction was based on alleged admissions and confessions as well as scientific evidence. Certain vital non-disclosures relevant to both these issues which were 'at the heart of the appeal' were withheld from disclosure by the West Yorkshire Police, the staff of the Director of Public Prosecutions, the prosecution's psychologist and the prosecution's former scientists. The non-disclosure led to the

16 Cmnd 8092, HMSO, 1981.

17 Royal Commission on Criminal Justice Report (Cmnd 2263, HMSO, 1993).

18 L Bridges, 'Normalising injustice: the Royal Commission on Criminal Justice' *Journal of Law and Society*, Vol 21, 1994, p 20.

19 *R v Hill and Others (Guildford Four Case), The Times*, 23 Oct 1975, 27 Feb 1977 and 20 Oct 1989.

20 *R v Maguire and Others (Maguire Seven Case)* [1992] 2 All ER 433; (1992) 94 Cr App R 133.

21 Luban, *op cit*, fn 1, p 60.

quashing of the conviction. In the case of the Cardiff Three,[22] their convictions in 1990 for the murder of a prostitute were overturned in December 1992 when it was referred to the Court of Appeal, who expressed horror at the evidence of oppression revealed on the police interview tapes.[23]

When one reads this list of miscarriages of justice and the grounds for quashing the convictions, one is bound to ponder carefully Luban's contention that 'persons accused of crime enjoy no advantages whatever no matter how many rights the courts and legislatures have apportioned them'. This statement is somewhat extreme, but there is no doubt that the position is thoroughly unsatisfactory. It is, however, fair to observe that all miscarriages here referred to occurred before PACE. The Human Rights Act of 1998 may well serve to ensure less glaring cases of miscarriage in the future.

THE POSITION OVERSEAS

In the Caribbean, what we find is that the police still have wide constitutional discretions which can be (and usually are) exercised arbitrarily and not normally in favour of the accused. A classic example can be found in the regime under s 5(5) of the Antigua and Barbuda Constitution for dealing with a person detained upon suspicion of having committed a criminal offence. The section reads as follows:

> A person who is arrested or detained—
>
> (a) for the purpose of bringing him before the court in execution of the order of the court; or
>
> (b) upon reasonable suspicion of his having committed or being about to commit a criminal offence under any law and who is released shall be brought before the court within 48 hours after his detention and, in computing time for the purposes of this sub-section, Sundays and public holidays shall be excluded.

It happens frequently that the police in Antigua and Barbuda find it necessary to detain someone suspected of committing an offence on a Wednesday not on the Thursday but on the Friday. In this way the suspect can be held in a police cell until Monday – normally a total of 72 hours – thus rendering the 48 hours prescribed in the Constitution nugatory. If the Monday is a bank holiday (and there are some of these that fall on a Monday), the suspect can be held until the Tuesday, that is, for nearly 100 hours – more than twice the constitutional limit!

One further point of disadvantage for the criminal defendant is that in most countries the status and quality of criminal defence lawyers tend to be low in comparison with corporate and civil defence attorneys; this means that the best material does not usually represent criminal defendants.[24] An even further

---

22 *R v Parris, Abdullahi and Miller* [1993] 97 Cr App R 99.

23 In writing this section I have profited from reading Walker and Starmer (eds), *Miscarriages of Justice: A Review of Justice in Error* (London, Blackstone Ltd, 1999) which is the *locus classicus* on this issue and a treasure-house of data on the subject of miscarriages of justice.

24 See G Arthur Martin's article, 'The role and responsibility of the defense advocate' [1990] 12 Crim LR 376, where at p 379 it is stated that criminal defence lawyers risk being identified with their clients in the public mind and even in the view of their colleagues.

disadvantage in England is that those who are sent to assist such persons at police stations are often young, inexperienced practitioners who, for one reason or another, do not want to maintain adversarial relations with the police and, therefore, tend to adopt a conciliatory attitude, sacrificing principle for good relations with the authorities. In that way there is a failure zealously and conscientiously to guard the interests of the beleaguered client.[25]

HOW DO THE ETHICS OF THE DEFENCE ATTORNEY STAND IN NEWLY-INDEPENDENT COUNTRIES?

All the relevant Codes of Ethics in these jurisdictions uniformly provide for a lawyer (or attorney-at-law, as they are now styled) in most overseas territories who undertakes the defence of a person accused of crime to use 'all fair and reasonable means to present every defence available at law' in the pursuit of that defence.[26] The Codes also articulate an obligation by the attorney to accept the retainer 'regardless of his own personal opinion as to the guilt of the accused'.[27]

Quite apart from the Codes, however, most of the newly-independent jurisdictions provide clear constitutional guarantees of an ethical nature to the criminal defendant. In setting them out below, reference will be made to the Constitution of Antigua and Barbuda. Under that Instrument the defendant is:

(1) to be given a fair hearing within a reasonable time by an independent and impartial court established by law (s 15(1));

(2) presumed to be innocent until the contrary is proved by a judge or jury OR until he pleads guilty (s 15(2)(a));

(3) to be informed of the nature of the offence in a language he understands (s 15(2)(b));

(4) to be given adequate time and facilities for the preparation of his defence (s 15(2)(c));

(5) to be permitted to defend himself in person or (at his expense) by a lawyer of his choice (s 15(2)(d));

(6) to be given the right to call witness in his own defence and to cross-examine the witness or witnesses for the prosecution (s 15(2)(e));

(7) entitled to be furnished an interpreter free of charge (s 15(2)(f));

(8) entitled to elect to be tried by a jury when charged on information in the High Court (s 15(2)(g));

(9) entitled, on payment of the prescribed fee, to a copy of any record of the proceedings made by or on behalf of the Court (s 15(3));

(10) not to be held guilty of a criminal offence on account of any act or omission which did not, at the time it took place, constitute such an offence (s 15(4));

(11) not again to be tried for an offence for which he has been tried by a duly established court and either convicted or acquitted (s 15(5));

25 See M McConville, J Hodgson, L Bridges and A Pavolovic, *Standing Accused: The Organisation and Practices of Criminal Defence Lawyers in Britain* (Oxford, Clarendon Press, 1994).

26 See, for instance, the OECS Code, r 20; Barbados 23; Antigua 23.

27 See Barbados 28; Trinidad and Tobago 25.

(12) not to be tried for a criminal offence if he shows he has been pardoned for that offence (s 15(6));

(13) not to be compellable to give evidence at his trial (s 15(7)); and

(14) to be tried in public (s 15(9)).

Most post-independence Codes also make provision for withdrawal by counsel, and once again one finds a posture of indulgence and concern, although it should be pointed out that the rules relating to withdrawal refer to both criminal and civil matters.

The rules are set out in identical form in all Caribbean Codes. I will, therefore, only cite the provisions from Trinidad & Tobago.[28]

Rule 34 of Part A of that Code permits an attorney-at-law to withdraw from employment where a fee arrangement with the client has broken down; or the attorney's ability to work with colleagues dictates that the best interest of the client will be served by withdrawal; or when the client freely assents to the termination; or where for reasons of the attorney's mental or physical condition or other good and compelling reason it is difficult for the lawyer to carry out his employment effectively; or where there is conflict which arises because of the lawyer's association with another client whose interest conflicts with that of the client from whom the attorney is withdrawing.

It will not, however, be feasible to withdraw until the attorney has taken reasonable steps to avoid foreseeable prejudice or injury to the rights of the client including giving due notice; allowing time for employing a replacement, handing over all necessary property, subject to any lien the attorney may have over such property; complying with all applicable laws and, where appropriate, securing the permission of the court where the hearing of the matter has commenced. In the event of withdrawal, the attorney must refund to the client such part of the fees, if any, already paid as may be fair and reasonable.[29]

In other circumstances, an attorney may withdraw forthwith from employment or from a matter pending before a tribunal where the client insists upon his attorney representing a claim or defence that he cannot conscientiously advance; where the client seeks to pursue a course of conduct which is illegal or which will result in deliberately deceiving the court; where a client has in the course of the proceedings perpetrated a fraud upon the tribunal and on request by the attorney has refused or is unable to rectify the same; where the lawyer's continued employment will involve him in a violation of the law or of a disciplinary rule; where the client by any other conduct renders it unreasonably difficult for the attorney to carry out his employment effectively or with the rules of law and professional ethics; or where for any good and compelling reason it is difficult for counsel to operate effectively.[30]

28 Schedule 3 (Trinidad & Tobago Code of Ethics) of the Legal Profession Act 1986. Rules (the Code) are made under s 35 of this Act.

29 *Ibid*, r 12 of the Code (Pt B).

30 *Ibid*, r 13 of the Code (Pt B).

THE PROSECUTION

In trying to define the duty of a prosecutor in a criminal case, we find one consistent theme always recurring, expressed in this sense: it is not the duty of the prosecution to seek a conviction but to see that justice is done.

The actual words of several Codes in the Eastern Caribbean are as follows: 'When engaged as a public prosecutor the primary duty of an attorney-at-law is not to secure a conviction but to see that justice is done and to that end he shall not withhold facts tending to prove either the guilt or innocence of the accused.'[31]

The Code in the Cayman Islands puts it this fuller way:

> While it is the duty of prosecuting counsel to use every known fact to support the prosecution, there is also a corresponding responsibility to advise the defence of any facts, information or documents which may be of assistance to the defence or which may be of use in mitigation. In the event that a defendant is found guilty or has pleaded guilty prosecuting counsel also has a responsibility to advise the defence of any relevant factors known to the prosecution but not to the defence which might be used in mitigation.[32]

One can only hope that such a civilised form of behaviour will be followed generally in dealing with criminal defendants. In this connection, prosecutors everywhere will also do well to heed these words of Rand J in the Canadian case of *Boucher v R* [1955] SCR 16 at pp 23–24:

> The role of prosecutor excludes any notion of winning or losing; his function is a matter of public duty than which in civil life there can be none charged with greater personal responsibility. It is to be efficiently performed with an ingrained sense of the dignity, the seriousness and the justness of the judicial proceedings.[33]

FUNCTIONS OF PROSECUTORS

Charles Wolfram sees prosecutors as 'the only governmental officers responsible for obtaining convictions of the guilty in litigated criminal cases' who also 'bear alone the state's considerable responsibility to see that no innocent person is prosecuted, convicted or punished'. He finds this dual role to be 'in marked contrast to the nature of the defence function'.

Accordingly he equates the prosecution's position to that of a judicial officer – 'one of the most psychologically difficult tasks that lawyers are asked to perform'. He thus sees the prosecutor conceptually as a client-less lawyer but with several important constituencies – including the police, the judges and the victim. If a client is to be identified, Wolfram considers it would be the public.[34]

---

31 See Codes as follows: OECS, r 14; Barbados, r 18; Antigua, r 14; Trinidad, r 14.

32 See the Cayman Islands Law Society Code, Preliminary Draft, r 9.02.

33 Quoted in MacKenzie, *op cit*, fn 8, at Chapter 6.1.

34 See Wolfram, *op cit*, fn 11, pp 759–61, 13.10–13.10.2.

WHO PROSECUTES? TO WHOM RESPONSIBLE?

Prosecutors tend to be lawyers only. In many countries in the common law world they may sometimes be members of the police, as they are in the Caribbean in the case of minor offences. But even when they are not lawyers, they act in the name of a Director of Public Prosecutions (DPP) who is usually an office enshrined in the constitution.

In Caribbean constitutions, this officer is appointed on the advice of respective Judicial and Legal Services Commissions and dismissible by the same method, after a tribunal appointed by the particular Head of the Judiciary has satisfied himself there is a *prima facie* case for dismissal. The Director of Public Prosecutions in most territories does not take his orders from any other person or authority – although in two jurisdictions the Attorney-General is competent to give him directions in respect of offences relating to official secrets, mutiny or incitement to mutiny or of any offence relating to a right or obligation of the country under international law.[35]

The intention is that there should be the same (or substantially the same) degree of independence as with judicial appointments. In small newly-independent jurisdictions, the independence of these executives is more apparent on the books than real and it all boils down to the integrity of office holders. If they are prepared to act fairly and impartially in the performance of their important functions, they can make a genuine difference to the administration of justice.

THE FAIRNESS OF THE TRIAL

The overriding duty of the prosecution in a criminal trial is that a defendant accused of a crime should be accorded a fair trial. This requirement was recently underscored in a case[36] that came before the Privy Council from the Cayman Islands and the issues in that trial relate so much to unfairness and prejudice that it is considered useful to deal here with the decision at some length.

The appellant stood trial in the Grand Court in the Cayman Islands on a criminal indictment involving four counts of theft and one count of obtaining a valuable security by deception. His trial lasted 41 days and is said to have been the longest criminal trial in the history of the Cayman Islands. At the conclusion of the trial before Williams J and a jury he was on 8 August 1997 convicted on all counts, sentenced to 4½ years' imprisonment and ordered to pay compensation. The

35 See for instance s 89 of the Antigua and Barbuda Constitution. See also s 79A of the Barbados Constitution, which has a somewhat longer list of matters on which the Attorney-General can give directions to the Director of Public Prosecutions. In addition to those mentioned above, directions may be given on matters relating to piracy; trading or otherwise dealing in slaves; foreign enlistment; publications calculated to interfere with peaceful relations of Barbados with foreign states; high treason, treason, misprision of treason, treachery; sedition; official secrets and unlawful oaths.

36 *Barry Victor Randall v The Queen*. Judgment delivered on 16 April 2002 (Privy Council Appeal No 22 of 2001).

appellant appealed against conviction and sentence on 13 August 1998 and in December 1998 the Court of Appeal dismissed his appeal against conviction on counts 1 to 4, allowed his appeal against conviction on count 5 and dismissed his appeal against sentence. The appellant renewed his appeal against conviction and sentence before the Judicial Committee of the Privy Council, who reluctantly allowed the appeal on the ground that there were such substantial departures from good practice as to deny the appellant a fair trial.

The Board acknowledged that the case against the appellant was strong but expressed the view that:

> ... the right of a criminal defendant to a fair trial is absolute. There will come a point when the departure from good practice is so gross, or so persistent, or so prejudicial, or so irremediable that an appellate court will have no choice but to condemn a trial as unfair and quash a conviction as unsafe, however strong the grounds for believing the defendant to be guilty. The right to a fair trial is one to be enjoyed by the guilty as well as the innocent, for a defendant is presumed to be innocent until proved to be otherwise in a fairly conducted trial.

The appellant's complaint of unfairness fell under four heads, of which we will refer only (in the interest of brevity) to one, viz that prosecuting counsel repeatedly interpolated prejudicial comments while examining prosecution witnesses; repeatedly interrupted the cross-examination of prosecution witnesses, often with prejudicial comment; repeatedly interrupted the examination-in-chief and re-examination of the appellant; interpolated prejudicial comment in the course of his cross-examination of the defendant; and interrupted the judge in the course of his summing up.

Their Lordships illustrated this particular complaint with four full pages of examples which also included interruptions and aspersions made by the prosecuting officer on the motives and conduct of the appellant and of defence counsel.

Their Lordships were not amused and had this to say about the conduct of the case:

> Prosecuting counsel conducted himself as no minister of justice should conduct himself. The trial judge failed to exert the authority vested in him to control the proceedings and enforce proper standards of behaviour.

Regrettably he allowed himself to be overborne and allowed his antipathy to both the appellant and his counsel to be only too manifest.

This case furnishes a classic example of how not to conduct a prosecution and is one that should be brought to the notice of judges and prosecutors in the common law world. It also provides guidance as to how a reviewing court (in this case the Court of Appeal) should assess the evidence when defence counsel presents a large number of complaints regarding the prosecution's case. Here the Court of Appeal had asserted that of the 79 instances listed in the notice of appeal, only three had been 'earnestly pursued'. It was also said that of the eight passages critical of the trial judge's conduct, only three had been pursued. On this aspect the Privy Council commented charitably as follows:

> In presenting an appeal based on criticisms of many separate passages in a very lengthy transcript counsel is faced with considerable difficulties in presentation and the court is also faced with difficulties in considering the full ambit of the criticism and the large body of material which supports it. There may have been a degree of misunderstanding between counsel and the court as to the number of instances upon which the appellant was relying, but the Board understands that no complaint made by the appellant was abandoned. Therefore, for whatever reason, it is clear that the Court of Appeal did not adequately examine the matters relied on by the appellant. After its fuller and more detailed consideration the Board is satisfied that the decision of the Court of Appeal on this issue cannot stand.

It was in these circumstances that the Privy Council expressed regret that it found itself in disagreement with the view taken by the Court of Appeal on the principal issue in the appeal.

The Board ended on this euphemistic note: 'It is apparent from the judgment of the Court that it did not give full consideration to a large number of the appellant's complaints, including a number of the more serious.'

When one considers that the Cayman Court of Appeal comprised three of the most brilliant and experienced numbers of the Caribbean judiciary, viz Henry P, Georges and Kerr JJA, one cannot avoid a tinge of regret that this matter was allowed to reach the Privy Council in London, who were surprisingly able to find more time to peruse the bulky transcripts than their Caribbean brethren. Is this because of pressure of work on the part of their Cayman Islands colleagues or is it because the system in the region's judiciaries permits latitude to the prosecutor and judge that British colleagues find impermissible? We can only hope it is the former – regrettable as that would be. However, the alarm bells rung by the Privy Council should be heard throughout the Caribbean now that our long-outstanding Court of Justice is shortly to be inaugurated in early 2005.

POLICE POWERS VIS-À-VIS SUSPECTS AND PERSONS CHARGED

The matter of police powers in relation to a suspect has long been the subject of controversy in England and elsewhere. The Police and Criminal Evidence Act (PACE) 1984 and its Codes of Practice were intended to govern the treatment of suspects in police custody but empirical studies reveal that, although there have been minor improvements, the police generally tend to exercise their powers in an oppressive manner, whether it be on the occasions of questioning the suspect[37] or video-taping interrogations[38] or stopping, searching or arresting[39] or of the exercise of the suspect's right to legal advice.[40]

37 See David Roberts, 'Questioning the suspect: the solicitor's role' [1993] Crim LR 368–73.

38 See Mike McConville, 'Videotaping interrogations: police behaviour on or off camera' [1992] Crim LR 532–48.

39 See Andrew Sanders, 'Rights, remedies and the Police and Criminal Evidence Act' [1998] Crim LR 833/834.

40 *Ibid*, p 835.

Discussing the issue of the provision of advice and assistance to suspects in police stations, David Roberts makes the point that those legal advisers who undertake this work 'responsibly and courageously' will no doubt find it a 'disagreeable and solitary calling'. In his view the junior counsel involved find the task even more difficult because they are not sure what their proper role is when it comes to regulating the content of the interviews. Roberts then makes the following statement which is applicable to much that the police do with a suspect between detention and charging:[41] 'Where ambiguity reigns, the dominance of the police is likely to be reinforced, because it is they who have control over the interviewing environment and because there is no realistic immediate remedy which a legal adviser might pursue when the police overstep the mark.'

Two other writers writing about police malpractice after PACE have had this to say:[42]

> It is hardly surprising that the police have little more respect for PACE and COP than they did for the Judges' Rules ... The Police have a history of law-breaking that flourishes as never before ... Police malpractice is not indiscriminate but it has self-imposed limits (relating to a sense of morality or danger) rather than limits imposed by law. Law breaking in itself seems to be of little concern to the police.

The position in England is at the beginning of the 21st century being replicated in countries overseas in so far as police deviance is concerned. Unfortunately, there is little empirical evidence available in the latter to establish ethical breaches or cases of police brutality, but from time to time judges have spoken out strongly about police malpractice and there are many cases where in serious criminal matters such breaches have led to the courts holding that a confession was not voluntary.

Irregularities occur most often when the prosecution is carried out by the police, the vast majority of whom are non-lawyers. Although some police prosecutors may have much experience in prosecuting, they clearly do not have knowledge of the fine points of evidence and the interpretation of statutes. Moreover, they invariably consider that it is their business to try and secure convictions by any means, especially when they find themselves up against highly skilled lawyers appearing for the defence.

NEGOTIATED JUSTICE

PLEA BARGAINING

This arrangement is American in concept, Wolfram seeing it as 'an illustration of the reach and limits of prosecutorial discretion', the legitimacy of which is accepted by the US Supreme Court. Professor Goldstein also considers that judges should develop 'a common-law set of limits on plea bargaining and that hearings

41 See Roberts, *op cit*, fn 37, p 373.

42 See Andrew Sanders and Lee Bridges 'Access to legal advice and police malpractice' [1990] Crim LR 494.

be made potentially more adversarial by giving crime victims a formal role in them'.[43] The arrangement is structured and explicit: counsel meets the judge in chambers to review the evidence. The judge indicates what reduction in the sentence he would countenance if the defendant pleads guilty and the judge's views are then communicated to the defendant.

The principle is that pleas should not be negotiated for reasons of expediency when the defendant does not consider he is guilty.[44]

Although there are those who feel that plea-bargaining should be introduced into the English system as a means of shortening the process, the fact remains that it has not. There can at the present be no bargaining as to sentence[45] in the English judicial system, although credit for a plea is now enshrined by statute in England by s 48 of the Criminal Justice and Public Order Act 1994.

A prosecutor in the US has a wide discretion in deciding the number and nature of charges to be pressed and the length and type of sentence to be recommended on conviction. He is under no obligation, once he agrees to recommend a certain sentence, to explain his reasons to a judge or to make the recommendation 'enthusiastically'.[46] Nor may he resort to race or religion in deciding whether to negotiate or what plea to offer, although it is constitutionally proper for the prosecution to increase the charges if an offered plea is refused.[47] Alternatively, a prosecutor is not forbidden to overcharge an accused person with more offences than he has collected evidence for, or even with more serious offences than the evidence warrants.[48]

English law differs fundamentally from American law, which gives a prosecutor considerable latitude in this matter of plea bargaining.

THE JURY

No discussion of the ethics of the criminal process would be complete without some consideration of the jury system. There is some uncertainty as to its origins, but the regime dates its beginnings from the time of the feudal system of 9th century France from which it was transported in a different guise to the Anglo-Saxon world. Initially it was said – under the feudal regime – to be a tool of social

43 Wolfram, *op cit*, fn 11, p 769. Wolfram considers a plea bargain as essentially a contract and points out that whereas a prosecutor is under no obligation to embark on the process, once an agreement has been reached he is not at liberty to resile from it. This is also the position in Canada.

44 See MacKenzie, *op cit*, fn 8, 6.5.

45 *R v Turner* [1970] QB 231. See also two articles by Paul Thomas in [1969] Crim LR 79 and [1970] Crim LR 559, in which the writer makes the statement that the Court of Appeal [1970] 2 All ER 281 seems to suggest that a 'controlled' form of plea bargaining could play a useful part in dispensing justice. In the 30 years since the decision, the arrangement has not become, however, popular, although pleading guilty to a lesser crime than originally charged is normally permissible.

46 See *US v Phillips Petroleum Co*, 435 F Supp 622, p 640 and *US v Benchimol*, 105 S Ct 2103.

47 *Bordenkircher v Hayes* (1978) 434 US 357; 98 S Ct 663 L Ed 2d 604.

48 See Wolfram, *op cit*, fn 11, pp 769 and 770.

control, since the jury was then actual witnesses to the crime. After 1066 it became in England a mode of trial and has remained so to this day.

Sir Henry Maitland avers that trial by ordeal (outlawed since the 13th century) was originally preferred to the jury system, which, however, won the day as time went by. Accordingly, by the end of the 15th century, the jury were no longer witnesses but a body of citizens chosen at random to decide whether those who professed to having witnessed the crime were to be believed or not. By the 17th century the jury came to be regarded as the best check on the royal judges who were doing the bidding of the Stuart Kings.

It was in that context that the revolting New World Americans came to enshrine both in their federal and state constitutions trial by jury – their intention being that the juries were to stand up to the judges who were controlled by a hostile British Government. The jury thus became symbols of the popular cause. When the Americans attained independence, one provision in the Constitution was to this effect: 'In all criminal prosecutions the accused shall enjoy the right to a speedy and public trial, by an impartial jury of the State and district wherein the crime shall have been committed' (Art 6).

In Britain the jury system has for generations been extolled as the most precious right possessed by the ordinary Englishman. For the great Sir William Blackstone, it was variously regarded as 'the glory of the English law'; 'the most transcendent privilege which any subject can enjoy or wish for'; 'the benchmark of liberty'; and 'the palladium of justice'. In more recent days Lady Kennedy of the Shaws QC, a distinguished practitioner in the field of criminal law, declared: 'Seeing the courts in action and participating in that process maintains public trust and confidence in the law.' Lord Devlin proclaimed that the jury system is 'the lamp which shows that freedom lives'. One Liberal Democrat peer sees the jury as 'the great bulwark of freedom in this country'. For the indomitable Lord Denning: 'It is a lesson which has been handed down from one generation to another during the last 800 years. The people of England, by sitting as jurors, have taken an active part in the administration of justice.' The whole attitude of the English towards the jury system is encapsulated in the following pithy statement by Lord Denning in his book *What Next in the Law*, from which the above passage is also taken, at p 33. Here is Lord Denning's homely remark: 'I have always been a firm believer in trial by jury. Somehow it is ingrained in me. As it is in most Englishmen.'

Later on in the book, at p 146 there is a caption in which he speaks of 'The golden age of trial by jury' (the 19th century was that age).

In his *Review of the Criminal Courts in England and Wales* published in October 2002, Lord Justice Auld, on p 137 of his Report, states that 'in England and Wales there is no constitutional right, nor indeed any kind of general right, to judge and jury – only a general obligation to submit to it in indictable cases'.

By far the most rational and closely reasoned exposition I have come across on the vulnerability of the jury system in the light of present-day circumstances has recently been given in an Address delivered by Sir Louis Blom-Cooper QC on 22 October 2003 to the British Academy of Forensic Sciences at the Royal College of Physicians in London. It is so logical and cogent that I have felt constrained to draw heavily upon it in this section.

The jury is empowered to return any verdict in the teeth of both law and fact and there is no judicial power to reverse such a verdict, no matter how perverse it may be. It is described by Sir Louis as 'the oddity of (the) institution politically unaccountable in an age insistent upon audit and accountability': the jury being in a position to decide 'the guilt of an accused by way of an unarticulated verdict proclaimed in never more than three syllables'. He aptly characterises the verdict as 'an oracular utterance devoid of any ratiocination'.

After explaining the composite and symbiotic nature of the function of the judge and jury in a criminal cause or matter and stipulating the circumstances in which a judge may withhold a matter from a jury, he ventures the opinion that the jury is no protection of our liberties. In this assertion he has the firm support of Professor Glanville Williams, that great authority in criminal law, who confirms that most of the great pronouncements on constitutional liberty from the 18th century onwards have been the work of judges, either sitting in appellate courts or giving directions to juries, and that the assumption that political liberty at the present day depends upon the jury is 'merely folklore'.

Sir Louis Blom-Cooper goes to the heart of the matter in posing the following question: 'Stripped of all the rhetorical response that comes trippingly off the protagonist's tongue, does the jury as a mode of criminal trial provide as good, if not a better, quality of justice than other modes, primarily trial by professional(s)?' He continues: 'That is the question: not whether trial by jury is a fundamental freedom or God-given right to the English.'

The lack of empirical studies on the matter is regretted because since 1981 a statutory ban has been placed on jury research and because even before then it was considered improper (if not a contempt of court) for jurors to reveal what took place in the secrecy of the jury room. One study is relevant – that by Baldwin and McConville – on the subject of jury trials in England which found evidence of strong disagreement between professionals and juries over certain convictions.[49] The study revealed that more than five per cent of persons found guilty by a jury were thought by professionals 'to have been convicted in questionable circumstances, a statistic which the authors regarded as the most disturbing arising from their study'.

The Runciman Commission of 1993 found that judges and prosecutors considered jury convictions as running counter to the evidence or the law in 2% of cases.

49 Baldwin and McConville, *Jury Trials* (Oxford, Clarendon Press, 1979).

In a criminal matter, the jury is the exclusive decision-maker and Sir Louis asks rhetorically: 'Has the jury the equipment and ability to see through all the potential defects of the criminal process?' He answers that question in a manner that must commend itself to those of us who examine the issue without emotion, viz: 'Its failure to discriminate between the correct and incorrect result must constitute an ever-present worry to the administrators of criminal justice.'

In the Diplock courts in Northern Ireland, juries were not empanelled but the cases were heard by a single judge when dealing with terrorist offences. Notwithstanding such a departure it has been agreed in most quarters that these trials were most successful and commanded the respect of the lawyers appearing in them. Such an arrangement pointed the way to reform. The most pressing problem today affecting the jury system is that in returning their verdict, a jury is not required to give reasons for reaching that verdict. Indeed, it is fair to say that since jurors are not legally qualified they cannot in difficult cases be expected to furnish coherent reasons for their verdict. Take the case of *Boreman* [2000] 1 All ER 307, in which the trial judge found it necessary to direct the jury on murder, causation, self-defence, provocation, the effect of intoxication on the specific intent in a murder trial and the 'all important matter of joint enterprise'. How can a jury of laymen be expected to understand legal terminology sufficiently to formulate coherent reasons for a verdict? Indeed, there is considerable uncertainty as to how juries reach their decision, in the absence of empirical evidence.

It is on those grounds that constitutional lawyers must now consider fundamentally whether the jury system fulfils the requirement of a fair trial under Art 6 of the Human Rights Act of 1998, the terms of which are also enshrined in most modern-day constitutions. One must seriously consider whether the statement of Lord Justice Henry in *Flannery v Halifax Estate Agency* [2000] 1 WLR 377 is not equally applicable to the jury. This is what the learned Lord Justice said: 'A requirement to give reasons concentrates the mind. If it is fulfilled, the resulting decision is much more likely to be soundly based on the evidence than if it is not.'

That was a case in which a new trial was ordered on the ground that the trial judge had failed to provide reasons for preferring the evidence of one expert witness to that of another. And yet how often in criminal cases – concerning gun crimes, for instance – are jurors called upon to make similar preferences for reasons which need not be revealed? That is the problem posed for juries in the common law world in the face of the firmly entrenched principle that the giving of reasons in judicial adjudication is an essential feature of due process and of justice.

Reform is, however, on the cards. Even a dedicated protagonist of the system like the late Lord Denning was ready to admit this. We live in a new technological age and what was good for the 12th or 13th century is no longer good for our time. Modern constitutions now give new rights to the citizenry.

One must therefore accept the felicitous assessment of Sir Louis, who puts it in this way:

> The jury is the high point, the apotheosis of amateurism, potentially a recipe for incompetence and unbridled bias. The mood of civilized systems of criminal justice increasingly demands professionalism from those operating the trial process. I do not mean to be contemptuous of the amateur's ability to judge human conduct, only the task of evaluating evidence in the court-room, which is a job for professionals, not for occasional amateurs. We should be able to trust those trained to be judges. Jerome Frank, in his *Courts on Trial* 1950, p 252, said, 'It is, I think, wiser to trust a competent, honest judge, with a trained intuition, than twelve inexperienced laymen'. The cases brought to the criminal courts often nowadays invite a sophisticated approach to the undertaking and appreciation of recondite expert evidence, particularly on scientific and technical issues.

In 1859, the celebrated judge Sir James Fitz-James Stephen, writing on jury trials, expressed a view that few spectacles were more ridiculous and incongruous than to witness 12 individuals with no scientific knowledge trying to grapple with matters in which eminent scientists are in conflict with one another in evidence adduced in court. 'How', he trenchantly asked, 'can ordinary tradesmen and farmers who have never been accustomed to give sustained attention to any subject whatever for an hour together, be expected to weigh evidence the delivery of which occupies many days and which bears upon subjects which can only be described in language altogether new and foreign to their understanding?'

Technology has made lengthy strides in the 145 years since Mr Justice Stephens wrote those words. International financial transactions for example, have moved apace and become infinitely more complex. Information technology has become a science. It stands to reason that if justice is to be done, criminal trials involving such transactions must today be undertaken by specially trained judges – either sitting alone or with assessors.

Public opinion, supported by such objective expert views as that of Lord Justice Auld, will in time no doubt bring about the establishment of special tribunals to hear cases of fraud. In that respect I can do no better than quote Sir Louis again (what he says being applicable worldwide):

> We need to start educating the British public that the gradual dismantling or even ultimate disappearance of its cherished institution will not be disastrous. It will in fact bring clarity and purpose to a civilised process of ensuring justice to both prosecutor and prosecuted.

In a very revealing article by Matthew Lewin in the English newspaper *The Independent*,[50] the writer indicated that his recent service on English juries had had his faith in the system 'severely battered'. He suggested that jurors should have more hands-on training (when they arrive to serve) than the brief inaudible video he experienced. He castigated the quality of personality selected to serve. Most professionals like architects, doctors and dentists secure exemption; what they leave is the 'salt of the earth' individual. However, the trouble with these persons is that many of them do not speak good English and are unable to understand the clearest directions from a judge. There is a lamentable lack of ability to collate evidence or organise facts and they tend to arrive at facts in a random and

50 4 February 2004, p 17.

haphazard manner – 'seldom relating their convictions to the body of evidence they had heard'. Lewin also blamed some judges for not appreciating the level of understanding of jurors – referring to one judge who made a number of references to the 'sophistication of 21st century jurors'.

Many jurors came with anti-police and anti-prosecution prejudices. They came with what he styled 'a mission to acquit' and to shun the idea of conviction even in the face of the most cogent evidence. Lewin also came across a juror who, after a drug offence trial, admitted to him that he had himself been a small-time drug dealer. When later Lewin found the same juror on another drug related trial, he reported the matter to the court and had that jury discharged.

We must, therefore, like Lewin, welcome the announcement that British ministers were about to consult on the idea of permitting research on jury deliberations and impropriety and on allowing appellate tribunals to probe what takes place in the jury room. This is the type of reform that is long overdue and one can only hope for further large-scale reviews of the entire system.

If the criminal process which we have discussed at such length in this chapter is to maintain its credibility, we will need as lawyers and non-lawyers to shake off the ingrained sentimentality and myth that have so beset us over the years and which have made us so wedded to a jury system that has evidently been gradually outliving its usefulness.

CONCLUDING COMMENTS

In the Speech from the Throne, before the Parliament at Westminster in 2002, the Queen referred to 'a commitment to reform and re-balance the criminal justice system to deliver justice for all and to safeguard the interests of witnesses, victims and communities'.

This re-balance implies that the pendulum has swung too far in favour of the defence in a criminal trial, and more attention should be directed to the interests of victims and witnesses and *less* to the defendant.

One school of thought propounds that the inquisitorial system applied in other European countries like France is more appropriate than the adversarial as a way of arriving at the truth. The present English establishment thinks the aim should be to retain the adversarial system, but to carry out a programme of reform to redress the balance in the way discussed below.

We have reviewed in some detail how the two sides in a criminal matter are pitted against each other with the judge playing the role of an umpire to ensure fairness in dealing with the witnesses and in keeping both the prosecution and defence lawyers under control. There are those who contend that there is no better way of deciding whether an accused person is innocent or guilty. One writer,[51] David Corker, points out that this is not a matter to be considered from the 'management consultancy or top-down perspective' or assessed from the viewpoint of performance indicators. Rather, it should be addressed from a

51 Luban, *op cit*, fn 1, p 60.

historical context in which the defence rights were conferred by the common law to establish some degree of equality of arms. Corker cites a growing chorus of observers as being disillusioned with the adversary system which is blamed for no longer serving either justice or the victims of crime. He attributes to these observers the allegation that 'overall the current system of criminal trials is no longer a search for the truth and can too easily be undermined by defence ploys'.

When careful thought is given to the two systems, the contrast between the inquisitorial regime of Continental Europe and the English adversarial system is more illusory than real. Both are inherently adversarial. The real difference between them is in the powers of fact-finding. In the English system, fact-gathering is by the police without any direct judicial input; fact-finding is a matter exclusively for the judge at trial. In Europe, fact-finding is an ongoing process which begins via the *juge d'Instruction* from the moment the criminal event occurred.

It is clear that the New Labour Government is obsessed with the 'need for speed' in obtaining convictions and with reducing costs while paying lip service to the plight of victims. This view is reinforced by the tenor of an article written in late 2002 by the then Minister of State for Criminal Justice, in which he announced the intention of the British Government 'to modernise and improve the criminal justice system' by impending legislation on the lines of proposals published in a White Paper *Justice for All*.

The Minister believes that he should ensure there be the disclosure of the prosecution and defence case at an early stage which he claims would avoid time-wasting adjournments and encourage guilty defendants to plead guilty and set contested cases on the right course. He hopes 'to improve prosecution disclosure and to reduce the scope for tactical manoeuvring by the defence'. He would look at 'enhancing the requirements of the defence statement and (requiring) judges to alert the defence to inadequacies in defence statements'. He aims at 'speedier, simpler and quality justice where the guilty defendant can see no longer advantage or real disadvantage in playing the system in the hope something will turn up'.

Finally the Minister comes out into the open when he declares: 'But in some areas the pendulum has swung too far in favour of the protection of the defendant to the detriment of justice.'[52]

If the Minister's idea of a 'level playing field' is accepted in this peculiar situation and takes root in Britain, one can only express the hope that the new approach against the protection of the defendant in criminal justice will not blindly be followed in the rest of the common law world, but that they will continue to see that justice is done to all those accused of crime. Justice should never be sacrificed on the altar of speed.

The next chapter will look at alternative dispute resolution.

52 See article by Lord Falconer, 'Rebalancing the system' in *New Law Journal*, Vol 152, No 7057, 22 November 2002, p 1742. See also a useful summary of the new Criminal Justice Act 2003 by Professor Michael Zander in *New Law Journal*, Vol 153, No 7106–1778/9.

CHAPTER 11

ALTERNATIVE DISPUTE RESOLUTION

CURRENT THINKING ON THE SUBJECT

The matter of dispute resolution is at the heart of legal ethics. We have become so acculturated to the idea of having our disputes referred to a court environment that we tend to doubt there is a better – and more economical – way. We tend to think of the courts whenever a dispute arises – it is a culture of trial by combat to which we subscribe. The result is that there is much stress, expense and delay, the lawyers being the principal beneficiaries. How many of us have stopped to consider whether there is a more rational way? How many of us have realised that most of the forms of action deployed by our legal advisers today were devised since Norman times in England? Indeed, one writer has said that even though the forms of action in some cases may have been buried, they still rule us from the grave.[1]

My own experience is that the ordinary litigant feels strongly that if a lawyer is not prepared to go to court to fight every inch of the way, he is not worth retaining. His stocks as a lawyer are judged from his predisposition to fight, to be aggressive, and to be confrontational when dealing not only with his opponent but even with the judge. He is of course also expected to adopt a totally hostile attitude towards the client on the other side, as well as towards his witnesses. Counsel must ask no quarter: he must also give none. In short, one does not go to court to solve a disputed problem – one's objective is to fight a battle and to win it.

Lawyers tend to be rated according to how many cases they win and how many accused persons they 'get off', not on their knowledge of the law or on their integrity. And they do nothing to explode these myths. It is not often realised that a litigant succeeds because he simply happens to be on the right side of the law and because he has a strong case on the facts.

There is also the aspect that in a system of adversarial advocacy, there is always the danger that opulence carries the day. The wealthy multi-national defendant has the resources to retain high-powered lawyers and expensive experts, whereas the indigent plaintiff who has been injured or otherwise disadvantaged by the defendant's machinery is either unable to hire a lawyer at all or, if he is able, must settle for an inexperienced advocate whose fees are minimal. In other words it is a question of how much justice the litigant can afford.

---

1 See an admirable article by Professor Deborah Rhode, 'Ethical perspectives on legal practice', *Stan LR*, Vol 37, 1985, which states:

'The adversary system's extensive procedural protections generate frequent opportunities for evasion, harassment, and delay. In large-scale litigation principal pathologies include endless wrangling over peripheral issues, as well as over- and under-production of discoverable material.'

See also a fully reasoned article by Professor Carrie Menkel-Meadow, 'Another view of legal negotiation: the structure of problem solving'; and an equally interesting article by the same author entitled 'What Trina taught me: reflections on mediation, inequality, teaching and life'.

When the contest is thus so uneven, the result is that the passive presiding judge or the jury is likely to be misled – if he or she is not wary – by the advocacy skills of the more seasoned performer – 'full' (as he may well be) 'of wise saws and modern instances'. The experienced performer is sure to have access to more up-to-date case material from his firm's more elaborate and extensive library to be able to persuade the court in his favour. It is in such circumstances that William Simon claims that litigation becomes a game or ritual with perspectives which relieve the process of any necessity to generate fair or rational results.[2] In this connection Professor Rhode, after making her point about the way litigation is regarded, continues with this telling statement:[3]

> Such a normative climate easily gives rise to the attitude expressed by one British barrister (Lord Cross of Chelsea):
>
>> It is sometimes more fun to have a bad case than to have a good one for it tests your powers of persuasion more severely. Certainly I have seldom felt better pleased than when I persuaded the court to come to a decision which I was convinced was wrong.

A further point to be examined is the extent to which the adversary system assists in arriving at the truth, and the answer is found partly in the felicitous words of Deborah Rhode in the same article:

> Carefully scripted court performance often bear limited resemblance to the actual facts triggering the dispute. And conventional techniques of witness selection and preparation can easily yield guided tours down memory lane with pre-determined destinations clearly in view.

THE POSITION IN ENGLAND: ARE LAWYERS BEING CONVERTED?

English litigation has from time immemorial been based on excessive orality, but there has been in recent years an attempt to lessen that orality and to depend upon skeleton arguments and other case papers. In England the buzzword these days has been 'case-management' since the Civil Justice Review of 1988. The judge has become much more proactive than he previously was in directing how the proceedings should move along at the interlocutory stage and even when the matter reaches the court. This approach has been concretised by the reforms introduced by Lord Woolf, the Lord Chief Justice of England and Wales at the time of writing.

There can be no dispute that the adversarial paradigm in litigation is usually both lengthy and expensive. The result is that justice is not a virtue shared equally by the rich and the poor (as has already been pointed out). It is on this account

2 See William Simon, 'The ideology of advocacy: procedural justice and professional ethics', *Wisconsin LR*, 1978.

3 See Rhode, *op cit*, fn 1.

that English judges today are showing such interest in ADR – in the words of a legal commentator, 'talking themselves out of a job'.[4]

The commentator spoke of Lord Irvine, the Lord Chancellor, reminding judges of the fact that the Tony Blair Government intended to use ADR in all suitable cases, provided there is agreement by the other side. The analyst also referred to an annual essay competition launched by Lord Phillips of Worth Matravers, the Master of the Rolls, with the theme 'To litigate or mediate', for which law students will compete and in respect of which a first prize of £1,000 is being offered by the Civil Justice Council.

Rosenthal put a question to the Master of the Rolls as to whether the courts would actually order parties to resort to ADR, to which Lord Phillips replied in the affirmative, drawing attention to a case in which the Court of Appeal had ordered a retrial and in which the Master of the Rolls had urged the parties to consider ADR rather than go through the agony of the new trial (it was a case of clinical negligence).

The legal commentator in the same article revealed that in the previous year (2000/01) the English Court of Appeal had recommended mediation in 69 cases, of which 30% settled. There are, however, some legal experts who contend that an individualistic approach to bringing parties to the negotiating table via ADR is to be preferred as likely to be more effective than general invitations at an early stage in the litigating process.[5]

Before proceeding further with our discussion, it should be pointed out that ADR in England embraces not only civil matters but also family cases – sometimes referred to as family dispute resolution (FDR). There is even talk of ODR (online dispute resolution) to which reference will later in this chapter be made.

A further point to note is that although ADR/FDR is normally voluntary, once an agreement is made at a pre-trial settlement hearing, known as an FDR appointment, it is not open to the party who makes a commitment to change his mind. Thus, in a 2002 case[6] a husband, having at such a hearing agreed to give his wife a divorce settlement of £3.5 million out of his £13 million fortune, subsequently decided to change his mind. His wife applied to the High Court for the making of a final order in the terms agreed at the FDR hearing on 3 August 2001. The judge at first instance held that the husband was not bound by the agreement, but his decision was overruled by the Court of Appeal which held that a binding agreement was reached in the FDR settlement and ordered that the husband pay not only the £3.5 million but also the costs of £250,000.

4 See Joshua Rosenberg's informative article in the *Daily Telegraph* of 24 July 2001, p 18, in which he outlines attitudes to ADR as follows: lawyers ('some of the most senior Silks') are retraining as mediators. Judges are 'enthusiastic converts to alternative methods of dispute resolution'. He cites Lord Woolf, the Lord Chief Justice, as saying that litigation can be a disaster 'not only for neighbours who have to sell their homes to pay for the cost of going to court, but also for large companies whose executives are diverted from the work they should be doing'.

5 See article entitled 'The Lawbiter' at p 547 of the *New Law Journal*, Vol 152, No 7027, 12 April 2002. In this article it is noted that in the Commercial Court, over a four-year period, there has been 30 orders for ADR, of which it was undertaken in a little under one-half of the cases with a settlement rate of 52%.

6 *Rose v Rose* [2002] All ER (D) 269 (Feb).

The courts are also beginning to show a disposition to give effect to clauses specifically referring disputes to ADR. In the case of *Channel Tunnel Group LW v Balfour Beatty Construction Ltd* [1993] AC 334, the court was asked to stay the proceedings brought in pursuance of a provision in a contract which required disputes to be referred to a panel and then – only if necessary – to arbitration in Brussels. Lord Mustill considered that it was within the inherent jurisdiction of the court to stay proceedings brought before the House of Lords 'in breach of an agreement to decide disputes in some other way'. He considered that it made for 'the orderly regulation of international commerce for a commercial institution to abide by a system of dispute resolution to which it has agreed'. The House upheld the clause and granted the stay.

It is significant that this decision was concretised in s 9(2) of the Arbitration Act of 1996.

Christopher Newmark has assessed the recent case of *Cable & Wireless plc v IBM UK Ltd* [2002] All ER (D) 277 in this useful way:[7]

> Until the *Cable & Wireless* decision, those drafting dispute resolution clauses have been uncertain as to the degree of specificity or certainty that is required in order to render their clauses enforceable. Most held the view that it was at least necessary to have a prescribed date on which a negotiation or mediation process was to terminate if unsuccessful, so as to ensure that the clause could not be criticised for locking the parties into an unending negotiation.

Although it was suggested in that case that the procedure to be employed in order to comply with the clause was unclear, the judge (Coleman J) considered otherwise. Since there was reference in the clause to the Centre for Excellence in Dispute Resolution (CEDR), the judge concluded that CEDR mediation and procedures were intended. However, he ruled that even if he had not reached that conclusion, the proper requirement for satisfying endorsement of the clause was present, namely, 'the obligation to mediate was expressed in unqualified and mandatory terms'. This particular case contained a clause providing for negotiation, then ADR, before litigation could take place, although it also oddly stated: 'However, an ADR procedure which is being followed shall not prevent any Party or Local Party from issuing proceedings.'

The judge derived support for his determination from a decision of the Court of Appeal, *Dunnett v Railtrack* [2002] All ER (D) 314 (Feb), in which it was laid down that a court should further the objective of the CPR to encourage ADR, to which priority and pre-eminence should be given in the settlement of disputes.

It should also be borne in mind that Pt 44 of the CPR requires that a matter to be taken into consideration in the award of costs is unreasonable refusal of, or unreasonable conduct during, ADR proceedings. It was on this basis that Mr Rose in *Rose v Rose*[8] (already referred to) was called upon to pay costs amounting to £250,000.

---

7 See Christopher Newmark's article 'In praise of ADR', *New Law Journal*, Vol 152, 13 December 2002, 1896, in which this aspect of ADR is eruditely dealt with.

8 See fn 6 and accompanying text.

It is very much in keeping with the present era that ADR should have a special place in the scheme of things when the question of access to justice is being considered. Lord Woolf, the present Lord Chief Justice of England and Wales, put the matter in proper perspective when he made the following pronouncement at the Tom Sargant Memorial Lecture on 19 November 1996:[9]

> I have made 303 recommendations in my report but my major ambition goes beyond the individual reforms. It is to change the culture of civil justice from one which is excessively adversarial, disproportionately expensive and unequal and therefore inaccessible to the majority of our citizens to one which approaches the resolution of disputes in a rational and proportionate manner and regards the weapon of litigation as the ultimate deterrent – a deterrent not to be used except as the last resort because the consequences of doing so even after the implementation of my reforms will be largely unpredictable.

The new culture to which Lord Woolf refers is undoubtedly spreading throughout the Commonwealth, and after looking at what is happening in metropolitan countries we shall address the extent of which ADR is taking root in several Commonwealth countries.

ADR IN DEVELOPED COUNTRIES

THE US

ADR has a long history in the US, where it was in recent times put on the statute book by the Federal Arbitration Act of 1925 – later adopted in 1955 by the National Conference of Commissioners on Uniform State Laws as the Uniform Arbitration Act. By 1982, according to one assessment, 94.2% of all civil cases filed in the federal courts were settled out of court. In the criminal field, only 14.8% of federal cases reached the trial stage, the vast majority having been disposed of by way of negotiated plea bargains. In divorce matters, too, there is a heavy accent on negotiation, especially in respect of settlement of property and maintenance as well as child support and custody. Lawyers are more and more equipping themselves to serve as mediators, but it is feared that, without proper training and re-orientation, lawyers will not make good negotiators since by original training they tend to have an adversarial mindset running counter to the whole spirit of ADR. In Wolfram's view, whenever lawyers become mediators, two stereotypes of mediation are likely to come into play – the competitive and the accommodative or co-operative.[10] It would clearly be desirable, therefore, that non-lawyers should also be the negotiators, since what is expected of a mediator is an attitude of neutrality and not partisanship.

9 See the substance of Lord Woolf's Tom Sargant Memorial Lecture referred to in the *New Law Journal*, p 1701. In the case of *Hurst v Leming* [2002] CP Rep 59, Lightman J described ADR as being 'at the heart of today's civil justice system'.

10 Wolfram, 1999, pp 713–30.

However, there can be no doubt that in recent years the US has provided enlightened leadership in supporting all forms of ADR. Indeed, it is said that the fastest growing sub-group of the American Bar Association is the section on dispute resolution which is collaborating with the American Arbitration Association on rules of ethics for arbitration and due process protocols for arbitration and mediation.

The American stand has obviously influenced the English and Canadians and we will now consider the position in those countries.

ENGLAND

The English legislation on the matter of arbitration in its most modern form is to be found in the 1996 Arbitration Act which, in the words of one enlightened commentator, 'was intended to assure judicial respect for the autonomy of the arbitral process and to enhance the finality of arbitral awards'.[11] In this connection the judiciary accepts the limitations to judicial review enshrined in s 68 of the 1996 Act which also enables arbitrators 'to enjoy greater freedom than ever to fashion procedure appropriate to the circumstances of a particular dispute'.[12] In so far as the applicable appeal regime is concerned, that writer has quite rightly observed that the regime created by s 69 of the Act 'stands out as an anomalous feature of a modern pro-arbitration jurisdiction'.[13]

Two other writers on the subject have given their joint views on the procedural status of arbitration as follows:[14]

> Arbitration can and should be a flexible and efficient procedure for determining disputes. At its best it will be cost-efficient and quick. At its worst it will be more expensive and slower than litigation but without an effective right of appeal. Which of these outcomes prevails is in the hands of the tribunal and the parties.

CANADA – INTERNATIONAL ARBITRATION

Canada provides a striking example of a country making a determined effort to utilise mediation services, often at no cost to the parties, instead of the formal costly proceedings before the courts. Before giving some account of these domestic measures, we should – in the interest of completeness – refer to Canada's position in so far as international arbitration is concerned.

Although internally arbitration and other alternative measures have for years been employed, international arbitral methods came into their own after 1986, when the federal government acceded to the Convention on the Recognition and Enforcement of Foreign Arbitral Awards – otherwise known as 'the New York

---

11 Shackleton, 'Challenging arbitration awards, part II: procedural irregularity', in *New Law Journal*, Vol 152, No 7058, 29 November 2002, p 1816.

12 *Ibid*, p 1817.

13 Shackleton, 'Challenging arbitration awards, part III: appeals on questions of law', in *New Law Journal*, Vol 152, No 7059, 6 December 2002, p 1835.

14 Foyle and Singh, 'Arbitration: an introduction to the procedure', in *New Law Journal*, Vol 152, No 7049, 27 September 2002, p 1418.

Convention'. Thereafter the federal parliament and all provincial and territorial governments passed legislation based on the UNCITRAL Model Law on International Commercial Arbitration and thereby implemented the New York Convention.

There is, however, one convention which has not been ratified by Canada. It is the Convention on the Settlement of Investment Disputes between States and Nationals of Other States, otherwise referred to as 'the Washington Convention'. This Convention was opened for signature on 18 March 1965 on behalf of the states members of the International Bank for Reconstruction and Development. It entered into force on 14 October 1966. As of 31 December 2002, 148 states had signed the Convention, while 132 of them had duly delivered their instruments of ratification. The Canadian Government has all along felt itself inhibited from signing because of the objections of Quebec and Alberta.

This then is the Canadian position on international conventions relating to arbitration.

We must now examine what has been happening in other aspects of internal alternative dispute resolution (ADR).

CANADA – MUNICIPAL ADR

Since 1993, the Federal Provincial Territorial Working Group on Dispute Resolution continued to be a forum for practitioners of dispute resolution in identifying solutions to the problems encountered by all the provincial and territorial governments. The result is that a decade later every province has family mediation arrangements of one kind or another. For instance, in British Columbia, the Provincial Court (Family) Rules passed in 1998 provide more early settlement opportunities and ensure more efficient case management. There is a project underway in five Family Justice Registries under which before the litigants actually appear in court, they meet with a Family Justice Counsellor to be briefed about available services including mediation. The Child, Family and Community Service Act permits parties voluntarily to choose mediation for the resolution of child protection disputes. The mediation services are free and delivered by child protection mediators.

In Manitoba, mediation services are available on a voluntary basis in civil matters and since 15 January 2001 Family Conciliation (Manitoba Family Services and Housing) has offered comprehensive mediation services as a means of providing an alternative to court action in matters of divorce where minor children are involved.

In Ontario, the Dispute Resolution Office (DRO) is a focal point for providing consulting services, neutral third party services, training, information and referral in dispute resolution, the office being staffed by highly qualified professionals dedicated to promoting efficient systems of alternative dispute resolution.

In the Northwest Territories, there are private sector mediators in family law matters and, although in the Yukon Territory there is no court-attached mediation programme, mediation is carried out on a voluntary basis.[15]

NEWLY-INDEPENDENT AND OVERSEAS DEPENDENT TERRITORIES

The position on the use of ADR in these countries varies widely and is largely dependent on resources.

In some countries, like Bermuda, which is a thriving British colony, there is frequent resort to it, since parties realise it is the best way of ensuring quick resolution of their disputes. The fact is that, despite valiant efforts on the part of the judiciary in that island, the civil lists continue to be clogged.

On the other hand, ADR is seldom resorted to in the Cayman Islands – another wealthy colonial financial centre – where a litigant can often get a civil suit in the courts resolved within six months of its being filed.

In Jamaica, there has of recent years been a noticeable increase in applications to have disputes resolved by alternative means. The applications are made more often by the litigants themselves rather than by the courts.

There is, however, provision under the Magistrates Court (Amendment) Rules 1999 for a judge, where in the course of proceedings he considers it desirable, to refer a matter to mediation and adjourn the proceedings to enable attendance on a mediator. Such mediators may, under the Rules, be appointed by the Chief Justice on the recommendation of the Dispute Resolution Foundation.

The same Rules also make provision for small claims to be heard at a special sitting of the Resident Magistrates' Court appointed for the purpose and it is only if the judge hearing a small claim action considers the matter would be more appropriately heard at a regular sitting of the Resident Magistrates' Court that it may be transferred to that tribunal.

Jamaica has also passed legislation[16] to try by mediation persons charged with the following offences:

- unlawful wounding;
- assault;
- assault occasioning actual bodily harm;
- certain offences under the Trespass Act;
- certain offences under the Town and Communities Act;
- any offence under the Litter Act;
- certain offences under the Malicious Injuries to Property Act; and
- an offence under the Noise Abatement Act.

15 Much of the material in this section on Canada is drawn from a document entitled 'Cross Country Snapshot of Dispute Resolution' put out by the Canadian Forum on Civil Justice, Spring 22.

16 The Criminal Justice (Reform) (Amendment) Act 2001, s 16 and Sched 2.

Once again, the Chief Justice has the power to appoint 'approved mediators'[17] and a mediation order made under the Act operates to suspend the trial of the offence. The order may limit the time within which the mediation may be completed as well as the time within which a report on the mediation is to be submitted setting out whether the mediation took place, whether agreement was reached, the terms of the agreement and suggestions for a date to be fixed for the court to make the necessary order. If the matter has not been resolved, the court is to proceed to try it.[18] The new Civil Procedure Code Law makes provision for disputes to be resolved by ADR at the various stages of the proceedings. The Alternative Dispute Resolution Foundation (ADRF) has additionally undertaken to provide community based mediation services in various parishes across the country.

Trinidad & Tobago has likewise embraced alternative resolution arrangements in both civil and criminal matters. In 1998, the Community Mediation Act was passed and it has since been amended by an Act No 45 of 2000. These enactments were followed by the Community Mediation Regulations of 2000. The position in Trinidad & Tobago follows closely that set out for Jamaica in that there exists availability for mediation in certain minor criminal offences, but it also covers civil and family matters.

In St Lucia, where the OECS Supreme Court had its headquarters, a court-annexed mediation referral scheme was initiated in a pilot stage brought into being by a Practice Direction (2/2002) issued by the Chief Justice Sir Dennis Byron. The first six months of the project was a resounding success, after which the scene was set for similar programmes in the British Virgin Islands, Anguilla, Montserrat, St Kitts and Nevis, Antigua and Barbuda, Dominica, St Vincent and the Grenadines, and Grenada. By the end of 2004, an expert from the Law School in Trinidad had trained lawyers in all the countries in the OECS.

The Government of Malaysia has expressed itself as being very interested in developing alternatives to the adversarial court regime. In 1978, a Regional Centre of Arbitration was set up and studies are underway to arrive at a comprehensive programme of mediation and conciliation in settling disputes in the Federation.[19]

17 *Ibid*, s 16(3).

18 *Ibid*, ss 5 and 6.

19 See letter on my files dated 30 November 2002 from the Attorney-General of the Federation of Malaysia.

One other country which has made much use of ADR is Singapore. In that country the Singapore Mediation Centre (SMC) conducts mediation for civil and commercial disputes. The following chart shows the number of cases mediated by the SMC over the five-year period 1997–2001:

Year	1997	1998	1999	2000	2001
No of cases mediated	110	170	159	198	147

Mediation in Singapore is carried out in the subordinate court for civil, family and criminal matters, the services in civil cases being provided for claims up to $250,000. The following charts show the number of civil cases mediated for the same five-year period 1997–2001:

Year	1997	1998	1999	2000	2001
No of cases mediated[20]	3,428	3,943	4,550	5,651	4,850[21]

In respect of family matters, counselling and mediation services are provided for divorce cases, custody and access of children, maintenance and division of matrimonial property. An estimated 10,000 cases are mediated annually in the subordinate courts.

In so far as criminal matters are concerned, mediation services exist for certain types of criminal complaints, viz relational disputes, public mischief, affray and simple assault. An estimated 1,000 criminal cases are mediated annually.

Turning now to arbitration, the Singapore International Arbitration Centre (SIAC) provides facilities and a panel of arbitrators for international and domestic commercial disputes. The SIAC utilises its own rules of arbitration largely based on the Uncitral Arbitration Rules and the Rules of the London Court of International Arbitration. The following chart shows the number of cases arbitrated by the SIAC over the five-year period 1997–2001:

Year	1997	1998	1999	2000	2001
No of cases arbitrated[22]	58	89	89	83	100

20 These figures (kindly provided by the Attorney-General of Singapore for the author) have been extracted from the Subordinate Courts Annual Reports and relate primarily to the cases mediated by its Primary Dispute Resolution Centre.

21 This figure serves the period 1 January to 30 September 2001.

22 Figures also provided through the Singapore Attorney-General by the Singapore International Arbitration Centre.

In South Africa, certain civil cases may – under the provisions of the short process courts and mediation in certain Civil Cases Act 1991 – be heard by mediators and adjudicators appointed by the Minister of Justice from persons whose names have been submitted to the Minister by the Association of Law Societies, the General Bar Council and the Ministry of Justice. Such officials are subject to the administrative control of the magistrates in the districts they serve.

In the case of mediation, after a summons for the institution of civil proceedings has been issued or during the actual hearing of the case but before judgment, the parties or their legal representatives may give notice to the clerk of the court that they wish the matter in question to be referred for mediation (s 3(1)(a)).

Within 14 days of the receipt of such notice (or of the adjournment if the hearing has begun), the clerk of the court shall summon the parties before a mediator (s 3(1)(c)) for an interview and investigation with a view to effecting an out-of-court settlement. Even if a full settlement cannot be reached, it is permissible for the parties to arrange to simplify the issues; amend the pleadings with a view to an intended or further trial; make admissions of fact, thereby avoiding the necessity of adducing evidence at the trial; limit the number of witnesses to attest at a trial; or take any action which may contribute to the expeditious and cost-saving disposition of the case (s 3(1)(b)).

Subsequent to this interview and investigation, the mediator issues an order, s 3(2), from which there is *no* appeal (s 3(7)).

An adjudicator is given similar functions under the Act but he must not be in the service of the state and he holds office at the minister's pleasure (s 6). He must have at least five years' uninterrupted service as an advocate or attorney or as a magistrate (s 7).

In the short process courts, there is flexibility in procedure. Thus, steps can be taken, in consultation with the parties, which may lead to the expeditious and cost-saving disposition of cases, including the abandonment of any rule of evidence (s 10(1)). Evidence to prove or disprove a fact in issue may be given in writing or orally.

Although no appeal lies from orders of mediators or adjudicators, proceedings may be brought under review of the Supreme Court where there is an absence of jurisdiction; or where there is an interest in the cause, bias, malice or corruption; or in the event of gross irregularity in the proceedings (s 12).

The most important aspect of this form of alternative resolution is that the state 'case manages' the dispute and matters are not allowed to drift in the manner common in ordinary court procedures. There is much to commend such a system if justice is not to be unduly delayed.

THE LAWYER AS MEDIATOR

A word should be said here about the lawyer's duty as mediator. It is common ground that when a lawyer serves in such a capacity, he is not acting for either party and it is vital that the parties should be so informed. Nor is he to bring pressure to bear on any side and he should encourage the parties to seek counsel's independent advice at every step of the way if that becomes absolutely necessary. Under no circumstances should he assume the mantle of legal adviser while serving as mediator. A mediator should be an unbiased impartial person who does not try to decide a case or to impose a settlement. He is asked to help with the negotiations by both parties and in the event that they fail to come to some common understanding, they are still free to take the matter to court for a judicial determination.

ONLINE DISPUTE RESOLUTION (ODR)

One final form of dispute resolution, which is an outgrowth of the internet, is online dispute resolution (ODR).

This is essentially a type of 'documents only' arbitration in which the contentions of the respective parties are set out online with supporting documents. An arbitrator is also selected by the service provider. After online consultation with the parties reviewing the respective representations, the provider makes an award (as mediator) via a secure online server.

The matter then proceeds as follows:

- Party A completes a form identifying the parties to the dispute as well as the nature thereof and what is sought to be achieved.
- The service refers this form to Party B to see whether that party is willing to participate.
- Once both agree to mediation, they set out the ground rules by which the process will continue.
- The mediator then communicates to both parties either simultaneously or separately in an effort to settle.

The great advantage in this form of dispute resolution is that no scheduling court programme is required, since the internet site is open on a 24-hours-a-day, seven-days-a-week basis.

The learned writer[23] who has advanced these novel ideas also points out that: 'Access is extremely flexible – participants can access the service at home or at work and there is no need for either the disputants or third party to travel to a neutral venue – a feature of particular advantage to cross-border disputes.' It is further pointed out that settlement 'can be extremely quick and costs kept to a minimum'.

23 Bryan Clarke, Lecturer in Law, Heriot Watt University. The material here is drawn from his article entitled 'ODR: the new kid in town' *New Law Journal*, Vol 152, 15 November 2002, p 1711.

Obviously, there is also the downside to such a procedure. The disputants do not have an opportunity of a face-to face encounter and are unable to observe the reactions of each other to the other's suggestions or counter-proposals. The author of the article suggests that 'video conferencing techniques offer the possibility to replicate at least some of the nuances of face-to-face communications', although he also concedes that 'the costs involved and limited accessibility to such technologies may often prove prohibitive'. The problem of security has also been addressed, since it is always possible for hackers to intercept email communications, and the suggestion has been made that encryption software might be utilised.

The writer of the article considers that, just as lawyers are beginning to accept ADR after some hesitation, it is possible they will also come to embrace ODR – a view I respectfully share. There may well be a bright future for ODR, as technology improves, and as the legal profession weighs the economy of the arrangement against the costliness of litigation.

PRIVILEGE AND ADR

Privilege does not normally attach to correspondence in civil proceedings where lawyers simply act as intermediaries, but whenever a negotiated settlement or compromise is being attempted, statements made in such proceedings are generally marked 'Without Prejudice' and are protected by privilege. In fact, even if the correspondence is not so marked, privilege will attach so long as it can be shown that an attempt is being made to settle out of court.[24]

If the negotiations succeed there would of course be no difficulty in the parties to the settlement utilising the correspondence as evidence of the agreement.[25]

ALTERNATIVE AVENUES OF HELP IN THE UK

There are Citizens Advice Bureaux in existence all over the UK where consultations are free. There are also referral schemes where solicitors offer clients, free of cost, a consultation for an initial half-hour. In addition, there are about 50 law centres with shop-window offices where free legal advice is offered to the poor, but these centres are of limited value since they cannot compete with practising lawyers in divorce matters or in the drafting of conveyances or in taking cases of serious personal injury. As a result, they concentrate on immigration, employment, housing and welfare matters. Trade unions also offer legal help to their members, not on the same basis as legal plans that one finds in the US Organisations like the Automobile Association, the Consumers Association and the National Association for Mental Health likewise offer free legal assistance, mainly to their members. The Bar's Free Representation Unit gives assistance at tribunals and Criminal Injuries Compensation Authority hearings. The Bar and

24 See *South Shopshire District Council v Amos* [1986] 1 WLR 1271.
25 *Tomlin v Standard Telephones & Cables Ltd* [1969] 1 WLR 1378.

the solicitors provide *pro bono* services. These represent only a small sample of the alternative ways in which people's legal problems are solved.

SMALL CLAIMS AND SHORT PROCESS TRIBUNALS

Since 1973, a small claims procedure was also introduced in England, operating within the county courts under which system the district judges assumed the role of arbitrators in informal proceedings. Lawyers do not usually attend these hearings though they are in no way excluded. In most cases, the loser does not meet the winner's costs although reimbursement of a successful party's daily wage may be ordered.

The procedure was further extended by an arrangement which came into effect on Lord Woolf's reforms being implemented in 1999. Under this new arrangement, claims of £5,000 and under were allocated to a small claims track – the limit being reduced to £1,000 in the case of personal injury or house disrepair cases. In this system the parties sit informally around a table in the judge's room and there are none of the formalities which attend a full-blown performance in a court.

If the judge considers it desirable to hear the evidence of an expert witness, he or she may so order, both parties in such a case being encouraged to utilise the services of that expert as a means of saving costs. If the judge considers a particular matter too complicated for the small claims court, he is at liberty to refer it to be dealt with by a 'fast-track', a procedure streamlined to deal in open court with claims up to £15,000.

The English arrangements are similar to the short process courts which operate in South Africa in civil cases with the help of adjudicators and mediators from whose determination there is no appeal, except for such fundamental defects as a lack of jurisdiction and a charge of bias or corruption.

CONCLUSION

In this chapter we have attempted very briefly to trace the development of ADR in England and North America, observing that traditional court proceedings tend to die hard. We have also examined ADR's beginnings elsewhere. The lawyers, no less than the litigants, clearly feel they should have their day in court, and this is hardly surprising since advocates are accustomed to receiving handsome fees especially when they represent opulent clients. Happily the signs are that more and more practitioners worldwide are preparing themselves to become proficient in the field of arbitration and mediation. In the Caribbean, ADR is taught to law students where it is an examinable elective in the academic stage at the Faculty of Law in Barbados as well as in the Hugh Wooding Law School in Trinidad, ie, at the professional stage, where, however, it is not a subject that counts for credit.

We have outlined the flaws in the adversary system. It is a system that does not necessarily uncover the truth, nor does it normally solve the bulk of the litigant's problems. We have looked briefly at the English forms of adversarialism and considered the effects upon it of Lord Woolf's proposals for reform of the court system. We have also examined the attention being given throughout the common law world to appropriate forms of dispute resolution – mediation, arbitration, family dispute resolution (FDR) and even online dispute resolution (ODR), now in its infancy. In other words we have in the process seen whether governments and the legal profession are heeding Lord Woolf's suggestion to 'change the culture of civil justice'.

We have tried to summarise the extent to which ADR has affected international negotiations as well as municipal contractual arrangements in England and in Canada. We have examined arbitration and mediation efforts in a limited number of Commonwealth countries, notably Singapore, Malaysia and the Caribbean. We have considered the alternative efforts of small claims courts in England and South Africa. We have seen the readiness of such jurisdictions as Bermuda, Barbados, Trinidad & Tobago, Jamaica and the OECS to consider replacing formal court proceedings by mediation and arbitration. We have also briefly looked at the effect of professional privilege on ADR.

The tendency under the new dispensation is to simplify procedures and make them more readily available by methods outside the court system; there can be no doubt that these alternative arrangements offer many advantages. They are less formal, less costly and offer the citizenry much swifter results. They involve those concerned in a collaborative way in the solution of their problems.[26] They create a situation in which the complainant and the defendant are far more likely to end up on speaking, if not on friendly, terms. But more germanely: the new arrangements concern themselves with solutions rather than with 'winning the case'.[27]

26 See a characteristically sound article by Professor Carrie Mendel-Meadow entitled 'The trouble with the adversary system in a postmodern, multicultural world', in *William and Mary Law Review*, Vol 38:1, 1996, in which the author pleads that changes to the adversary system must be a root-and-branch affair: 'a cultural change is required and that is not easy to legislate.'

27 See AK Fiadjoe, *Alternative Dispute Resolution: A Developing World Perspective* (London, Cavendish Publishing, 2004). Dr Fiadjoe's new book provides a stimulating and scholarly treatise of a subject growing in significance and importance in the developing world.

CHAPTER 12

EPILOGUE

In this work I have made an attempt to situate the lawyer in a new globalised environment in the 21st century to show the extent to which legal ethics and professional liability have become matters of concern to be addressed with anxious care.

I have suggested that there is a crisis in the sense that there are at present many ethical tensions between the solo practitioner (who prescribes to one form of ethics) and the practitioner in a large law firm (who prescribes to another). Some lawyers cannot understand why the law should not be regarded as a business, while others consider such an approach heretical. Some lawyers consider altruism should be an important part of their agenda, while others consider increasing their earnings should be paramount. Some lawyers consider advertising is necessary in order that the public should get access to justice: some violently oppose advertisement as unprofessional and dismiss indignantly the access argument. Some see the urgent need to protect the man accused of crime from the heavy-handedness of the state: others consider that there is too much indulgence for the criminal and too little for the victim. Some consider there is too much talk about the 'corporate lawyer' and too little about the 'people's lawyer'.

In all this, I have shown that there are certain issues in which the profession has developed some common ground. There is widespread agreement that the lawyer should no longer be singled out as being immune from suit for negligence in the course of his professional duties; that the profession must be made accountable to the public it serves and for whose business its members assume responsibility. I have reviewed the extent to which lawyers can be sued not only in contract and in tort, but also for breaches of trust. I have examined how in special circumstances they are liable to pay wasted costs to an opponent's client.

I have considered the extent to which governments scrutinise the self-regulation so dear to the hearts of the profession and reviewed disciplinary regimes as part and parcel of the process of accountability to which its members are today subjected. I have tried to show the part legal and judicial codes of ethics play in the matter of self-regulation and towards reminding the profession of its duties to the clients, to the courts, to their colleagues and to the public.

I have probed in some depth the responsibilities of the lawyer to keep inviolate the confidences his client shares with him while at the same time surveying the extent to which as legal adviser a strenuous attempt must be made to avoid conflicts of interest in an environment in which conflicts are increasingly likely to occur – even on the bench with judges and magistrates.

I have devoted an entire chapter to the ethics of the criminal process recalling that we live in an age of drug trafficking, money laundering and terrorism as a result of which the lawyer must understand the laws governing these ills and his or her role not only in preserving the confidences of his or her client but especially in serving the public interest. The lawyer must also understand the role of the police in the criminal process while not unwittingly allowing him or herself to fall prey to any oppressive police practices. I have suggested that the jury system should be reformed.

An effort has also been made in this book to urge that, operating in the public interest, we must rid ourselves of the mindset of adversarial confrontation and turn to a culture of mediation and conciliation as a means of settling disputes. We need to think more of solving problems than of defeating an enemy.

When I told one of my very senior 'unlawyerly' friends that I was spending a year of my retiring years writing this book on the ethics of the legal profession, he expressed his sympathies and suggested that it would either have to be a very short book or a very long one trying to convince the public that if the subject of my discourse does exist, the public cannot recognise it! While not entirely doubting my friend's scepticism, I decided to take a middle course, viz to write a book that is neither inordinately short nor too long. The reader will see that I have attempted to state that legal ethics do exist but that, although human frailty abounds in good measure in the profession, we must not lose hope that our members have the capacity if they exort the will to help to make the world a more altruistic place in which to live.

But what must the lawyers do to show that they can shake themselves out of the rut into which they have fallen? They must first recognise that they are in a rut. Then how to try and get out of it. Sol Linowitz provides an answer, praying in aid support from another distinguished ethicist, Geoffrey Hazard. This is what Linowitz suggests as the way out:[1]

> In Geoffrey Hazard's terms, lawyers must find ways to 'fantasize' about themselves and their profession – to see and thus to create the possibility of a legal profession that is once again independent, willing to sacrifice money for pride, eager to reassert its role as the guarantor of rights. To make the contribution only lawyers can make to the future of our country and the world, we must accept rather than simply assert our responsibilities. When we look at our fellows and we decide whom we respect, civic leadership shall count for more than hourly rate, the sense of justice for more than a record of victories at trial, service to those who need the law for more than representation of those who merely use the law. The fault is not in our stars but in ourselves.

It is that 'sense of justice' that dictates the final exhortation which concludes this work.

Throughout this book I have urged that the lawyer is in the unique position vis-à-vis his or her clients, viz that he or she is heir to a sacred trust which he or she must not betray. And when our labours cease, how will we know whether we

1 Linowitz, *The Betrayed Profession: Lawyering at the End of the Twentieth Century*, 1994, pp 244–45. Copyright (c) 1994 by Sol M Linowitz and Martin Mayer. Originally published by Charles Scribner's Sons. Reprinted by permission of Curtis Brown Ltd.

have fulfilled that trust? Although it may be considered a counsel of perfection, the ideal implicit in what Lord Brougham famously described as the proud boast of Augustus should be our aim, viz although we may have found law dear, we should have left it cheap; although we may have found it a sealed book, it should have been left a living letter; although we may have found it the patrimony of the rich, it should have been left the inheritance of the poor.

Such lofty ideals, however, would call for complete rethinking or what Professor Carrie Menkel-Meadow refers to as 're-conceptualisation' of the role of lawyers in advancing her thesis that we need to change our whole approach to lawyering, that approach involving a new 'ethic of care'.

We must address our business not with charity but with understanding – putting ourselves in others' shoes. After all: 'altruism is implicated in many of the reasons for becoming lawyers: to eradicate poverty and human suffering, to seek equality, to promote justice, to facilitate peaceful and effective conflict resolution, to promote mutually and socially advantageous transactions, or simply "to help others" – all motivations that go beyond professional self-interest.'[2]

It is that ethic of care that motivates us when we embark on *pro bono* work; when we endeavour to mediate rather than litigate; and when we make a sincere effort to appreciate and empathise with the problems of our opponent as we would do for our clients. It should be our driving force when we decide as lawyers never to mislead the court and to make every relevant case available, even if such authority serves to strengthen the opponent's case. It should govern our willingness to act *pro bono* on appeal if we feel convinced that a client has been wrongly convicted or that in some other way he or she has been denied justice. It should impel us to bring to the court's notice mitigating factors in favour of a defendant convicted of a criminal offence. If we feel constrained to withdraw from representation in a suit because the client insists in urging that we put forward a defence which amounts to a fraud on the court or some other illegality, we should take the step to withdraw only when we are satisfied that the client has secured alternative competent representation.

If we find it difficult to make this type of commitment to the profession of our choice, we would serve humanity better if we should transfer our labours to another corner of the vineyard, since the community would consider that we have failed to live up to the noble ideals we have espoused.

In the course of writing the preceding chapters, I could not resist many personal reflections going back 50 years. While serving as a magistrate many years ago I was constantly exercised over the number of occasions when persons appeared before me charged with petty theft and similar crimes who were driven to criminal conduct simply because of want. They were clearly the victims of the conditions in which they lived, but the range of punishment was usually circumscribed. In some cases, a youngster would be required by statute to serve a term of imprisonment if he committed a particular offence a second time. There

2 See Professor Carrie Menkel-Meadow's fascinating article 'Is altruism possible in lawyering?', in *Georgia State University Law Review*, Vol 8, 1992, 385 at p 414.

was no provision, for instance, for community service. The police were seldom interested in the surroundings from which the accused came or any such environmental factor. There was no provision – as there is today – for mediation in respect of certain minor crimes.

Later on, as general counsel for three international corporations operating in several Caribbean jurisdictions, I saw the folly and undesirability of taking to court many of the actions brought against the corporations and took every available opportunity to settle out of court. There is no doubt that lawyers have a special responsibility towards third parties, especially when those parties are the victims of the actions of powerful multinationals. Further, victims should always be given special consideration when crimes of violence are committed.

The legal profession needs to become a more compassionate and helping profession so that, as Professor Menkel-Meadow puts it, 'we can begin to think of "helped" souls just as the medical profession thinks of "cures"'.[3]

In the course of closely examining a piece of sculpture which I commissioned to depict the lawyer when I was writing my first book on the history and status of the legal profession in 1978,[4] I was struck by the fact that the sculptor produced not one person, but two. The lawyer (as depicted) stood erect with wig and gown, while a smaller figure clung smugly to his back as if afraid, and pleading to his patron: 'I must lean upon you and expect you to come to my aid.' The erect protecting figure gazes ahead from a single piercing eye of justice, but etched in the zericote wood there is a deep question mark, which begins in his stomach and extends to his spine. This question mark seems to invite three questions, viz:

> Since I owe a triple allegiance to the courts, the client and the public, how do I properly serve all these interests, if I am to be effective?
>
> To what extent is it my business to solve the problems before me by trying to arrive at the truth?
>
> Would it not be wise if in the end I serve only the cause of justice?

These are the issues the lawyer must forever strive to resolve today while realising that 'the old order changeth, yielding place to new'.

Our profession will not go wrong if its members take to heart the following advice from Professor Menkel-Meadow:[5]

> At the present time the legal system and its ethical codes do try to make each person an island entire of herself, perhaps with her lawyer as her Robinson Crusoe or Man Friday. It would be better to think of ourselves as the ships to save those lost and deserted souls on those islands of legal trouble if only because we realise that we might ourselves one day be the person on the island.

---

3 *Ibid*.

4 Phillips, *The Evolving Legal Profession in the Commonwealth* (Dobbs Ferry, NY, Oceana Publications, 1978).

5 See Menkel-Meadow, *op cit*, fn 2, p 419.

BIBLIOGRAPHY

GENERAL WORKS

Abel, RL and Lewis, Philip SC, *Lawyers in Society – An Overview*, Berkeley and Los Angeles, CA: University of California Press, 1995.

Ashworth, Andrew, 'Ethics and criminal justice', in Cranston, Ross (ed), *Legal Ethics and Professional Responsibility*, Oxford: Clarendon Press, 1995.

Auburn, Jonathan, *Legal Professional Privilege: Law and Theory*, Oxford: Hart Publishing, 2000.

Berlins, Marcel and Dyer, Clare, *The Law Machine* (5th edn), London: Penguin Books, 2000.

Billins, Roger, *Solicitors' Duties and Responsibilities*, London: Sweet & Maxwell, 1999.

Boon, Andrew and Levin, Jennifer, *The Ethics and Conduct of Lawyers in England and Wales*, Oxford and Portland, OR: Hart Publishing, 1999.

Brown, Peter Megargee, *Rascals: The Selling of the Legal Profession*, New York: Benchmark Press, 1989.

Carlin, J, *A Study of the NY City Bar*, NY: Russell Sage Foundation, 1966.

Cohen, Henry, *History of the English Bar*, London: Sweet & Maxwell, 1929.

Cranston, Ross (ed), *Legal Ethics and Professional Responsibility*, Oxford: Clarendon Press, 1995.

Cripps, Yvonne, *The Legal Implications of Disclosure in the Public Interest*, London: Sweet & Maxwell, 1994.

Denning (Lord), *What's Next in the Law*, London: Butterworths, 1982.

Dezaley, Yves and Sugarman, David, *Professional Competition and Professional Power – Lawyers, Accountants and the Social Construction of Markets*, London and NY: Routledge, 1995.

Evans, Hugh, *Lawyers' Liabilities*, London: Sweet & Maxwell, 2002.

Evans, Keith, *Advocacy in Court: A Beginner's Guide*, London: Sweet & Maxwell, 2000.

Fiadjoe, AK, *Alternative Dispute Resolution: A Developing World Perspective*, London: Cavendish Publishing, 2004.

Flenley, William and Leech, Tom, *Solicitors' Negligence*, London: Butterworths, 1999.

Galanter, Marc and Palay, Thomas, 'Large law firms and professional responsibility', in Cranston, Ross (ed), *Legal Ethics and Professional Responsibility*, Oxford: Clarendon Press, 1995.

Griffiths, JAG, *The Politics of the Judiciary*, London: Fortuna Press, 1992.

Hagan, John and Kay, Fiona, *Gender in Practice. A Study of Lawyers' Lives*, Oxford: OUP, 1995.

Halliday, Terrence C and Karpik, Lucien, *Lawyers and the Rise of Western Political Liberalism*, Oxford: Oxford Socio-Legal Studies, Clarendon Press, 1997.

Houle, CO, *Continuing Learning in the Professions*, San Francisco, California and London: Jossey Bass, 1980.

Jackson, R and Powell, J, *Professional Negligence*, London: Sweet & Maxwell, 2001.

Kronman, Anthony T, *The Lost Lawyer: Failing Ideals of the Legal Profession*, Cambridge: CUP, 1993.

Law Society, *The Guide to the Professional Conduct of Solicitors*, 1999.

Linowitz, Sol M with Mayer, Martin, *The Betrayed Profession: Lawyering at the End of the Twentieth Century*, NY: Charles Scribner's Sons, Maxwell and MacMillan, reprinted by Curtis Brown Ltd, 1994.

Luban, David, 'Speculating on justice: the ethos and jurisprudence of contingency fees', in Parker, Stephen and Samford, Charles (eds), *Legal Practice*, Oxford: Clarendon Press, 1995.

Luban, David, *Lawyers and Justice: An Ethical Study*, Princeton, NJ: Princeton University Press, 1988.

MacKenzie, Gavin, *Lawyers and Ethics: Professional Responsibility and Discipline*, Canada: Carswell, A Thomson Company, 2001.

McConville, M, Hodgson, J, Bridges, L and Pavolovic A, *Standing Accused. The Organisation and Practices of Criminal Defence Lawyers in Britain*, Oxford: Clarendon Press, 1994.

McConville, M, Sanders, A and Leng, R, *The Case for the Prosecution*, London: Routledge, 1991.

Megarry, RE, *Lawyer and Litigant in England*. Published under the auspices of the Hamlyn Trust, 1962.

Nakajima, Chizu and Sheffield, Elizabeth, *Conflicts of Interest and Chinese Walls*, London: Butterworths, 2002.

Nelson, Robert, Trubek, David and Solomon, Rayman, *Lawyers' Ideals/Lawyers' Practices: Transformations in the Legal Profession*, Ithaca and NY: Cornell University Press, 1992.

Nicolson, Donald and Webb, Julian, *Professional Legal Ethics: Critical Interrogations*, Oxford: OUP, 1999.

Nunez-Tesheira, Karen, *The Legal Profession in the English Speaking Caribbean*, Kingston, Jamaica: Caribbean Law Publishing Company, 2001.

O'Dair, Richard, *Legal Ethics: Text and Materials*, London: Butterworths, 2001.

Orkin, MM, *Legal Ethics*, Toronto: Cartwright, 1957.

Parker, Stephen and Sampford, Charles (eds), *Legal Ethics and Practice Contemporary Issues*, Oxford: Clarendon Press, 1995.

Phillips, Sir Fred, *The Evolving Legal Profession in the Commonwealth*, Dobbs Ferry, NY: Oceana Publications, 1978.

Pollard, Duke, *The Caribbean Court of Justice: What It Is and What It Does*, Guyana: Caribbean Community Secretariat, 2000.

Rhode, Deborah L (ed), *Ethics in Practice: Lawyers' Roles Responsibilities and Regulations*, Oxford: OUP, 2000.

Sarat, Austin (ed), *Everyday Practices and Trouble Cases*, Evanston, Illinois: Northwestern University Press, American Bar Foundation, 1998.

Stager, David AA and Arthurs, Harry W, *Lawyers in Canada*, Buffalo and London: University of Toronto Press (published in association with Statistics Canada), 1990.

Thorne, Frederic C, *Law Relating to Solicitors*, London: Butterworths, 1988.

Thurman Arnold, *The Symbols of Government*, New Haven, CT: Yale University Press, 1935.

Tur, Dr Richard, 'Family lawyering', in *Legal Ethics and Legal Practice*, Oxford: Clarendon Press, 1995.

Tyrrell, Alan and Zahad, Yakub (eds), *The Legal Professions in the New Europe*, London: Cavendish Publishing, 1996.

Walker, Clive and Starmer, Keith, *Miscarriages of Justice: A Review of Justice in Error*, London: Blackstone Press, 1999.

Wolfram, Charles, *Modern Legal Ethics (Hornbrook Series Student Edition)*, St Paul, MN: West Publishing Co, 1999.

OFFICIAL PUBLICATIONS, ARTICLES AND OTHER DOCUMENTS

Adams, AM (1989), 'The legal profession, a critical evaluation', 93 Dickenson LR 652.

Allan, TRS (1987), 'Legal privilege and the principle of fairness in criminal trials', Crim LR 449.

Arthurs, Harry W (1994), 'Notes on the crisis in the Canadian legal profession'. International Journal of the Legal Profession, Vol 1, No 3.

Arthurs, Harry W and Kreklewich, Robert (1996), 'Law, legal institutions and the legal profession in the new economy', Osgoode Hall LJ, Vol 34, No 1.

Arthurs, Harry W (1997), 'Globalisation of the mind: Canadian ethics and the restructuring of legal fields', in Journal of Law and Society' Vol 12, No 2 .

Arthurs, Harry W (1998), 'Why Canadian Law Schools do not teach legal ethics', in *Ethical Challenges to Legal Education and Conduct*, Oxford: Hart Publishing.

Arthurs, Harry W (1999), 'A global code of legal ethics', in *Legal Ethics*, Vol 2, Pt I, Oxford: Hart Publishing.

Arthurs, Harry W (2001), 'The world turned upside down: are changes in political economy and legal practice transforming legal education and scholarship or vice versa?' International Journal of Legal Education, Vol 8, No 1.

Arthurs, Harry W (2001), 'Twentieth Anniversary volume: legal education, knowledge and access', the Windsor Yearbook of Access to Justice, Vol XX 35.

Arthurs, Harry W (2002), 'Poor Canadian legal education so near to Wall Street, so far from God', in Osgoode Hall LJ, Vol 38, No 3.

Atkinson, Roy (1995), 'A dissenter's commentary on the professionalism crusade', 74 Tex LR 259.

Belof, Michael J (2002), 'Recusal of judges: the UK experience', Journal of Commonwealth Lawyers' Association, Vol II, No 3, p 15.

Bridges, Lee, (1994), 'Normalising injustice: the Royal Commission on Criminal Justice', 21 Journal of Law and Society.

Brown, Ewan (2002), 'Legal professional privilege and the Revenue', in NLJ, Vol 152, 5 July 2002.

Burger, Chief Justice Warren (1995), 'The Decline of Professionalism': remarks adapted from 23rd Annual John F Sonnett Memorial Lecture, delivered at Fordham University School of Law, 23 January 1995.

Canadian Judicial Council (1998), Ethical Principles for Judges.

Clarke, Bryan (2002), 'ODR: the new kid in town' in NLJ, Vol 152, 15 November 2002, 1710.

Code of the Bar Council (2000), General Council of the Bar of England and Wales.

Daniels, Ronald J (1992), 'The law firm in an efficient community', 37 McGill LJ 801.

Daniels, Ronald J (1993), 'Growing pains: the how and why of law firm expansion', 43 University of Toronto LJ 147.

Dezalay, Yves (1991), 'Territorial battles and tribal disputes', MLR, No 54, 794.

Falconer, Lord (2002), 'Re-balancing the system', NLJ, Vol 152, 1742.

Flood, John (1989), 'Megalaw in the UK: professionalism or corporatism? A preliminary report', 64 Ind LJ 569.

Foyle, Andrew and Singh, Saira (2002), 'Arbitration: an introduction to the procedure', NLJ, Vol 152, 27 September, 1417.

Freedman Munroe H (1966), 'Professional responsibility of the criminal defence lawyer: the three hardest questions', 64 Mich LR 1469.

Greenbaum, EH (1996), 'Development of law firm training programs: coping with a turbulent environment', 3:3 International Journal of the Legal Profession 315.

Hazard Jr, Geoffrey C (1991), 'The future of legal ethics', Yale LJ, Vol 100, 1238.

McConville, Mike (1992), 'Videotaping interrogations: police behaviour on or off camera', Crim LR 532.

McHale, JV (1989), 'Confidentiality: an absolute obligation?', MLR, Vol 52, 715.

McKenzie, Ian, Morgan, Rod and Reiner, Robert (1990), 'Principle and voluntary attendance at the police station', Crim LR 22.

Martin, G Arthur (1970), 'The role and responsibility of the defence advocate', Criminal Law Quarterly 377.

Mason, Stephen (2002), 'Lawyers and the duty of confidentiality in an electronic age', NLJ, Vol 12, 3 May, 664.

Menkel-Meadow, Carrie (1984), 'Towards another view of legal negotiation: the structure of problem solving', UCLALR, Vol 31, 754.

Menkel-Meadow, Carrie (1985), 'For and against settlement: uses and abuses of the Mandatory Settlement Conference', UCLALR, Vol 33, 385.

Menkel-Meadow, Carrie (1990), 'Lying to clients for economic gain or paternalistic judgment: a proposal for a golden rule of candour', University of Pennsylvania LR, Vol 138, 761.

Menkel-Meadow, Carrie (1992), 'Is altruism possible in lawyering?', Georgia State University LR, Vol 8, 385.

Menkel-Meadow, Carrie (1996), 'The trouble with the adversary system in a postmodern, multicultural world', William and Mary LR, Vol 38, 5.

Menkel-Meadow, Carrie (1997), 'Ethics in ADR representation: a road map of critical issues', *Dispute Resolution Magazine*, Winter 1997.

Menkel-Meadow, Carrie (1997), 'What Trina taught me: reflections on mediation, inequality, teaching and life', Minnesota LR, Vol 81, 1413.

Menkel-Meadow, Carrie (1997), 'Ethics in alternative dispute resolution. New Issues, no answers from the adversary conception of lawyers' responsibilities', South Texas LR, Vol 38, 407.

Miller, Richard (2002), 'What is the future of legal aid?', NLJ, Vol 152, 15 March, 386.

Miller, Richard (2002), 'Legal aid: back to business as usual', NLJ, Vol 152, 12 April, 545.

Millett (Lord) (1998), 'Equity's place in the law of commerce', 114 LQR 214.

Modernising Justice, presented to Parliament by the Lord Chancellor December 1998.

Newbold, ALE (1990), 'The crime/fraud exception to legal professional privilege', Modern LR, Vol 53, 472.

Newmark, Christopher (2002), 'In praise of ADR', NLJ, Vol 152, 13 December.

O'Connor, Patrick (1992), 'Prosecution disclosure: principle, practice and justice', Crim LR 464.

Passmore, Colin (2000), 'Privilege update', NLJ, Vol 150, 11 February.

Passmore, Colin (2000), 'Search warrants and privilege', NLJ, Vol 150, 1 December.

Passmore, Colin (2001), 'Privilege update', NLJ, Vol 151, 16 February.

Posner, Richard A (1998), 'Professionalism', 40 Arizona LR 1.

Rawlins, Hugh (2000), 'The Caribbean Court of Justice: the history and analysis of the debate', Georgetown, Guyana: CARICOM Secretariat.

Rhode, Deborah L (1985), 'Ethical perspectives on legal practice', 37 Stan LR 589.

Rhode, Deborah L (1991), 'An adversarial exchange on adversarial ethics: text, sub-text and context', 41 Journal of Legal Education 30.

Rhode, Deborah L (1991), 'Ethics by the pervasive method', 42 Journal of Legal Education 31.

Rhode, Deborah L (1991), 'Gender and professional roles', 63 Fordham LR 39.

Roberts, David (1993), 'Questioning the suspect: the solicitor's role', in Crim LR 368.

Rosenberg, Joshua (2001) article on ADR in *Daily Telegraph*, 24 July 2001, p 18.

Royal Commission on Criminal Justice, Lord Runciman's Report 1991 (Cmnd 2263, HMSO, London).

Royal Commission on Criminal Procedure, Lord Phillips' Report 1981 (Cmnd 8092, HMSO, London).

Sanders, Andrew (1988), 'Rights, remedies and the Police and Criminal Evidence Act', Crim LR 802.

Sanders, Andrew and Bridges, Lee (1990), 'Access to legal advice and police malpractice', Crim LR 494.

Schroeder, Justice Walter (1963), statement made in Lecture entitled 'Some Ethical Problems in Criminal Law', Law Society of Upper Canada Special Lectures.

Shackleton, Stewart (2002), 'Challenging arbitration awards – jurisdiction', NLJ, Vol 152, 22 November, 1746.

Shackleton, Stewart (2002), 'Challenging arbitration awards – procedural irregularity', NLJ, Vol 152, 29 November, 1816.

Simon, William H (1978), 'The ideology of advocacy: procedural justice and professional ethics', Wisconsin LR 19.

Simon, William H (1993), 'The ethics of criminal defence', Mich LR 1703.

Thomas, Paul, articles on plea bargaining in [1969] Crim LR 79 and [1970] Crim LR 559.

Woolf, Lord (1996), commentary on Tom Sargant Memorial Lecture, NLJ, Vol 146, 19 November .

Zander, Michael (2002), 'If conditional fees, why not contingency fees?', NLJ, Vol 152, 24 May, 747.

LEGAL AND JUDICIAL CODES

LEGAL

(1) Antigua and Barbuda Code under s 21 of the Legal Profession ('LPA') in Act 1997 (No 9 of 1997).

(2) Bahamas Bar (Code of Professional Conduct) Regulations made under s 40 of the Bar A Ch 44).

(3) Barbados Code of Ethics of the Disciplinary Committee made under the LPA (Cap 370A).

(4) OECS (less Antigua and Barbuda and St Lucia) Code of Ethics.

(5) St. Lucia Code of Ethics of the Council of the Bar Association made under s 35 of the Legal Profession Act 2000 (No 31 of 2000).

(6) Trinidad & Tobago – Code of Ethics of the Council of the Law Association made under s 354 of the LPA 1986 (No 21 of 1986).

(7) Belize Legal Profession (Code of Conduct) Rules 1991 made under s 18 of the Legal Profession Act 1988.

(8) Ghana.

(9) Malaysia.

(10) Mauritius.

(11) New Zealand.

(12) Singapore.

(13) South Africa.

JUDICIAL

(1) Guyana.

(2) Kenya.

(3) Mauritius.

(4) Nigeria.

(5) Organisation of Eastern Caribbean States (OECS).

(6) Pakistan.

(7) South Africa.

(8) Uganda.

INDEX